Economic Growth, Material Flows and the Environment

ADVANCES IN ECOLOGICAL ECONOMICS

Series Editor: Jeroen C.J.M. van den Bergh, *Professor of Environmental Economics, Free University, Amsterdam, The Netherlands*

Founding Editor: Robert Costanza, *Director, University of Maryland Institute for Ecological Economics and Professor, Center for Environmental and Estuarine Studies and Zoology Department, USA*

This important series makes a significant contribution to the development of the principles and practices of ecological economics, a field which has expanded dramatically in recent years. The series provides an invaluable forum for the publication of high quality work and shows how ecological economic analysis can make a contribution to understanding and resolving important problems.

The main emphasis of the series is on the development and application of new original ideas in ecological economics. International in its approach, it includes some of the best theoretical and empirical work in the field with contributions to fundamental principles, rigorous evaluations of existing concepts, historical surveys and future visions. It seeks to address some of the most important theoretical questions and gives policy solutions for the ecological problems confronting the global village as we move into the twenty-first century.

Titles in the series include:

Economic Growth, Material Flows and the Environment

New Applications of Structural Decomposition Analysis and Physical Input–Output Tables

Dr. Rutger Hoekstra

Department of National Accounts,
Statistics Netherlands,
Voorburg, The Netherlands

ADVANCES IN ECOLOGICAL ECONOMICS

Edward Elgar
Cheltenham, UK • Northampton, MA, USA

Published by
Edward Elgar Publishing Limited
Glensanda House
Montpellier Parade
Cheltenham
Glos GL50 1UA
UK

Edward Elgar Publishing, Inc.
136 West Street
Suite 202
Northampton
Massachusetts 01060
USA

A catalogue record for this book
is available from the British Library

Library of Congress Cataloguing in Publication Data

Hoekstra, Rutger, 1974–
    Economic growth, material flows and the environment : new application of
    structural decomposition analysis and physical input–output tables /
    Rutger Hoekstra.
        p. cm– (Advances in ecological economics)
Thesis (Ph.D.)–Free University, Amsterdam, 2003.
Includes bibliographical references and index.
ISBN 1-84542-189-2
    1. Environmental economics–Mathematical models. 2. Sustainable
development–Mathematical models. 3. Natural resources–Mathematical models.
4. Materials management–Economic aspects. I. Title. II. Series.
Hc79.E5H635 2005
333.7'01'5195–dc22   2005047120

ISBN 978 1 84542 189 2

Dedicated to Suzanne and Cas

Contents

Tables

Figures

Abbreviations

BaU	Business-as-usual
CBS	Centraal Bureau voor de Statistiek (Statistics Netherlands)
CPB	Centraal Planbureau (Netherlands Bureau of Economic Policy Analysis)
EKC	Environmental Kuznets curve
FDL	Final demand level (effect)
FDM	Final demand mix (effect)
HIOT	Hybrid input–output table
IO	Input–output
IDA	Index decomposition analysis
I–M–P	International material–product (chain)
IOC	Input–output coefficients (effect)
IS	Import substitution (effect)
KLEMO	K (Capital), L (Labor), E (Energy), M (Materials), (O) (Other)
LCA	Life cycle assessment
MB	Mass balance
MFA	Material flow analysis
MIOT	Monetary input–output table
M–P	Material-product (chain)
NAM	National accounting matrix
NAMEA	National accounting matrix including environmental accounts
PIOT	Physical input–output table
RAS	Not an abbreviation. An updating method for IO tables.
SAM	Social accounting matrix
SDA	Structural decomposition analysis
SEEA	System of environmental and economic accounting
SFA	Substance flow analysis
SNA	System of national accounts
STREAM	Substance Throughput Related to Economic Activity Model
SUT	Supply and use tables
TC	Technological change (effect)
TMR	Total material requirement
UN	United Nations

Symbols

Below, the most frequently used symbols of this book are listed. Upper case letters are used for matrices and lower case letters indicate vectors or scalars. Each of these symbols is used in combination with a variety of subscripts and superscripts, which are explained in the relevant chapters. Note that, throughout the book, bold is used to indicate physical variables, while normal is used for monetary or hybrid variables (that is, vectors which have data in several units). Hybrid variables are distinguished by an asterisk.

A	Intermediate input coefficients
b	Imports
C, c	Household consumption
D, d	Raw material extraction (D denotes determinant effects in Chapter 7)
E, e	Emissions to nature
F, f	Investments
g	Supply and use totals for industries
H, h	Sector share
K, k	Primary inputs
L	Leontief inverse
m	Absolute value of policy indicator
n	Intensity coefficient of policy indicator
p	Prices
q	Output
R, r	Use of residuals
S, s	Stocks
u	Value-added coefficient
U	Use matrix
v	Value added
V	Supply matrix
W, w	Supply of residuals (w are decomposition weights in chapters 6 and 7)
Y, y	Final demand
Z	Intermediate inputs

Preface

This book is based on my PhD thesis, which was completed in 2003 at the Free University in Amsterdam. I would like to express my gratitude to Prof. Dr Jeroen van den Bergh for his knowledgeable, creative and enthusiastic supervision. Our fruitful cooperation led to several co–authored articles in scientific journals. I would also like to acknowledge my other colleagues at the Free University, particularly Marco Janssen with whom I collaborated extensively during this period. I am also grateful to the members of the MUSSIM (Materials Use and Spatial Scales in Industrial Metabolism) project for the feedback that they gave me. Furthermore, I would like thank the Dutch Organization for Scientific Research (NWO) for funding our project.

The data that are used in this book were created by myself and the National Accounts department of Statistics Netherlands. I am grateful to Sake de Boer, Jan van Dalen, Robert Poort, Henk Verduin, René Jolly, Frank Blaauwendraat, Cees van der Ende, Coen Lavina, Rinus Monsieurs, Sandra Schaaf, Renée Spronk and Wim Tebbens for their contributions towards the construction of the physical supply and use tables that are discussed in Chapter 5. Sake, in particular, played an invaluable part in introducing me to the world of national accounts, as well as giving feedback on my work.

During my years as a PhD student I have had the privilege of meeting, cooperating and receiving feedback from many other scientists and policy researchers. For their feedback on this book and other collaborative work, I thank: Erik Dietzenbacher, Bart Los, Adam Rose, Steven Casler, Annemarth Idenburg, Hein Mannaerts, Bert Steenge, Harmen Verbruggen, Cees Withagen, Bert Balk, Henri de Groot and Marcel Boumans.

The author thanks Springer for permission to reprint 'Structural decomposition analysis of physical flows in the economy' (*Environmental and Resource Economics*, 2002, with van den Bergh – Chapter 6) and Elsevier for 'Comparing structural and index decomposition analysis' (*Energy Economics*, 2003 with van den Bergh – Chapter 7). The author is fully responsible for the text of the publication: the text does not necessarily correspond with the official point of view of Statistics Netherlands.

Last but not least I would like to acknowledge the support of friends, family and my wife Suzanne during this period in my life.

Rutger

1. Introduction

1.1 MOTIVATION AND APPROACH

Economic activities affect the environment in many ways. Of the most serious environmental and resource problems, many are related to the extraction and emission of materials and substances. Industrial processes require non-renewable raw materials, such as metal ores and fossil fuels, which leads to the depletion of existing resource stocks. Moreover, excessive use of renewable resources, such as wood and fish, can lead to a collapse of ecosystems and extinction of species. At the same time, the use of resources in the economy results in wastes and emissions, which cause environmental problems such as global warming, acid rain, eutrophication, and the depletion of the ozone layer.[1]

Clarification of the relationship between the economy and materials flows is essential for a good understanding of environmental problems and policies to resolve them. The structure of an economy consists of different elements, such as technology, sector structure, consumption patterns, investments, import and export. Each of these is related, in its own way, to physical flows[2] of raw materials, products and wastes. Physical flow patterns are therefore affected by changes in the economic structure. This book contributes to an understanding of the relationship between structural change and physical flows, and thereby helps to clarify the relationship between the economy and the environment.

The methods used in this book are based on the input–output (IO) framework. An IO table usually records the flows of goods and services of an economy. These tables are useful for environmental-economic analysis because the individual components of the economic structure are distinguished, and, moreover, they can be constructed in monetary, physical or hybrid units. A physical IO table (PIOT) records the physical flows associated with the economic activities, including the extraction of materials from nature and emissions to the environment. Chapters 2 to 5 elaborate on the construction and application of physical input–output tables, monetary and hybrid IO tables (MIOTs and HIOTs respectively) for environmental analysis.

The effect of structural change on physical flows can be studied using

1

environmental structural decomposition analysis (SDA). This method requires historical IO data and information on material throughput for at least two years. SDA is capable of analyzing the impact of economic growth, technological changes, shift in consumption patterns and international trade effects. Chapters 6 to 9 present technical innovations of environmental SDA, and apply these to the HIOTs constructed in Chapter 5.

The work reported here is part of a long academic debate in which the relationship between the economy and the environment has been studied from a wide range of theoretical and empirical angles. Three topics in the literature are relevant to this book: namely, the 'growth debate', economic models that include material flows, and economic-environmental accounting frameworks. These are discussed in Sections 1.2, 1.3 and 1.4, respectively.

1.2 THE GROWTH DEBATE

An important question motivating this book is can economic growth continue indefinitely given the constraints set by the natural environment? Whereas some argue that this is possible (Beckerman, 1999), others are more pessimistic (Daly, 1999). Growth optimists expect that the positive correlation between economic growth and environmental pressure will, and already is, reversing. Growth pessimists believe that, in the very long run, this will turn out to be impossible. This section provides a short introduction to the debate (for an overview and assessment of the debate, see van den Bergh and de Mooij, 1999). An overview of empirical studies related to material flows is provided in Cleveland and Ruth (1997).

The world is currently in a phase of long-term economic expansion. Maddison (2001) estimates that this started around AD 1000 in Western Europe. Around the end of the eighteenth century and the beginning of the nineteenth century, the rate of economic growth increased significantly.[3] Although economic growth is regionally different and can vary in the short term, the overall picture is clearly one of expanding global economic output.[4] Moreover, the growth in economic output since the Industrial Revolution has coincided with increases of resource use and waste emissions to the environment.

There is hardly any question that there are environmental limits to the amount of physical flows that an economy can extract and emit. The Earth's natural system is limited in physical size, which implies that resources are finite. Furthermore, the environment is a combination of biotic and abiotic components, which is not infinitely stable. The implication of environmental limits is that long-term growth can only occur if environmental pressures remain within these boundaries. Hence, Daly (1977, 1991) advocated a 'steady-state economy', in which the main objective is to minimize the use of materials and energy.

The growth debate relates to the concept of sustainable development, which 'ensure[s] that it meets the needs of the present without compromising the ability of future generations to meet their own needs' (WCED, 1987: p. 8).[5] While the concept of sustainable development sets the goal, the growth debate discusses the prospects of achieving this outcome. The differing viewpoints can be supported by various methods.[6]

Integrated world models have been used to assess the sustainability of economic growth. The report to the Club of Rome, *The Limits to Growth*, by Meadows et al. (1972) is well known because of the prediction of imminent resource depletion. Duchin and Lange et al. (1994) developed an IO model of the world, which uses technological projections to show that current developments are unsustainable.

Another line of research is based on the second law of thermodynamics, the entropy law. To sustain a system, a constant supply of low-entropy material and energy input are required, while high-entropy wastes should be emitted (Boulding, 1966; Georgescu-Roegen 1971). Furthermore, this type of analysis led to the idea that material use is not likely to be reduced to zero, because of the dissipative use of some materials and the almost infinite amounts of energy required for 100 per cent recycling rates.

A line of empirical research that has led to significant debate is the Environmental Kuznets Curve (EKC). These studies are based on cross-sectional or time series data, which show an inverted U-shape relationship between economic output and environmental pressures. The implication is that the environment is a luxury good, which receives more attention beyond a certain threshold of income or wealth.[7] However, this black-box approach does not explain the mechanisms that achieve this outcome. Doubts have, therefore, been raised over the robustness and generality of the EKC. Moreover, it has been suggested that relinking[8] occurred in the late 1980s (de Bruijn and Opschoor, 1997; de Bruijn and Heintz, 1999).

Decomposition analysis can be used to obtain insights into the black-box of the EKC. These analyses are used to study the impact of structural change on environmental pressures using historical data. Country-level and sector-level decomposition is usually referred to as index decomposition analysis (IDA) (Ang and Zhang, 2000), while decomposition of the IO model is called structural decomposition analysis (SDA) (Rose and Casler, 1996; Rose, 1999; Hoekstra and van den Bergh, 2002). SDA is capable of detailed analysis of the influence of structural change on environmentally-relevant physical flows.

So how does this book contribute to the growth debate? Historical SDA is used to understand the driving forces of the physical economy. It assesses the impact of changes in technology, consumption, international trade and investment on physical flows. The empirical results of SDA studies are reviewed to see if these provide insight into the growth debate. So far, the SDA literature has focused almost exclusively on energy and energy-related emissions. This book contains an SDA study of material flows, which decomposed the use of iron and steel and plastic products in the Netherlands for the period 1990–1997. The results of this analysis are used as input in forecasting and backcasting scenario analyses, leading to projections of physical flows for the period 2030.

1.3 ECONOMIC MODELS OF MATERIAL FLOWS

Since this book studies the material throughput of the economy, this section pays attention to economic models that include physical flows. More complete overviews are given in Ruth (1993, 1999) and Kandelaars and van den Bergh (2001).

Material flow models generally incorporate the mass balance (MB) principle. Utilization of this principle has a long history in environmental and ecological economics (Ayres and Kneese, 1969; Ayres, 1978; Perrings, 1987; Ruth, 1993). MB is derived from the first law of thermodynamics, which states that energy is always conserved. Although mass can be converted into energy and vice versa, this only occurs in nuclear fission and fusion.[9] In all other physical processes, mass and energy are conserved separately. MB therefore applies to nearly all system boundaries and spatial scales on earth. The economic implication of MB is that the physical inputs into an economy must equal the sum of output of wastes and stock changes of materials and products in the economy.

The economics of environmental and resource problems studies the physical input to and output from economies. A central concept in environmental and resource economics is neoclassical production functions. It does not, however, guarantee consistency with MB. Daly (1999: p. 640) provides an eloquent example of the inconsistency of MB and traditional production functions in economics: given a fixed amount of eggs, flour and sugar, 'the function says we could make our cake a thousand time bigger if the cook simply stirred faster and used a bigger oven'. If the term 'bigger' refers to the value of the cake, which is what most production functions do, a thousand-fold increase is possible because economic science has set no limit to the value that can be derived from a fixed amount of material. However, if the production function measures the physical size of a cake, it should incorporate MB. Several publications have introduced production functions that are consistent with MB (Georgescu-Roegen, 1971; Gross and Veendorp, 1990; van den Bergh and Nijkamp, 1994; and van den Bergh, 1999).

Material flow analysis (MFA) and substance flow analysis (SFA) record the flow of physical inputs and outputs of a system. MB is the guiding principle for both these approaches. MFA has been used to study the material throughput of production processes, cities and national economies. SFA is similar to MFA, but focuses on one or more specific substances (van der Voet, 1996)

Material-Product (M-P) chain analysis tracks the material flows that are associated with the life cycle of one or more products (Opschoor, 1994). Unlike MFA and SFA, product flows are included, which allows for the economic analysis of prices, costs and benefits (Kandelaars, 1998). Van Beukering (2001) introduced the concept of an international material-product (I-M-P) chain, which includes international flows of materials and products. Life cycle assessment (LCA) is a specific type of M-P chain analysis that assesses the environmental consequences of a product's life cycle (Guinée, 1995). It is often used to choose between two alternatives, on the basis of their environmental repercussions.

'Industrial metabolism' (Ayres and Simonis, 1994) and 'industrial ecology' (Allenby and Richards, 1994; Socolow et al., 1994; and Graedel and Allenby, 1995) are modern concepts in the analysis of physical flows. 'Metabolism' is a biological metaphor that reflects the fact that industrial processes require materials and energy to function and that they inevitably generate wastes and emissions. The 'ecology' metaphor illustrates that an industrial process cannot be viewed in isolation because it is linked to many other systems. The goals of these conceptual frameworks are to identify opportunities for reducing resource use and emissions.[10] Because these approaches study industrial processes from the perspective of the complete system, it is possible to identify when environmental problems are shifted rather than being solved.

Macroeconomic models can also analyze physical flows. For example, STREAM (Substance Throughput Related to Economic Activity Model) was developed by the Netherlands Bureau for Economic Policy Analysis (CPB) to investigate seven bulk goods for the Netherlands and Western Europe. It is a partial equilibrium model, which can analyze the economic and environmental consequences of certain policies (Mannaerts, 2000).

IO models have been used in physical flows analysis on national or other spatial scales. They have been applied to analyze energy use (Bullard III and Herendeen, 1975; Casler and Wilbur, 1984; Miller and Blair, 1985: Ch. 6), CO_2 emissions (Proops et al., 1993), and material flows (Ayres, 1978). A more complete discussion of environmental applications of the IO model is presented in Section 2.4.[11]

The policy goals of material flow models relate to the growth debate and sustainability. The aim is to reduce environmental problems while maintaining economic growth. In the context of material flows this is sometimes translated into the aim of 'dematerialization'.[12] This occurs if resource use decreases (absolute dematerialization) or increases at a lower rate than average income per capita (relative dematerialization). Note that the latter leads to increasing environmental pressures.

This book employs the hybrid IO approach to model physical flows. This model specification uses multiple units. Monetary and physical data can therefore be analyzed simultaneously, which allows for the examination of dematerialization.

1.4 ECONOMY-ENVIRONMENT ACCOUNTS

Frameworks for the accounting of economic-environmental relationships date back to the late 1960s. Many are based on an IO structure. Cumberland (1966) proposes a regional IO table that includes the environmental benefits and costs of industries and final demand categories. The difference between these costs and benefits is proposed as an indicator of environmental pressure, which can be used to formulate regional development objectives.

Daly (1968) summarizes the link between humans and non-human systems as shown in Table 1.1. Quadrant (2) describes interactions between economic processes. Inputs are obtained from non-human sources (3), while material throughput leads to emissions (1). Finally, the interaction between the natural processes is recorded in quadrant (4). The framework is discussed in the context of a hybrid IO model, in which the human and non-human outputs are measured in several different units. Isard (1972) pays special attention to the ecological relationships in quadrant (4). He applied this in a case study of a marina.

Table 1.1 A basic economy-environment account

From	To	
	Human	Non-human
Human	(2)	(1)
Non-human	(3)	(4)

Source: Daly (1968, p. 401)

Victor (1972) introduces an economy-environment framework that couples monetary supply and use tables (SUT) to 'ecological commodities'. The emission and extraction of these ecological commodities is recorded per economic commodity and industry.

A well-known accounting and modelling framework is the augmented Leontief model (Leontief, 1970; Leontief and Ford, 1972). Rows of pollutant emissions data were added to the standard IO model, and corresponding abatement sectors were added as columns. The analysis is, therefore, restricted to quadrants (1) and (2) of Table 1.1. However, quadrant (3) could easily be included.

These frameworks have inspired a range of physical and environmental national accounts, culminating in the System of Environmental and Economic Accounting (SEEA, 2002), which are satellite accounts of the System of National Accounts (UN, 1993). Many of the SEEA accounting frameworks employ physical units: for example, economy-wide MFA, the national accounting matrix with environmental accounts (NAMEA), physical supply and use tables (SUT), physical IO tables (PIOTs), and resource accounts.

Economy-wide MFA, also known as 'bulk-MFA', is the application of the MFA method on the national level (Adriaanse et al., 1997; WRI, 2000; Eurostat, 2001). These studies estimate the mass of raw materials, products and waste emissions of an economy. They include estimates of 'hidden flows', such as mining overburden and erosion. These data provide valuable information about the material flows in economies. However, bulk-MFA *indicators* have been proposed as measures of sustainability. For example, the Total Material Requirement (TMR) adds all material flows extracted and imported, as well as hidden flows, into a single indicator. Bulk materials are aggregated, irrespective of their environmental characteristics. Even authors who are generally supportive conclude that measures such as TMR are 'not very good indicators for environmental pressure' (Kleijn, 2001: p. 8). Nevertheless, these type of indicators continue to attract a lot of attention.

The NAMEA approach combines the monetary national accounting matrix (NAM) and environmental data (de Haan, 2004).[13] It registers the emissions of polluting substances as well as the extraction of oil and natural gas. Physical units are used to record the emissions and extraction data, which are used to calculate the contribution towards specific environmental themes such as global warming and acidification.

This book discusses and elaborates on the PIOT framework, which is an economic-environmental accounting framework that has been implemented for several countries as well as for the European Union. A PIOT describes the flows of materials, products and wastes associated with economic activities. It records quadrants (1), (2) and (3) of Table 1.1 in physical units, which implies that it can serve as a source of data for environmental IO analysis. This book distinguishes between three types of PIOTs: the basic, extended and full PIOT. The basic PIOT is based on the work by Stahmer et al. (1997) and is similar to the traditional monetary IO table. The extended PIOT proposed by Konijn et al. (1995) introduced the innovation of splitting the production processes into structural and auxiliary components (see Chapter 4 for details). Finally, the full PIOT is the attempt by this book to integrate and elaborate on the insights of the basic and extended PIOT by including all aspects of material flows including wastes, packaging, recycling, landfilling and incineration.[14]

1.5 OBJECTIVES

This book aims to contribute to a better understanding of the relationship between economic growth, structural change and the material flows of the economy. By doing so, the relationship between the economy and the environment becomes clearer. The specific objectives are:

1. Explore and elaborate the physical IO tables (PIOTs) as an economic-environmental accounting framework.
2. Investigate structural decomposition analysis (SDA) as a tool to identify the influence of structural change on physical flows. In particular,
    a. compare methods and techniques used in SDA with other decomposition methods;
    b. develop forecasting and backcasting scenario analysis based on SDA results.
3. Construct hybrid IO tables (HIOTs) for iron and steel and plastic products for the Netherlands for 1990 and 1997.
4. Investigate the structural changes that have contributed to the use of iron and steel and plastics in the Netherlands for the period 1990–1997.

1.6 OUTLINE

The organization of this book is as follows. Chapter 2 introduces IO tables and models for economic and environmental analysis. The theoretical aspects of constructing IO tables from SUT are discussed briefly in Chapter 3. Chapter 4 reviews the PIOT literature, and proposes a new PIOT framework. Chapter 5 describes the process of constructing HIOTs for iron and steel and plastics in the Netherlands (1990 and 1997). Applications of SDA to environmental issues are reviewed in Chapter 6. In Chapter 7, the techniques used in SDA are compared with those used in index decomposition analysis, so as to transfer techniques between the two methods. The data from Chapter 5 is analyzed with SDA in Chapter 8. The results of this are subsequently used in forecasting and backcasting scenario analyses in Chapter 9. Chapter 10 concludes.

NOTES

1. Material flows are indirectly related to other environmental problems as well. For example, oil spills are the result of the necessity to transport this physical substance. Excessive logging can lead to a loss of biodiversity. Policies that reduce the use of oil and wood therefore reduce these environmental risks.
2. The terms 'physical flows', 'material flows', 'physical throughput' and 'material throughput' will be used interchangeably to refer to the movement of physical substances. The term 'throughput' was proposed by Daly (1977).
3. Estimates differ as to when rapid growth began. For example, Mokyr (1999) estimates the transition to have occurred around 1760, while Maddison (2001) suggests that it was around 1820.
4. It has been suggested that short-term productivity growth started to slow down from the mid-1970s (Griliches, 1994).
5. There are different interpretations of sustainability. 'Strong sustainability' has been defined as non-decreasing stocks of economic and environmental capital. 'Weak sustainability' only requires the total capital stock not to decrease, thus allowing for substitutability of environmental and economic capital (see, for example, Turner et al., 1992).
6. Van den Bergh and de Mooij (1999) distinguish five perspectives in the growth debate: 1) The 'immaterialist' asserts that economic growth is undesirable; 2) the 'pessimist' believes that economic growth cannot continue indefinitely; 3) the 'technocrat' believes that sustained economic growth can be supported by technological solutions; 4) the 'opportunist' assumes that ultimate collapse is inevitable given the nature of human beings; and 5) the 'optimist' argues that economic growth is a necessary condition for the improvement of environmental quality.
7. Grossman and Krueger (1995) find that for almost every pollutant the turning point is below \$8000 per capita. This threshold varies for each pollutant.
8. Relinking is the increase of environmental pressures with economic growth.
9. This relationship is expressed in Einstein's famous equation $E = mc^2$.
10. This has led to the idea of 'industrial parks', such as the one at Kalundborg, Denmark, based on the principles of industrial ecology. In these parks, spatial proximity allows companies to close materials cycles and gain competitive advantages, notably because waste by-products can be used by other firms (Chertow, 2000).
11. Some publications compare or combine different models. For example, MFA/SFA, LCA and partial equilibrium models are compared in Bouman et al. (2000), and LCA and IO analysis in Lenzen (2001); Heijungs and Suh (2001) and Suh (2004b).
12. 'Delinking' and 'decoupling' are used to refer to the more general phenomenon of the reduction of environmental pressure relative to economic output. Dematerialization is specifically used in relation to material flows.
13. See also the special issue on NAMEA of *Structural Change and Economic Dynamics*, 1999, Vol. 10.
14. Frameworks that are not discussed in detail in Section 1.4 are Richardson (1972), Johnson and Bennet (1981), and Schaffer (2001).

2. Input–Output Tables and Models

2.1 INTRODUCTION

The history of input–output (IO) tables and modeling dates from 1936, when Wassily Leontief published his article 'Quantitative input and output relations in the economic system of the United States' in the *Review of Economics and Statistics* (Leontief, 1936). This article discusses the construction of an economic transactions table that Leontief based on the *Tableau Economique*, proposed by the physiocrat François Quesnay in 1758. The latter framework was designed to register the flow of money between landowners, farmers and artisans.[1] Leontief applied and adjusted this idea, producing a 41-sector table for the United States, which subsequently became known as an 'IO table'.

The IO table records all transactions associated with economic activities. Leontief also developed the first IO models, which are based on the IO table. His 1941 book introduced the assumptions that led to the now well-known IO model (Leontief, 1941). The most modern mechanical calculators available at the time were used to solve the set of simultaneous equations of the IO model for the years 1919 and 1929. The subsequent development of the IO framework has been driven by its two application fields: accounting and modeling.[2]

IO tables, and derived frameworks, such as supply and use tables (SUT) and the Social Accounting Matrix (SAM), are used by statistical bureaus as frameworks for constructing National Accounts. The 'System of National Accounts' (SNA) Handbook recommends the use of SUT, rather than IO tables, for National Accounts (UN, 1968, 1993). The advantages of the SUT as an accounting framework, and their relationship with the IO table are discussed in Chapter 3. The SAM adds more information about financial flows to the SUT framework. Categories such as household income and labor are accounted for in greater detail than in the IO or SUT (Stone, 1961).

IO models are based on the data contained in an IO table. The assumptions of the IO model impose certain requirements on the IO table, which are discussed in this chapter. The IO model has been applied to many fields, including environmental issues. It is a popular tool for analysis because it has several attractive features. IO models allow for detailed models of the structure of the economy because of the disaggregated data that are contained in the IO table. Furthermore, an IO model is capable of assessing the direct and indirect demand effects, which makes it a useful tool to analyze economic changes. Moreover, IO models are based on straightforward assumptions, which make the model easy to apply and interpret.[3]

The organization of this chapter is as follows: the structure of an IO table is further examined in Section 2.2. Section 2.3 then discusses the interpretation and assumptions of the IO model. In Section 2.4, a survey of IO models that have been applied to environmental issues is presented. The hybrid model, which is used in this book, is discussed in Section 2.5. Section 2.6 concludes.

2.2 INPUT–OUTPUT TABLES

An IO table depicts the transactions associated with the production processes of an economic system. The input requirement of each production process is recorded, as well as the output of products. The table has a spatial dimension (county, state, region, country or supra-national region) as well as a time dimension (quarterly or annual). The production structure of the economy is split into production units (industry, commodity or activity). Production is defined as all goods and services that are intended to be sold on the market or used by the production unit itself, as well as goods and services produced by the government and non-profit organizations with paid employees (UN, 1993). This means that household work, for example, is not included.

Table 2.1 shows the structure of an IO table. The columns depict the input requirements of a production unit. Some inputs are purchased from other production units: these are the 'intermediate inputs', represented by matrix Z. Inputs that are not produced by other production units are called 'primary inputs' (matrix K). For example, the primary inputs of a monetary IO table are labor and capital depreciation. The total inputs of a production unit are given by the input vector q' (where q' is the transposed vector of q).

The rows indicate the destination of the outputs of the production units.[4] Some of the output goes to other production units (intermediate outputs Z). The remainder of the products is supplied to final markets, referred to as final demand (matrix Y). This includes categories such as private consumption, government consumption and exports. The total output for all sectors is given by the output vector q. The IO table is balanced: the sum of the inputs of a production unit is equal to the sum of its outputs. Equation 2.1 reflects this balance (where i represents the appropriate summation vectors):

$$Z' \cdot i + K' \cdot i = Z \cdot i + Y \cdot i = q \qquad (2.1)$$

Table 2.1 An input–output table

	Production units	Final demand	Total output
Production units	Z	Y	q
Primary inputs	K		
Total inputs	q'		

The IO table in Table 2.1 disaggregates the producers of the economy into 'production units'. There are three types of production units in the literature:

1. *Industry.* An industry-by-industry or institutional IO table is based on the organizational units of the economy.
2. *Commodity.* A commodity-by-commodity or functional IO table depicts the inputs and output of commodities, irrespective of the industry in which they are produced.
3. *Activity.* An activity-by-activity IO table is an analytical production unit proposed by Konijn (1994). An activity is the equivalent of a production process in the National Accounts.

These three types of tables are produced from SUT. Chapter 3 discusses the problems and procedures involved in producing these IO tables. In general, IO tables are associated with monetary values. Equation 2.1 is therefore usually expressed in financial terms: the total monetary value of the intermediate and primary inputs, which includes the profits or losses, is equal to the total monetary output. However, the IO framework lends itself to other measurement units as well. For example, IO tables can be produced in kilograms (the physical IO table (PIOT) discussed in Chapter 4) or Joules because of the mass balance principle and the law of conservation of energy.

2.3 INPUT–OUTPUT MODELS

IO models impose certain requirements on the IO table, because the data need to match the assumptions of the model. The IO model assumes homogeneous production: each production unit generates one commodity, and a commodity is produced only by one production unit. The first part of the assumption is dominant in standard microeconomic theory. For example, a traditional neoclassical production function usually specifies a single output of a production process. The issue of 'multiple production', that is the phenomenon that production units may produce several types of products, is often ignored in IO and other economic models.[5] However, methods have been developed to adapt the IO model to by-products (Stone, 1961; Londero, 2001). Wastes or emissions from production activities are typically by-products: they are clearly not the principal product of the production process, but are nevertheless intrinsically linked to the production technology. By-product models can be formulated to include scraps and waste (see for example Kagawa et al., 2002).

At the core of the IO model are the IO coefficients. These are grouped in the IO coefficients matrix A, defined in Equation 2.2 in matrix and scalar terms, respectively.

$$A = Z \cdot (\hat{q})^{-1} \quad \text{or} \quad A_{ij} = \frac{Z_{ij}}{q_j} \tag{2.2}$$

Here, Z denotes the intermediate input matrix,[6] while q is the output vector of Table 2.1. A 'hat' ($\wedge$) indicates that the vector has been diagonalized, that is the vector is transformed into a square matrix with the values of the vector on the diagonal. The IO coefficient matrix A_{ij} gives a technological description of the intermediate input–output structure: the quantity of intermediate input i that is required to produce one unit of output j. IO models assume that the elements of A_{ij} are constant. This *fixed coefficient assumption* implies that IO coefficients are independent of the level of output. In other words, the production relations exhibit constant returns to scale.

The Leontief production function of the IO model, which results from the fixed coefficient assumption, exhibits complementarity between inputs: output cannot be increased by substituting one input for another. This assumption deviates from most neoclassical production functions, which allow for substitution between inputs. However, some authors state that, for periods of 5 years (James et al., 1978) or even 10–15 years (Fankhauser and McCoy, 1995) the fixed coefficient assumption is acceptable.[7] Note that although the static IO model uses the fixed IO coefficients assumption, dynamic models may be produced by allowing for change in IO coefficients. Effect of changes in IO coefficients can be investigated using structural decomposition analysis (SDA), which is discussed in Chapters 6 to 9.

By rearranging Equation 2.1 and using Equation 2.2 to replace intermediate input matrix Z, Equation 2.3 is derived:

$$A \cdot q + Y \cdot i = q \qquad (2.3)$$

Rearranging this identity gives:

$$q = (I - A)^{-1} \cdot Y \cdot i \qquad (2.4)$$

Equation 2.4 is the best-known formulation of the IO model, where matrix *(I − A)*$^{-1}$ is usually referred to as the 'Leontief inverse'. Mathematically, the Leontief inverse can only be found if *(I − A)* is square and non-singular. An element of the Leontief inverse matrix assesses the direct and indirect effects of a change in final demand. When the final demand matrix is *Y*, then the production units produce *Y·i* to meet the demand. This is the direct demand. However, to produce this output, the production unit requires inputs of magnitude *A·Y·i*. This constitutes an increase in the demand for all production units that provide inputs. This extra demand will, in turn, have to be satisfied by more inputs: *A(A·Y·i)=A²·Y·i*, and so on. The IO model can therefore also be represented by Equation 2.5 (Miller and Blair, 1985):

$$q = (I + A + A^2 + A^3 + ...) \cdot Y \cdot i \qquad (2.5)$$

Mathematically, equations 2.4 and 2.5 are equivalent. Therefore, elements on the diagonal of the Leontief inverse are always equal to 1 plus the indirect requirements per unit output. The off-diagonal elements constitute indirect demand only. To illustrate the IO model, Box 2.1 presents an example.

The IO model is used in a number of applications. Two of these will be used in Chapter 4: namely, impact analysis and imputation to final demand. These are discussed in Box 2.2, which continues the example of Box 2.1.

2.4 ENVIRONMENTAL INPUT–OUTPUT MODELS

The IO model has been applied to many environmental issues (for overviews, see Miller and Blair, 1985: chs 6 and 7; Duchin and Steenge, 1999; and a special issue of *Economic Systems Research*, June 1998). The use of the IO set up as an economic-environmental account was discussed in Section 1.4

Box 2.1 A numerical example of the IO model

Consider the following monetary IO table:

MIOT	Materials	Services	Final demand	Total	Units
Materials	800	200	1000	2000	euro
Services	400	200	1000	1600	euro
Labor	600	600			
Profits	200	600			
Total	2000	1600			

The IO coefficient matrix A and the resulting Leontief inverse $(I - A)^{-1}$ are:

$$A = \begin{bmatrix} 0.400 & 0.125 \\ 0.200 & 0.125 \end{bmatrix} \quad (I - A)^{-1} = \begin{bmatrix} 1.750 & 0.250 \\ 0.400 & 1.200 \end{bmatrix}$$

The Leontief inverse shows that, if the final demand for materials increases by 1 euro, then the output of producers of materials increases by 1.75 euro, with direct demand equal to 1 euro and indirect demand being 0.75 euro. Furthermore, the additional indirect demand will lead to an increase of 0.40 euro in the output of the service sector. The IO model can be verified using Equation 2.4:

$$q = (I - A)^{-1} \cdot y$$
$$q = \begin{pmatrix} 1.750 & 0.250 \\ 0.400 & 1.200 \end{pmatrix} \cdot \begin{pmatrix} 1000 \\ 1000 \end{pmatrix} = \begin{pmatrix} 2000 \\ 1600 \end{pmatrix}$$

These frameworks provide a basis for IO models of environmental issues. An advantage of the IO model is that it is capable of accommodating several kinds of units simultaneously. Economic flows and materials flows can therefore be measured in monetary physical units, respectively. Models that use multiple units are referred to as 'hybrid' or 'mixed unit' models (see Section 2.5).

Impact analysis (see Box 2.2) can also be used to study the impact on environmental pressures (Konijn et al., 1995). Imputation to final demand (see Box 2.2) has been applied to energy analysis to investigate the embodied energy or carbon dioxide of final products. Bullard III and Herendeen (1975) describe the imputed energy requirements as the 'energy costs of goods and services'. Examples of imputation analysis are Wyckoff and Roop (1994), Wilting (1996), Battjes (1999), Machado et al. (2001), Tiwari (2000), Suh et al. (2002), and Suh (2004b).

Box 2.2 Impact analysis and imputation to final demand

Impact analysis (based on the example in Box 1.1)

This method can estimate the impact of an increase in final demand. For example, consider what would happen if the final demand for materials increased by 50% and the final demand for services increased by 20%. The impact of this change can be calculated as follows:

$$\Delta q = (I - A)^{-1} \cdot \Delta y$$

$$\Delta q = \begin{pmatrix} 1.750 & 0.250 \\ 0.400 & 1.200 \end{pmatrix} \cdot \begin{pmatrix} 500 \\ 200 \end{pmatrix} = \begin{pmatrix} 925 \\ 440 \end{pmatrix}$$

Impact analysis therefore predicts that the direct demand increase of 700 euro (= 500 + 200) will lead to an increase of output of 1365 euro (= 925 + 440). This implies that indirect demand relations are responsible for an increase of output of 665 euro (1365 − 700), which is nearly 50% of the total effect.

Imputation to final demand (based on the example in Box 1.1)

The use of inputs can be imputed to final demand. For example, the embodied labor and capital, both direct and indirect, that are required per unit of final demand can be assessed. Primary input coefficients are first calculated:

$$K \cdot (\hat{q})^{-1} = \begin{bmatrix} 0.300 & 0.375 \\ 0.100 & 0.375 \end{bmatrix}$$

Multiplying this by the Leontief inverse, the matrix of cumulated primary input coefficients is obtained:

$$\Phi = K \cdot (\hat{q})^{-1} \cdot (I - A)^{-1} = \begin{bmatrix} 0.675 & 0.525 \\ 0.325 & 0.475 \end{bmatrix}$$

The resulting matrix of direct and indirect demand for primary inputs indicates that 1 euro of final demand of materials embodies 0.675 euro of labor and 0.325 euro of profits. Other inputs or outputs, such as energy and emissions, can also be imputed to final demand.

The augmented Leontief model, proposed in Leontief (1970) and applied in Leontief and Ford (1972), is an accounting framework as well as a model. In this model, the emissions of pollutants are recorded in physical units in the intermediate demand matrix. The corresponding extra columns in the intermediate input matrix represent the cost structures of pollution abatement. The final demand of the pollution row indicates the tolerated level of pollution. Theoretical publications which discuss this model are Steenge (1978), Idenburg and Steenge (1991), Perman et al. (1996) and Luptacik and Böhm (1999).

IO models are suited to scenario analysis. Duchin and Lange et al. (1994) estimate technological developments to assess the sustainable scenario implicit in the Brundtland Report (WCED, 1987). They subsequently combine this with a 'World' model structure, which continues earlier work by Leontief et al. (1977). See also Idenburg (1993) for an extensive application of the World model to fuels in road transport. In the 'DEOS' model for the Netherlands, a monetary IO model is linked to data for nine types of emissions as well as inputs of water, wood and fish. The resulting model is used to optimize the value added, given a number of environmental targets for 2030 (Dellink et al., 1996). Other topics that are related to material flows and have been analyzed in IO models include remanufacturing (Ferrer and Ayres, 2000), recycling (Duchin and Lange, 1998), solid-waste management (Huang et al., 1994), logging of tropical wood (Hamilton, 1997), exhaustible resources (Kurz and Salvadori, 2000), and recycling (Nakamura, 1999).

This book covers four environmental applications of the IO framework. First, a physical IO table (PIOT) is discussed in Chapter 4. This is an economy-environment accounting framework that has recently been constructed for several countries. Second, structural decomposition analysis (SDA) is discussed in Chapters 6 to 8. SDA compares IO models for two different years in order to assess the effects of structural change on environmental emissions, energy use or material flows. Third, Chapter 9 presents forecasting and backcasting scenario analyses using the SDA results. Finally, hybrid IO models, which are used throughout chapters 4–9, are discussed in the next section.

2.5 HYBRID INPUT–OUTPUT MODELS

The 'hybrid' or 'mixed-unit' IO model accommodates multiple units. Each row of the hybrid IO table (HIOT) is recorded in its own unit of measurement. For example, Leontief (1966: p. 135) introduces a model in which outputs are measured in 'bushels of wheat' or 'yards of cloth'. The primary input of labor is expressed in 'man-years of labor'. Bullard III and Herendeen (1975) applied a hybrid model to energy analysis by expressing each of the rows of energy products in Joules. There are two advantages to a hybrid IO model: the hybrid coefficients often provide a better representation of technological requirements than monetary coefficients; and the hybrid model is consistent with mass and energy balance.

With regard to the first advantage, Bullard III and Herendeen (1975) and

Miller and Blair (1985) suggest that the hybrid coefficients provide a better description of the technological relationship between inputs and output, because monetary IO coefficients include price effects. The coefficients A_{ij}, shown in Equation 2.2, are a ratio of monetary values in the monetary IO model. In the hybrid model, different units may be used for the numerator and denominator. Consider the example of metal sheeting required for the bodywork of a car. The hybrid IO coefficient is shown in Equation 2.6.[8]

$$A^*_{met,car} = \frac{\text{kg of metal sheeting}}{\text{number of cars}} \qquad (2.6)$$

The monetary IO coefficient can be written as the product of the hybrid coefficient and the price ratio $p_{met,car}$ of the input and output, as shown:

$$A_{met,car} =$$
$$\frac{\text{kg of metal sheeting}}{\text{number of cars}} \times \frac{\text{price per kg of metal sheeting}}{\text{price per car}} = \qquad (2.7)$$
$$A^*_{met,car} \cdot P_{met,car}$$

The fixed coefficient assumption assumes that all IO coefficients A remain constant, irrespective of the level of output. Equation 2.8 shows which condition this implies for the hybrid IO coefficients, and Equation 2.9 does the same for the monetary IO coefficient:

$$\frac{dA^*_{met.car}}{dq^{car}} = 0 \qquad (2.8)$$

$$\frac{dA_{met,car}}{dq^{car}} = \frac{dA^*_{met.car}}{dq^{car}} \cdot P_{met,car} + A^*_{met.car} \cdot \frac{dp_{met,car}}{dq^{car}} = 0 \qquad (2.9)$$

Comparison of equations 2.8 and 2.9 shows that the fixed coefficient assumption is less restrictive for the hybrid coefficient. For the hybrid model the amount of metal sheeting required per car is assumed to remain constant. In the case of the monetary IO coefficient, an additional - restrictive - assumption is required: the price ratio of the input and output is assumed to be constant.[9]

The second advantage of the hybrid IO model is that it adheres to mass and energy balance principles. To show this, consider the four types of physical flows that are of interest to environmental analysis:

1. Physical extraction, such as mining, fishing, and logging.
2. Use of physical goods, such as plastics.
3. Supply of physical goods, such as fossil fuels.
4. Physical emissions, such as carbon dioxide.

These four types of physical flows can be linked to the hybrid or monetary IO models, as shown in Table 2.2. In each of these models, an intensity vector n or n_y is added to the standard IO model, which indicates, respectively, the intensity of the material flow per unit output or final demand. The models for the 'use of physical goods' and 'physical emissions' include a final demand term because goods are consumed and emissions are generated, respectively, by final demand components. For the sake of simplicity it is assumed that final demand does not lead to physical extraction and that the production sectors are the sole suppliers of physical products.

Table 2.2 Hybrid and monetary IO models

	Hybrid model	Monetary model
Physical extraction	$n^{*ext} \cdot \left(I - A^*\right)^{-1} \cdot y^*$	$n^{ext} \cdot \left(I - A\right)^{-1} \cdot y$
Use of physical goods	$n^{*use} \cdot \left(I - A^*\right)^{-1} \cdot y^* + n_y^{*use} \cdot y^*$	$n^{use} \cdot \left(I - A\right)^{-1} \cdot y + n_y^{use} \cdot y$
Supply of physical goods	$n^{*sup} \cdot \left(I - A^*\right)^{-1} \cdot y^*$	$n^{sup} \cdot \left(I - A\right)^{-1} \cdot y$
Physical emissions	$n^{*emis} \cdot \left(I - A^*\right)^{-1} \cdot y^* + n_y^{*emis} \cdot y^*$	$n^{emis} \cdot \left(I - A\right)^{-1} \cdot y + n_y^{emis} \cdot y$

Note: Asterisks denote a hybrid variable. The following superscripts are used: *ext*-physical extraction; *use*-use of physical goods; *sup*-supply of physical goods; *emis*-physical emissions.

An impact analysis of these models is illustrated in Box 2.3. Mass balance dictates that extraction of physical flows must equal emissions plus stock changes. Furthermore, the use of physical goods plus the stock changes must equal the supply of physical goods. Box 2.3 illustrates that the hybrid model always adheres to the mass balance principle, while the monetary model does not in the presence of non-uniform prices, that is when different customers pay different prices (Miller and Blair, 1985).[10]

So which units should be used in a hybrid specification? For many outputs there is a 'natural unit' of measurement, which is the unit that best describes the functionality of an input in technological processes or consumption. 'Best' means that the unit leads to IO coefficients that deviate least from the

Box 2.3 Mass balance in the hybrid IO and monetary IO model

Assume that the following HIOT underlies the MIOT of Box 2.1:

HIOT	Materials	Services	Final demand	Total	Units
Materials	40	20	50	110	kg
Services	4	2	10	16	service unit

The prices can be derived from the MIOT and the HIOT:

Prices	Materials	Services	Final demand	Total	Units
Materials	20	10	20	18.2	€/kg
Services	100	100	100	100	€/service unit

Also assume the following extraction and emissions data:

Physical flow	Materials	Services	Final demand	Total	Units
Extraction	130	0	0	130	kg
Emission	60	20	50	130	kg

As shown in Table 2.2, environmental analysis can focus on four issues: extraction, use, supply and emissions. The following intensity vectors n shown below are based on the data in this Box and Box 2.1.

$$n^{*ext} = \begin{pmatrix} 130 & 0 \\ 110 & 16 \end{pmatrix} \qquad n_y^{*use} = \begin{pmatrix} 50 & 0 \\ 50 & 10 \end{pmatrix} \qquad n^{*emis} = \begin{pmatrix} 60 & 20 \\ 110 & 16 \end{pmatrix}$$

$$n^{*sup} = \begin{pmatrix} 110 & 0 \\ 110 & 16 \end{pmatrix} \qquad n^{ext} = \begin{pmatrix} 130 & 0 \\ 2000 & 1600 \end{pmatrix} \qquad n_y^{use} = \begin{pmatrix} 50 & 0 \\ 1000 & 1000 \end{pmatrix}$$

$$n^{sup} = \begin{pmatrix} 110 & 0 \\ 2000 & 1600 \end{pmatrix} \qquad n^{*use} = \begin{pmatrix} 40 & 20 \\ 110 & 16 \end{pmatrix} \qquad n^{use} = \begin{pmatrix} 40 & 20 \\ 2000 & 1600 \end{pmatrix}$$

$$n^{use} = \begin{pmatrix} 40 & 20 \\ 2000 & 1600 \end{pmatrix} \qquad n^{sup} = \begin{pmatrix} 110 & 0 \\ 2000 & 1600 \end{pmatrix} \qquad n_y^{emis} = \begin{pmatrix} 50 & 0 \\ 1000 & 1000 \end{pmatrix}$$

Assume a 50% and 20% increase in the final demand for materials and services respectively (the same impact analysis as Box 2.2). The following results are obtained for the eight models of Table 2.2:

Physical flows	Hybrid model	Monetary model
Physical extraction	56.33 kg	60.13 kg
Use of physical goods	47.67 kg	49.00 kg
Supply of physical goods	47.67 kg	50.88 kg
Physical emissions	56.33 kg	58.25 kg

The results shows that mass balance only holds for the hybrid unit model, that is extraction = emission (both 56.33 kg) and supply = use (both 47.67 kg). The results also show that the mass balances for the monetary model do not hold. The reader should note that if there were uniform prices for materials, the mass balance for the monetary model would also hold.

fixed coefficient assumption. For example, the use of coal to produce electricity can be measured in kilograms or in Joules. Since coal comes in varying qualities, the hybrid coefficient of kilograms of coal per kWh of electricity is less likely to be constant than the embodied Joules in coal required per kWh of electricity. Furthermore, the function of the coal in this example is to produce energy. Joules are therefore the natural units.[11]

The hybrid model has a number of drawbacks. Production units of an IO table are inevitably aggregates. If the natural units of the sub-aggregates differ, this makes aggregate IO tables impossible from a theoretical point of view, that is the classification has to be very detailed. Alternatively, a less aggregated table, with 'second-best' natural units has to be accepted. Note also that the technological or demand characteristics of a product are often very difficult to capture in a single natural unit. For example, the demand for computers depends on multiple specifications of the machine. In this case, it might be adequate to use monetary units, which implicitly provide a value for these features, rather than to look for the elusive natural unit.

2.6 CONCLUSIONS

An IO table is used as an accounting framework and a source of data for IO modeling. The IO table is balanced, that is, the sum of the value of the inputs of a production unit equals the value of its total output. Two assumptions are required for IO modeling: namely, the homogeneous production and fixed IO coefficient assumptions. The model is capable of economy-wide analysis of the direct and indirect effects, in applications such as impact analysis and imputation to final demand. The IO model has been applied to a variety of environmental issues.

Monetary tables are most common in the IO framework, but an IO table can also be constructed in other units. IO models that are based on multiple units are referred to as 'hybrid models'. Each output in the IO model is measured in a natural unit which best reflects its technological or demand function. In this case, it provides a more accurate and time independent description of the technological relationships. The hybrid model performs better than the monetary IO model when there are non-uniform prices. The hybrid model is consistent with the mass balance principle in this situation. However, for uniform prices, both models perform equally.

NOTES

1. Kuczynski and Meek (1972) reproduce Quesnay (1766) and earlier *Tableau* versions.
2. Miller and Blair (1985) is the most commonly cited textbook on IO modeling. Rose and Miernyk (1989) provide a historical overview.
3. The IO method is no longer in the mainstream of economics. Up to the 1970s, articles on IO modeling appeared in most prestigious economic journals. This is no longer the case, despite the fact that IO models are widely applied. Los (2001) provides a brief discussion of this development as well as suggestions on how IO can recapture its position in economics.
4. IO tables record the origin and final destination of a transaction, without recording the transport and retail transactions. For example, a hammer is produced by a firm, sold to a store and then sold to a consumer. In this case, the IO table only records the sale of the hammer to the consumer. The sales and transport margins are assumed to be an input of the hammer-producing firm.
5. There are several types of multiple production (Konijn, 1994). A *subsidiary product* has a different technological production process from the principal product of an industry, for example, a food company that makes its own packaging. A *by-product* is unavoidably linked to the production of the principal product, for example, the production of gas by blast furnaces. *Joint products* occur when a production process does not have a clear principal or secondary product, for example, the production of meat and leather from cattle.
6. The model that uses the intermediate inputs is referred to as the 'open IO model'. In the 'closed IO model' some of the primary inputs and final demand categories are transferred to the IO coefficient matrix. For example, an IO model, which is closed with respect to households, includes the row of wages and the column of consumption (Miller and Blair, 1985).
7. Activity analysis, which was developed by Kantorovich and Koopmans simultaneously, can overcome the problem of fixed coefficients (see Ayres, 1978 and Kandelaars, 1998).
8. An asterisk is used to indicate a hybrid variable.
9. Strictly speaking, the fixed coefficient assumption could also imply that changes in the price ratio and hybrid coefficients cancel each other out exactly. This is, however, unlikely in reality.
10. Similarly, Miller and Blair (1985: Ch. 6) show that in the case of non-uniform prices the monetary IO model does not adhere to the energy conservation restriction of secondary and primary energy sources.
11. The natural unit may vary according to the production process in which the output is used. For example, fossil fuels can be used to produce energy or plastics. For the production of energy, their natural units are Joules, while for the production of plastics it is their mass. The hybrid model is not capable of multiple units in a single row of an IO table. For this example, the fossil fuel row would therefore have to be separated into two rows, to reflect these two functions of fossil fuels: energy and plastic production.

3. Constructing Input–Output Tables: Theory

3.1 INTRODUCTION

This chapter will describe the structure of monetary, physical and hybrid supply and use tables (SUT) as well as their conversion to input–output (IO) tables. The 'System of National Accounts' (SNA) handbook recommends using SUT as the basis for the National Accounts (UN, 1968, 1993). These tables are suited to the source statistics because they have an industry-by-commodity structure. Furthermore, they allow the recording of multiple products for a single industry. These advantages make them more suitable as accounting frameworks than IO tables. Many countries have, therefore, introduced these tables. For example, the Netherlands has constructed them for each year since 1987 (de Boer et al., 1999).

SUT can be converted to symmetrical IO tables, with industry-by-industry, commodity-by-commodity or activity-by-activity dimensions. These tables are produced by making assumptions about the technological or sales structure of the economy. However, these assumptions do not always correspond to the requirements of the IO model. Therefore, this chapter examines the necessary conditions to produce monetary, physical and hybrid tables that are consistent with the assumptions of the IO model.

The organization of this chapter is as follows. Section 3.2 presents the framework of the SUT. In Section 3.3 the different methods of constructing IO tables are discussed. Section 3.4 identifies four reasons for problems in constructing IO tables from SUT, illustrated by a numerical example. Section 3.5 concludes.

3.2 SUPPLY AND USE TABLES

In this section, SUT in monetary, physical and hybrid units are discussed. This introduction differs from traditional introductions of SUT because it distinguishes elements that are specific to material flows, such as residual by-products and emissions to nature. A monetary supply table, shown in Table

Table 3.1 A monetary supply table

Monetary supply	Industries	Total
Commodities	V'	q
Supply of residuals	W'	w
Total	g'	

Table 3.2 A physical supply table

Physical supply	Industries	Total
Commodities	V'	q
Supply of residuals	W'	w
Emissions to nature	E'	e
Total	g'	

3.1, records all goods and services that are produced by industries (matrix V').[1] Furthermore, industries sell residual by-products, such as scrap metal, to other firms (W'). The total quantity of each commodity is recorded in vector q (= $V' \cdot i$), while the total value of the supply of residuals is denoted by w (= $W' \cdot i$). Here i denotes a summation vector. The total value of the products made in each industry is recorded in vector g (= $V \cdot i + W \cdot i$).

The physical supply table records the physical outputs of industries. These include all physical commodities and residuals, whether they have economic value or not. Table 3.2 shows a physical supply table. The total physical output of each commodity is given by vector q (= $V' \cdot i$), while the total physical output of each industry is equal to vector g (= $V \cdot i + W \cdot i + E \cdot i$). The difference between the supply of residuals w (= $W' \cdot i$) and emissions to nature e (= $E' \cdot i$) is that the former type of waste by-products are supplied to other industries, while the latter are directly emitted to natural water, soil and air. Emissions to nature do not have a market price (although they may represent a social cost), while the residuals supplied usually have a price.

Table 3.3 A monetary use table

Monetary use	Industries	Final demand	Total
Commodities	U	Y	q
Use of residuals	R		w
Primary inputs	K		k
Total	g'		

Table 3.4 A physical use table

Physical use	Industries	Final demand	Total
Commodities	U	Y	q
Use of residuals	R		w
Raw materials	D		d
Total	g'		

Commodity balance (euro)	$V'i = Ui + Yi = q$	(3.1)
Industry balance (euro)	$i'V' + i'W = i'U = g'$	(3.2)
Commodity balance (kg)	$V\hat{\imath} = Ui + Yi = q$	(3.3)
Industry balance (kg)	$i'V' + i'W' + i'E' = i'U + i'R + i'D = g'$	(3.4)

The physical and monetary supply tables differ in a number of ways. The monetary matrix V' includes all transactions of goods and services in the economy. The physical industrial production matrix V' only records the output of physical commodities. This means that physical goods appear in both tables, while services, which are generally intangible commodities, are only registered in the monetary table. In the physical supply table, residuals are recorded in matrices W' and E'. In the monetary supply table only the wastes that are sold are recorded in matrix W'. Residuals can sometimes lead to costs, such as collection, landfilling and incineration charges. These costs are recorded as services in the monetary use tables. Eco-taxes, emission charges or permits could be recorded as primary inputs in the use table.

The use tables are discussed next. The monetary use table, shown in Table 3.3, records the use of commodities (U), residuals (R) and primary inputs (K) by each industry, as well as the consumption of commodities by final demand categories (Y). The use table is similar to an IO table, except that the use table has an asymmetrical industry-by-commodity structure. The monetary output value of commodities is recorded in vector q $(= U \cdot i + Y \cdot i)$, the total use of primary inputs in vector k $(= K \cdot i)$, the total use of residuals in vector r $(= R \cdot i)$, while vector g $(= U' \cdot i + R' \cdot i + K' \cdot i)$ denotes the total cost of the inputs required by each industry.

The physical use table records the physical inputs of commodities, residuals and raw materials, as shown in Table 3.4.[2] The physical output of each commodity is recorded in vector q $(= U \cdot i + Y \cdot i)$, the use of residuals in vector r $(= R \cdot i)$, the use of raw materials in vector d $(= D \cdot i)$, while vector g $(= U' \cdot i + R' i + D' \cdot i)$ records the mass of physical inputs per industry.

The monetary and physical use tables differ in several ways. Similarly to the supply tables, the monetary use table contains information on all goods and services in matrices U and Y, while the physical use table only includes physical commodities in matrices U and Y. Furthermore, the non-industrial inputs are different: primary inputs K in the monetary use table and raw materials D in the physical table. Industries require primary inputs, such as labor and capital goods depreciation, social charges and profits. None of these are recorded in the physical use table. On the other hand, raw materials are not recorded in monetary use tables, since these are supplied by nature. Both physical and monetary use tables record the use of residuals, the sum of which is equal to the sum of residuals supplied, that is, $r = w$ and $r = w$.

The SUT presented are balanced. This means that commodity totals (q or q) of the SUT are equal, as are the industry totals (g' or g'). The balance equations are given in equations 3.1 to 3.4. The fact that the commodity and industry dimensions of the SUT balance makes this a good accounting framework. SUT, both monetary and physical, are constructed using information from a variety of sources, such as production statistics, international trade statistics, labor accounts, waste statistics, capital accounts and consumer spending statistics. In the construction process, the balancing restrictions force comparison and adjustment of the data. Expert opinion on the relative quality of the different data sources is used to make these alterations.

The SUT are superior to IO tables for accounting purposes because the data that is available to national accounts is usually provided in commodity and industry dimensions. For example, for the production statistics, companies are asked to indicate the goods and services they supply and use, which leads to an industry-by-commodity account. Any conversion to a symmetrical IO table would require adjustment of the production statistics. The international trade accounts register the commodities imported and exported, which would make it difficult to integrate them in an industry-by-industry IO table. Primary input data, on the other hand, are recorded for each industry, making integration in a commodity-by-commodity IO table difficult.

SUT are further capable of recording multiple products of a single industry. Despite the superiority of SUT for accounting, their direct use in modeling is limited. The IO table is more attractive for modeling because of the symmetrical structure of intermediate demand, which allows the calculation of the Leontief inverse.

So far, SUT in monetary and physical units have been discussed. However, the supply and use framework is more versatile than this. Flows of goods and services can be measured in many other units, such as meters, square meters, cubic meters, Joules, kWh, liters, kilometers transported, surgical procedures performed, children taught, and scientific publications written. Section 2.5 discussed the idea that there is something like a 'natural unit', in which the output of each commodity can be measured. Recording each commodity in different units is also possible, and leads to a hybrid SUT, as shown in tables 3.5 and 3.6, respectively.

Table 3.5 A hybrid supply table

Hybrid supply	Industries	Output
Commodities	$V^{\bullet \prime}$	$q^{\bullet}$

Table 3.6 A hybrid use table

Hybrid use	Industries	Final demand	Output
Commodities	$U^{\bullet}$	$Y^{\bullet}$	$q^{\bullet}$

Assume each commodity row of the hybrid tables is expressed in its natural unit. For example, the supply of energy is expressed in Joules and the demand for water is expressed in cubic meters. Hybrid SUT do not have an industry balance since the inputs are all expressed in different units. Non-industrial inputs, such as the primary inputs of the monetary use table, are therefore not specified, although it is possible to add information, such as the number of workers. The commodity balance is shown in Equation 3.5:

$$V^{*'} \cdot i = U^* \cdot i + Y^* \cdot i = q^*$$ (3.5)

The hybrid specification is suited to IO modeling, but it is less suited for accounting applications, because it only balances for the commodity dimension. There are three types of SUT that balance both the commodity and industry dimensions. In this chapter, two have been discussed: the physical SUT in kilograms; and the monetary tables in current prices.[3] The third option would be SUT in energy units. Due to the conservation of energy, the input of energy must equal the useful output and energy losses.

3.3 CONSTRUCTING INPUT–OUTPUT TABLES[4]

Symmetrical IO tables are produced from SUT using a variety of approaches. In these transformation processes, the two tables are used to produce a single IO table. Essentially, the production units in the supply table are rearranged in such a way that only values on the diagonal remain. Simultaneously, assumptions are made about the input requirements of the production units and appropriate adjustments of the use tables are made. The use matrix is thereby transformed into an IO table.

In the conversion process, assumptions about the technology or sales structure of the economy are required. The sales structure is equal to the proportion of the output that is delivered to the intermediate and final demand categories. The symmetrical IO tables can have an industry-by-industry, commodity-by-commodity or activity-by-activity dimension. Four methods to produce commodity-by-commodity and industry-by-industry IO tables are summarized in Table 3.7. An activity-by-activity table will be discussed after the discussion of these four methods.

Each of these construction methods has problems. Approaches 1 and 2 are both industry-by-industry tables, which are based on market relations rather than the technological relations that are required by an IO model. Furthermore, the assumption of Approach 2, which is that an industry supplies its commodities to the consumers in the same proportions, is implausible. Approach 3 assumes that all commodities are made using the same production process, irrespective of where they are produced. But this assumption is rarely met in practice. However, an advantage of this approach is that, from a theoretical point of view, the commodity technology assumption corresponds to the fixed coefficients assumption of the IO model

(Konijn, 1994: p. 119). Approach 4 uses the assumption that all commodities made by an industry are produced in the same way, which is highly implausible. Furthermore, the industry technology assumption is inconsistent: multiplication of the resulting IO coefficients matrix by the supply matrix does not yield the use table.

Table 3.7 Approaches to produce symmetrical IO tables[5]

	Dimension	Assumption	Assumption in words
1.	Industry-by-industry	Fixed commodity sales structure	Each commodity has its own specific sales structure, irrespective of the industry by which it is produced[6]
2.	Industry-by-industry	Fixed industry sales structure	Each industry has its own specific sales structure, irrespective of its product mix[7]
3.	Commodity-by-commodity	Commodity technology	Each commodity is produced in its own specific way, irrespective of the industry by which it is produced
4.	Commodity-by-commodity	Industry technology	Each industry has its own specific way of production, irrespective of its product mix

Since the assumptions of Approach 3 are theoretically equivalent to the IO model, it is often regarded as the best IO table. However, when such tables are produced for real national economies, negative elements appear in the IO coefficients matrix. Before this phenomenon is considered, the mathematical formulation of the commodity technology assumption is discussed. This assumes that there is a production recipe for each commodity that is the same, irrespective of the industry in which the commodity is produced. The use table is therefore linked to the supply table by a production recipe matrix A, as shown in Equation 3.6:[8]

$$U = A \cdot V'$$ (3.6)

If V' is square[9] and non-singular then the system of simultaneous equations may be solved using Equation 3.7:

$$A = U \cdot \left(V' \right)^{-1}$$ (3.7)

The production recipe matrix A derived by Equation 3.7 is equivalent to the IO coefficient matrix of the IO model. However, when Equation 3.7 is applied to the SUT of the National Accounts, negative elements occur in the A matrix, and by extension in the intermediate input matrix Z. This is nonsense from an economic point of view: negative inputs of goods and services are not possible. Konijn (1994) mentions three reasons:

1. Measurement errors: all supply or use tables contain errors, because of measurement problems or human failing.
2. Heterogeneous production processes: identical commodities are produced differently in each industry.
3. Aggregation: commodities (or industries) with different production processes are aggregated.

An additional reason can be mentioned, namely:

4. Non-uniform prices: the monetary IO coefficients cause an incorrect allocation of inputs.

These reasons are illustrated using a numerical example in Section 3.4. Konijn's (1994) solution to the problem of negative elements is constructing an activity-by-activity IO table. An activity is, in essence, a production process. If a commodity is produced by two different production processes, then the activity-by-activity IO table would distinguish two activities. The number of activities is therefore equal to the number of principal commodities multiplied by the number of production processes for each commodity.

The procedure for constructing an activity-by-activity IO table differs from the methods discussed in Table 3.7. When aggregating the SUT to produce square tables, the similarity of the production processes is the basis for aggregation. When the commodity technology assumption is applied to the SUT, the negative elements are indications of where problems in the tables lie. The specific reasons for the presence of negative elements will then have to be identified. Sometimes, a solution of these problems requires additional information, such as knowledge about production technologies. Konijn (1994) presents an activity-by-activity, or 'homogeneous', IO table for 1987 for the Netherlands (a table for 1990 is presented in Konijn and de Boer, 1993).[10]

There are number of other methods to produce IO tables from SUT: the by-product, lump sum and transfer methods (see Konijn, 1994: sect. 5.3.3). Note also that national accounts departments, such as the Netherlands, use adapted version of the methods described in this section. Recently, Almon (2000) described a method to construct commodity-by-commodity IO tables without negative elements.[11] This procedure uses the following steps to produce the IO table:

1. The initial use matrix is assumed equal to the production recipe matrix.
2. The inputs required are estimated using this production recipe.
3. These inputs are subtracted from the industry column in the use table where it is a by-product, and is added to the industry column where it is the principal product.
4. If the amount of an input that is subtracted for a particular element is larger than the value in the use table, the subtracted amount scaled.
5. The resulting production recipe matrix is entered in Step 2, and the process is continued until the solution converges.

The resulting non-negative commodity-by-commodity IO table can be assessed by comparing the actual use table with the use table that is implied by the procedure. If the difference is large it indicates that there are still problems. Appropriate adjustments of the SUT are carried out to solve these issues, and the algorithm can be performed again. This iterative process is continued until the differences in the actual and implicit use tables are deemed to be acceptable. Vollebregt and van Dalen (2002) compared the construction of the activity-by-activity table, as proposed by Konijn (1994), and the Almon (2000) procedure, and found that both required additional information and both are time consuming. There is no quick method to produce an IO table that is consistent with IO modeling assumptions.

3.4 NEGATIVE ELEMENTS: A NUMERICAL EXAMPLE

This section identifies and discusses why the commodity technology assumption produces negative elements in commodity-by-commodity IO tables. Scheme 3.1 shows a numerical example with:

- Two commodities: materials (M Com) and services (S Com);
- Two industries: materials (M Ind) and service industry (S Ind);
- One primary input: labor;
- One final demand category: consumer (Cons).

As the scheme shows, the materials industry produces both materials (260 euro) and services (80 euro), while the services industry produces only services (240 euro). The IO coefficient matrix produced by the commodity technology assumption, as shown in Equation 3.7, is multiplied by the commodity output vector, to provide the intermediate input matrix shown in Scheme 3.1. The primary inputs are found by a similar procedure. The resulting IO table includes a negative element (−20 euro) for materials required in the production of materials. Why does this happen?

Scheme 3.1 Numerical example: supply, use and IO tables (in euro)

Supply	M Ind	S Ind	Total
M Com	260	0	260
S Com	80	240	320
Total	340	240	

Use	M Ind	S Ind	Cons	Total
M Com	10	90	160	260
S Com	120	60	140	320
Labor	210	90		
Total	340	240		

IO	M Com	S Com	Cons	Total
M Com	−20	120	160	260
S Com	100	80	140	320
Labor	180	120		
Total	260	320		

Note: Symbols used for schemes 3.1–3.6 and tables 3.8 and 3.9.

M Com	Material commodity
M Ind	Material industry
M Act	Material activity
S Com	Service commodity
S Ind	Service industry
S Act	Service activity
S1 Act	Production process (activity) that produces service 1
S2 Act	Production process (activity) that produces service 2
S Act1	Production process 1 (activity) that produces service commodity
S Act2	Production process 2 (activity) that produces service commodity
Cons	Consumption

Reason 1: Measurement Errors. The source of negative elements could be errors in the supply or use tables. Assume that the correct SUT are shown in Scheme 3.2. Comparing these with Scheme 3.1 shows that the errors in the use table caused the negative elements. Application of the commodity technology assumption to the correct SUT yields an IO table without negative elements. The table now has an activity by activity structure with a materials activity (M Act) and a service activity (S Act).

Reason 2: Heterogeneous Production Processes. It is possible that the production process of services in the materials industry differs from that of services made by the services industry. The type of services they both produce are, however, identical. There are three activities: materials activity (materials made in the materials industry); service activity 1 (services made in the materials industry); and service activity 2 (services made in the service industry). Assume that the correct SUT, which distinguish the different activities, are shown in Scheme 3.3. It is easy to verify that these SUT are equivalent to the industry-by-commodity tables in Scheme 3.1. Scheme 3.3 yields an activity-by-activity IO model without negative elements. Note that, in this case, the use table is actually the same as the IO table, because the supply table is already in diagonal form.

Reason 3: Aggregation. The third source of negative elements is the aggregation of different commodities (or industries). In the following example, it is assumed that there are two types of services that are produced by two production processes. There are therefore 3 activities: materials activity (production of materials); service activity 1 (the production of service 1); and service activity 2 (the production of service 2). Assume that the correct SUT are shown in Scheme 3.4. Again, it is easily verified that this is equivalent to the industry-by-commodity tables of Scheme 3.1. The correct SUT lead to a non-negative IO table.

Reason 4: Non-Uniform Prices. The last reason for the occurrence of negative elements is because of non-uniform prices, that is, where different consumers of a commodity pay different prices. To illustrate this situation, assume that Scheme 3.5 shows the correct SUT in hybrid units. Using the data from the SUT in Scheme 3.1 and the corresponding tables in Scheme 3.5, the prices can be derived. The prices are uniform for services, and non-uniform for materials. Materials are provided for 0.33 euro/kg to the materials activity, and for 1 euro/kg to the service activity and consumers. The hybrid SUT, shown in Scheme 3.5, lead to a non-negative hybrid activity-by-activity IO table, which is the same as the commodity-by-commodity IO table.

The numerical illustrations show the following sources for negative elements in the production of commodity-by-commodity IO tables:

1. Measurement errors: These occur in all National Accounts, but can be exposed by analyzing the negative elements of the IO table as well as by verification of the SUT with source statistics or external data.
2. Heterogeneous production processes: In practice, commodities are often produced by different production processes. These errors can be eliminated if each production process is assigned an individual activity. This requires additional information about the production technologies.
3. Aggregation: This problem is affected by the level of aggregation of the commodities and industries in the SUT. Extra information is required to estimate the production process of each commodity.
4. Non-uniform prices: This may occur in National Accounts. The influence of prices can be solved by creating hybrid SUT.

Scheme 3.2 Measurement errors (in euro)

Supply	M Ind	S Ind	Total
M Com	260	0	260
S Com	80	240	320
Total	340	240	

Use	M Ind	S Ind	Cons	Total
M Com	25	75	160	260
S Com	120	60	140	320
Labor	195	105		
Total	340	240		

IO	M Com	S Com	Cons	Total
M Com	0	100	160	260
S Com	100	80	140	320
Labor	160	140		
Total	260	320		

Scheme 3.3 Heterogeneous production processes (in euro)

Supply	M Act	S Act1	S Act2	Total
M Act	260	0	0	260
S Act1	0	80	0	80
S Act2	0	0	240	240
Total	260	80	240	

Use	M Act	S Act1	S Act2	Cons	Total
M Act	10	0	90	160	260
S Act1	0	10	0	80	80
S Act2	110	0	60	70	240
Labor	140	70	90		
Total	260	80	240		

IO	M Act	S Act1	S Act2	Cons	Total
M Act	10	0	90	160	260
S Act1	0	10	0	80	80
S Act2	110	0	60	70	240
Labor	140	70	90		
Total	260	80	240		

All four reasons can, and usually will, occur simultaneously (and perhaps in opposite directions). The absence of negative elements, therefore, does not necessarily mean that the resulting IO table is correct. The reasons listed above may be causing errors, but these may not be large enough or may be negated by another source, so that the values in the table remain positive.

Scheme 3.4 Aggregation (in euro)

Supply	M Act	S1 Act	S2 Act	Total
M Act	260	0	0	260
S1 Act	0	80	40	120
S2 Act	0	0	200	200
Total	260	80	240	

Use	M Act	S1 Act	S2 Act	Cons	Total
M Act	5	5	90	160	260
S1 Act	0	30	15	75	120
S2 Act	90	0	45	65	200
Labor	165	45	90		
Total	260	80	240		

IO	M Act	S Act1	S Act2	Cons	Total
M Act	5	7.5	87.5	160	260
S Act1	0	45	0	75	120
S Act2	90	0	45	65	200
Labor	165	67.5	67.5		
Total	260	120	200		

Scheme 3.5 Non-uniform prices (hybrid units: kg and units)

Supply	M Act	S Act	Total	Units
M Act	280	0	280	kg
S Act	8	24	32	unit

Use	M Act	S Act	Cons	Total	Units
M Act	30	90	160	280	kg
S Act	12	6	14	32	units

IO	M Act	S Act	Cons	Total	Units
M Act	5	7.5	160	260	kg
S Act	0	45	75	120	unit

Finally in this section, the numerical example from Scheme 3.1 will be used to illustrate the approach proposed by Almon (2000). This procedure, which is discussed in Section 3.3, ensures a positive outcome, as shown in Table 3.8. The fact that the results are the same as those for Scheme 3.2, the measurement errors example, is coincidental.

The use table that is implied by the results of the algorithm is provided in Table 3.9. This can be compared to the use table in Scheme 3.1. The two tables differ, which implies that any of the four reasons for negative elements are still causing problems. By analyzing the source data, the source of these errors can be identified. Appropriate adjustments of the SUT can be made and the algorithm rerun. Again the observed and implicit use tables are compared in an iterative process that continues until the differences are deemed to be acceptable.

Table 3.8 Results for the Almon (2000) procedure (in euro)

IO	M Com	S Com	Cons	Total
M Com	0	100	160	260
S Com	100	80	140	320
Labor	160	140		
Total	260	320		

Table 3.9 Implicit use table for the Almon (2000) procedure (in euro)

Implicit use	M Com	S Com
M Com	0	75
S Com	100	91

3.5 CONCLUSIONS

In this chapter, the theoretical aspects of the construction of IO tables from SUT have been discussed. Symmetrical IO tables with commodity-by-commodity and industry-by-industry dimensions are produced by making assumptions about the sales structure and technology. The commodity-by-commodity IO table, which is produced using the commodity technology, adheres to the assumptions of the IO model. However, when this approach is adapted to SUT, negative elements can occur. Four reasons for these negative elements were identified, namely: measurement errors, heterogeneous production processes, commodity aggregation and non-uniform prices. This chapter has also discussed the fact that the activity-by-activity table IO table proposed by Konijn (1994) adheres to the assumptions of the IO model, and does not have negative elements. However, this method requires additional information about production processes and is therefore time consuming.

NOTES

1. Capital letters denote matrices while lowercase letters refer to vectors. Bold font is used for physical variables throughout this book, while normal font indicates monetary values. Hybrid variables have normal font but are specified by an asterisk.
2. Stock changes are ignored in the supply and use tables of this chapter. The use and supply of residuals by final demand categories, as well as the use of raw materials by final demand, are also not included in the tables. These aspects are introduced in the physical IO table (PIOT) presented in Chapter 4.
3. Appendix 5.A provides an illustration to show that supply and use tables in constant prices do not balance.
4. This section is a brief introduction to the construction of IO tables. It draws heavily from Konijn (1994), which is a theoretical study into the construction of IO tables that are consistent with the assumptions of IO analysis. Readers are referred to Konijn (1994) and Konijn and Steenge (1995) for a more complete overview of the literature.
5. The mathematical formulations are shown in Table 5.7 in Konijn (1994: p. 112)
6. Sometimes referred to as the 'industry technology' application to the industry-by-industry IO table. Konijn (1994) argues that this terminology is inaccurate.
7. Sometimes referred to as the 'commodity technology' application to the industry-by-industry IO table. Konijn (1994) argues that this terminology is inaccurate.
8. The elements of the supply and use tables that are specific to material flows are not included in this derivation.
9. Squareness is an important issue. The number of commodities in the National Accounts often exceeds the number of industries. To make the supply table square, aggregation of the commodities is thus required. Equation 3.7 allows for a non-square use table, but this leads to a non-square IO table, which cannot be used in the IO model.
10. Eurostat has recently asked all member countries to produce homogeneous IO tables every five years, from 1995 onwards.
11. Almon (2000) presents a numerical algorithm that requires input from experts. Although it is a numerical procedure rather than a theoretical approach, it is discussed in this chapter because it has recently been proposed as a means of producing symmetrical commodity-by-commodity IO tables and is being considered by Eurostat for the production of symmetrical IO tables.

4. Physical Input–Output Tables

4.1 INTRODUCTION

In the last couple of decades, increasing attention on environmental issues has stimulated interest in environmental satellite accounts to complement the monetary National Accounts. A variety of accounts have recently been summarized in the 'System of Environmental and Economic Accounting' (SEEA, 2002). For a review of the literature on economy-environment accounting frameworks, see Section 1.4.

This chapter deals with physical input–output tables (PIOT), which is one of the physical accounts of the SEEA. This data framework records all physical flows associated with the economic system. The PIOT registers flows of physical products, extraction of materials from nature, the supply and use of wastes and residuals, emissions to nature and stock changes. Furthermore, a PIOT uses the same classification schemes for production activities as the monetary IO table (MIOT). This makes the combination of PIOT-MIOT suitable for environmental-economic analysis. Similar to the MIOT, a PIOT has an accounting and modeling function.[1] In this chapter, PIOTs which have been constructed for a variety of countries are reviewed, and two variants of the PIOT are distinguished: the basic and the extended PIOT. Furthermore, a third type of PIOT, the full PIOT, is proposed in this chapter. This chapter also presents a number of indicators and modeling applications of the PIOT data. The PIOT has two main advantages.

First, like the MIOT, the PIOT and physical supply and use tables (SUT) act as an integration framework for different data sources. Data for the PIOT are obtained from a variety of sources, such as energy accounts, waste accounts, production statistics and international trade statistics. The material balance principle provides an accounting identity that forces these different data sources to be confronted. This process leads to homogenization of classification schemes and data collection methods. Furthermore, it may expose errors in the different accounts.

Second, the construction of a PIOT can improve the corresponding MIOT because it depicts a different dimension of the economy. Some parts of the MIOT, where the source data are poor, can be improved by using insights from the PIOT. For example, the use of intermediate inputs is usually not backed by good production statistics. Monetary estimates can be improved by multiplying mass values from the PIOT by a price per kilogram. Furthermore, the use of physical units makes it easier to communicate with process engineers about the implicit technological relationships.

The organization of this chapter is as follows. Section 4.2 reviews the PIOTs that have been produced for five European countries and the European Union. In Section 4.3, the basic PIOT is introduced. Section 4.4 discusses the extended PIOT proposed by Konijn et al. (1995). In Section 4.5 this extended PIOT framework is elaborated to the full PIOT structure. To illustrate the full PIOT system, a numerical example is presented in Section 4.6. Section 4.7 discusses the environmental information that can be derived from the full PIOT. Input–output modeling applications of full PIOT data are discussed in Section 4.8. Section 4.9 concludes.

4.2 SURVEY

PIOTs exist for five countries: the Netherlands (Konijn et al., 1995; Konijn et al., 1997), Germany (Stahmer et al., 1997), Denmark (Gravgård-Pedersen, 1999), Italy (Nebbia, 2000) and Finland (Mäenpää and Muukkonen, 2001; Mäenpää, 2002). A preliminary PIOT for the European Union is based on information from the German and Danish PIOTs, scaled to EU levels (Giljum and Hubacek, 2001; Hubacek and Giljum, 2003).[2] The characteristics of these six studies are summarized in Table 4.1.

Four studies record the flows for 1990, while two account for 1995. The Dutch study introduced a PIOT, which is referred to in this chapter as an 'extended PIOT', while the rest used a 'basic PIOT' structure, which is similar to the MIOT structure.[3] The basic, extended and full PIOTs will be discussed in Sections 4.3 to 4.5. Most of the studies are focused solely on the accounting function of the PIOT, while the Dutch and EU PIOTs provide modeling applications as well. The disaggregation of the production structure ranges from five to 58 industries. The German, Italian, Finnish and EU PIOTs present tables only for the total mass of materials and products, while the Dutch and Danish studies report PIOTs for specific products. For example, the Danish PIOT distinguishes nine product types.

The PIOT is an accounting framework which should adhere to three conditions if it is to be used for environmental economic modeling:

1. The PIOT must adhere to economic (IO) modeling assumptions.
2. The PIOT must adhere to National Accounts definitions.
3. The physical flows should be relevant to urgent environmental problems.

Table 4.1 Review of PIOT studies

	The Netherlands	Germany	Denmark	Finland	Italy	EU
Year	1990	1990	1990, Air emissions for 1990-92	1995	1995	1990
Type	Extended PIOT	Basic PIOT	Basic PIOT	Basic PIOT	Basic PIOT	Basic PIOT
Aim	Accounting, modeling	Accounting	Accounting	Accounting	Accounting	Modeling
Production unit (no.)	Secondary materials (differs per material)	Industries (58)	Industries (27)	Industries (30)	Industries (5)	Industries (7)
Materials specified	Cement, concrete and concrete products; Plastics; Non-ferro metals; Paper and paper products; Iron, steel and zinc; Energy.	Total mass; Energy; Water; and Other materials.	Total mass; Animal and vegetable products; Stone, gravel and building materials; Energy; Metals, machinery, means of transport; Chemical products and fertilizers; Plastics and plastic products; Wood, paper and commodities thereof; Other commodities; Packaging.	Total mass.	Total mass; Carbon.	Total mass.
Comments	Introduces the extended PIOT. Monetary and physical accounts use different classifications. Models of materials use included.	3 material groups are distinguished. Inspired subsequent studies.	Distinguishes many materials and products flows.	Work in progress. Focused on: combustion, biological material flows and water content changes.	Aggregate study in terms of industry and material classification. Text is in Italian.	An estimate of a PIOT for the EU, based on the German and Danish PIOTs. Includes PIOT modeling exercises.

All these 3 conditions are important but, in our opinion, condition 3 leaves the most room for improvement in the current literature. It is imperative that a clear link is provided between the physical flows in an economy and the environmental pressures. Unfortunately most studies in Table 4.1, could improve upon the detail with which information on extraction, emissions and recycling are reported. For instance, the Dutch study provides detailed information about physical products, but it distinguishes only a few emissions and extraction categories, such as the 'balance of additions and subtractions'.

The German PIOT, which formed the basis for the subsequent PIOTs, distinguishes nine raw materials and eleven emission categories in the physical SUT.[4] However, the PIOT that is published distinguishes only two raw materials: produced and non-produced natural assets. Emissions are recorded solely for landfills, produced and non-produced natural assets. This information is disappointing from the point of view of environmental analysis. Note however, that this is mainly an issue of presentation. The data are often available, for example, in the other physical accounts of the German study, but are not reported in the main PIOT. The Italian and Finnish PIOTs publish aggregated waste and extraction categories. The Danish study provides one extraction, one recycling and seven emission categories. However, additional environmental information can be derived from the other PIOTs for specific materials.

The focus on aggregate material flow data is also common in the related field of bulk-MFA literature, which is discussed in Section 1.4. The bulk-MFA literature suggest (in our opinion erroneously) that aggregating the mass of different materials, irrespective of their environmental impact, can be used as indicators of sustainability. Regrettably it seems that the bulk-MFA literature has inspired PIOTs to focus on aggregate emission and extraction data. Furthermore, it also explains why some PIOTs studies reported in Table 4.1 focus (too) much on accurately estimating *all* physical flows in a material balance, instead of prioritizing those that are environmentally relevant.[5] For the PIOT to become a useful part of the environmental-economic toolkit, it should focus on its function as a data source for environmental IO models. This will only be achieved if it contains sufficiently disaggregated data on environmentally-relevant physical flows.[6]

4.3 THE BASIC PIOT[7]

The MIOT and basic PIOT, shown in tables 4.2 and 4.3 respectively, are similar to the monetary and physical use tables 3.3 and 3.4, except that the commodity-by-industry use table is converted into a symmetrical production process-by-production process (activity-by-activity) structure so that it adheres to IO modeling assumptions.

The residual by-products are recorded as negative inputs, which is consistent with the by-product IO model proposed by Stone (1961). If the by-product method is not used, the increase in demand for the by-product would erroneously lead to increased demand for the principal product. For example, output of metal products increases because of a demand increase for scrap.

Assume that both tables are consistent with the homogeneous production assumptions of the IO model: each production process is assumed to create one commodity and each commodity is produced by one production process. However, in addition to the principal product, some of the production processes generate wastes.

The basic PIOT accounts for material, product and waste flows associated with economic processes. Tables 4.2 and 4.3 distinguish α production processes, η types of primary inputs, β types of raw materials and γ types of residuals.[8] The basic PIOT and MIOT tables specify the same production processes and final demand categories. The intermediate matrix Z and $\mathbf{Z}$ and the final demand vector Y and $\mathbf{Y}$ have the same dimensions. However, the MIOT contains output data for all production processes, while the PIOT only records the flows of goods that have a physical dimension.[9] However, the PIOT records all residual by-products that are supplied to other production processes in the economy (W) or emitted to nature (E). The MIOT records only the supply of residuals that have a price (W). The use of residuals by production processes is recorded in matrix R and $\mathbf{R}$. The flows of wastes to the recycling, landfilling and incineration sectors as well as emissions to nature are further specified in the full PIOT of Section 4.5. Finally, both tables have different non-industrial inputs. For the MIOT these are the primary inputs K, such as labor and capital depreciation, while for the basic PIOT it is the extraction of raw materials that is recorded in matrix D.[10]

Note that the physical flows recorded in matrices D and E are not all environmentally relevant.[11] Many inputs and outputs have no or negligible environmental impact. For example, the use of oxygen in the combustion process of fossil fuels is not considered to be an environmental problem. Similarly, the emission of water in combustion processes is not a significant issue. Nevertheless, these flows are part of the PIOT that is complete.

The MIOT and basic PIOT exhibit financial and mass balance, depicted in equations 4.1 and 4.2 respectively.

$$Z' \cdot i_\alpha + K' \cdot i_\eta + R' \cdot i_\gamma - W' \cdot i_\gamma = Z \cdot i_\alpha + Y = q \qquad (4.1)$$

$$Z' \cdot i_\alpha + D' \cdot i_\beta + R' \cdot i_\gamma - W' \cdot i_\gamma - E' \cdot i_\gamma = Z \cdot i_\alpha + Y = q \qquad (4.2)$$

where i_α, i_β, i_γ, i_η, i_α, i_β, i_γ and i_η are the appropriate summation vectors.

Table 4.2 The MIOT

MIOT		Production processes			Final demand	Output
		1	...	*α*		
Production processes	*1*					
	...		*Z*		*Y*	*q*
	α					
Primary inputs	*1*					
	...		*K*			
	η					
Use of residuals	*1*					
	...		*R*			
	γ					
Supply of residuals	*1*					
	...		*−W*			
	γ					
Total			*q′*			

Table 4.3 The basic PIOT

Basic PIOT		Production processes			Final demand	Output
		1	...	*α*		
Production processes	*1*					
	...		*Z*		*Y*	*q*
	α					
Raw materials	*1*					
	...		*D*			
	β					
Use of residuals	*1*					
	...		*R*			
	γ					
Supply of residuals	*1*					
	...		*−W*			
	γ					
Emission to nature	*1*					
	...		*−E*			
	γ					
Total			*q′*			

Equations 4.3 provide the relationship between the basic PIOT and MIOT.

$$Z' = Z' \cdot \hat{p}_\alpha$$
$$Y' = Y' \cdot \hat{p}_\alpha$$
$$W' = W' \cdot \hat{p}_\gamma \tag{4.3}$$
$$R' = R' \cdot \hat{p}_\gamma$$

Vector p_α includes the prices of goods per unit mass, while p_γ is the vector of waste prices per unit mass. Note that there is no relationship between the MIOT and basic PIOT for production processes that do not produce a physical commodity. Therefore, the equations for Z and Y only hold for physical commodities. The monetary values of the services should be obtained directly from the MIOT.

4.4 THE EXTENDED PIOT

This section discusses the PIOT framework proposed by Konijn et al. (1995). The monetary and physical accounts of their set up are shown in Figure 4.1. For the monetary accounts an activity-by-activity MIOT is used (see Section 3.3). The physical accounts, which will be referred to as the 'extended PIOT', are split into several parts. The main innovation in Figure 4.1 is the distinction between 'use for transformation' and 'final use'. The former refers to physical inputs that are converted into other physical products. Final use is similar to the final demand concept in the monetary accounts. This is the final destination of a product where the consumer utilizes the services that the physical good provides.[12]

In the empirical applications presented in Konijn et al. (1995), the monetary and physical economies have different classifications. The MIOT has an activity-by-activity structure, while the intermediate final use has an activity-by-secondary materials classification, and the use for transformation has a secondary materials-by-secondary materials structure. In the applications provided, the disaggregation of the secondary materials is greater than that of the activity classification. This has the advantage of allowing the construction of detailed physical accounts, without having to adapt the MIOT. However, for a theoretical framework, there is no reason to use different classification schemes for the monetary and physical economies.

In Section 4.5, an adapted version of this extended PIOT is presented, which will be referred to as the full PIOT. The most important addition to the Konijn et al. (1995) framework is the further specification of recycling, residual flows, residuals and packaging. Different terminology is also introduced. Use for transformation is replaced by the 'structural production process', while intermediate final use is called the 'auxiliary production process'. These terms are chosen because they reflect the technological functions of materials in production processes. The terms secondary materials and primary materials are replaced by 'intermediate inputs' and 'raw materials', respectively. This is to avoid confusion with the more common use of 'secondary materials', namely to indicate recycled materials.

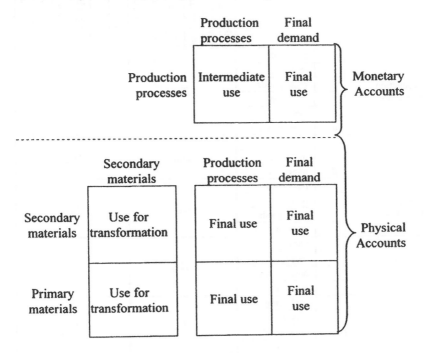

Figure 4.1 The extended PIOT with MIOT

4.5 THE FULL PIOT

In this section, the insights from the basic and extended PIOT framework, as well as other relevant aspects of material flows are combined. All aspects of extraction, products, packaging, recycling, waste and stocks are included, it will be referred to as a full PIOT. Table 4.4 shows the full PIOT framework with α production units, β types of raw materials, γ types of residuals, and δ types of stock changes. Three categories of goods (packaging, recycling and other goods) and three categories of services (landfilling, incineration and

Table 4.4 The full PIOT

Full PIOT			Structural production process							Auxiliary production process						
			I	...	...	...	...	α		I	...	...	...	...	α
			packaging	recycling	other goods	landfilling	incineration	other services		packaging	recycling	other goods	landfilling	incineration	other services
Production processes	I	packaging													
	...	recycling													
	...	other goods			Z_{str}							Z_{aux}			
	...	incineration													
	...	landfilling													
	α	other services													
Raw materials	I	materials													
	...	materials			D_{str}							D_{aux}			
	β	materials													
Use of residuals	I	packaging													
	...	recycling			R_{str}							R_{aux}			
	...	other goods													
	γ	materials													
Supply of residuals	I	packaging													
	...	recycling			$-W_{str}$							$-W_{aux}$			
	...	other goods													
	γ	materials													
Emissions to nature	I	packaging													
	...	recycling			$-E_{str}$							$-E_{aux}$			
	...	other goods													
	γ	materials													
Stock changes	I	packaging													
	...	recycling			$-S_{str}$							$-S_{aux}$			
	...	other goods													
	γ	materials													
Total					q'							0			

other services) are distinguished. Consumption is split into durable and non-durable goods. The relationship between the basic and full PIOT is provided by Equations 4.4. Variables of the basic PIOT are given on the left-hand side; full PIOT variables are provided on the right-hand side. The structural and auxiliary inputs are denoted by subscripts *str* and *aux*, respectively.

Table 4.4 (continued)

			Investment goods						Consumption		Total
			1	...	...	...	...	α	*1*	*2*	
			packaging	recycling	other goods	landfilling	incineration	other services	non-durable goods	durable goods	
Production processes	*1*	packaging									
	...	recycling									
	...	other goods			*F*				*C*		*q*
	...	incineration									
	...	landfilling									
	α	other services									
Raw materials	*1*	materials									
	...	materials							*D*$_{cons}$		*d*
	β	materials									
Use of residuals	*1*	packaging									
	...	recycling							*R*$_{cons}$		*r*
	...	other goods									
	γ	materials									
Supply of residuals	*1*	packaging									
	...	recycling			−*W*$_{inv}$				−*W*$_{cons}$		−*w*
	...	other goods									
	γ	materials									
Emissions to nature	*1*	packaging									
	...	recycling							−*E*$_{cons}$		−*e*
	...	other goods									
	γ	materials									
Stock changes	*1*	packaging									
	...	recycling			−*S*$_{inv}$				−*S*$_{cons}$		−*s*
	...	other goods									
	γ	materials									
					0				**0**		**0**

The final demand vector (*Y*) of the basic PIOT is the aggregate of the investments *(F)* and consumption (*C*) matrices. The relationship is simple: the only real difference is the distinction between the structural and auxiliary production processes, as proposed in the extended PIOT.

$$Z = Z_{str} + Z_{aux}$$
$$Y = F \cdot i_\alpha + C \cdot i_\alpha$$
$$D = D_{str} + D_{aux}$$
$$R = R_{str} + R_{aux} \qquad (4.4)$$
$$W = W_{str} + W_{aux}$$
$$E = E_{str} + E_{aux}$$

Four types of physical inputs and outputs of a production process can be distinguished: the structural production process, auxiliary production process, investment goods and unwanted physical inputs and outputs.

The structural production process encompasses all material flows that are associated with making the physical entity that is the physical good. The structural production process inputs are packaged product inputs (Z_{str}), raw materials (D_{str}) and use of residuals (R_{str}). The structural outputs are the products of the production process which are sold to other production processes (Z_{str}, Z_{aux} and F) or to consumers (C). However, not all structural inputs are converted to products. Residuals are supplied to other production processes (W_{str}) and emitted to nature (E_{str}). Stock changes are also possible (S_{str}). The mass balance of the structural production process equates the column sum to its row sum, as is shown in Equation 4.5. Note the special attention for packaging in the structural production process. Packaging is viewed as a structural input in the production process because it accompanies the finished product to the consumer. Since services do not produce physical commodities, there are no structural inputs for these production processes. The mass balance equation for the structural production process is:

$$Z_{str}' \cdot i_\alpha + D_{str}' \cdot i_\beta + R_{str}' \cdot i_\gamma - W_{str}' \cdot i_\gamma - E_{str}' \cdot i_\gamma - S_{str}' \cdot i_\delta =$$
$$Z_{str} \cdot i_\alpha + Z_{aux} \cdot i_\alpha + F \cdot i_\alpha + C \cdot i_\alpha = q \qquad (4.5)$$

The auxiliary production process includes all physical flows that are required to facilitate the production process, except those that are used in the structural production process. They also differ from investment goods because they are used within the accounting period of the IO table. The auxiliary production process uses packaged products (Z_{aux}) and raw materials (D_{aux}). Residuals (R_{aux}) can be used by, for example, the landfilling and incineration sectors.

These waste conversion processes store or transform these residual flows. The auxiliary outputs are residuals (W_{aux} and E_{aux}) and stock changes (S_{aux}). The mass balance equation for the auxiliary production process is provided in Equation 4.6.

$$Z_{aux}' \cdot i_\alpha + D_{aux}' \cdot i_\beta + R_{aux}' \cdot i_\gamma$$
$$-W_{aux}' \cdot i_\gamma - E_{aux}' \cdot i_\gamma - S_{aux}' \cdot i_\delta = 0 \qquad (4.6)$$

Investment goods are required in production processes. They facilitate production, but do not end in the products, which makes them similar to auxiliary inputs. However, investment goods are used over multiple periods. The physical balance for investment goods is shown in Equation 4.7. Packaged investment goods are supplied by other production processes *(F)*. However, in the matrix *F*, the rows for recycling and packaging are negligible. Similarly, raw materials or residuals are not used in the investment goods account.[13] On the output side, capital goods are written off and supplied to others in the economy (W_{inv}). These capital goods may be sold to other economic sectors, or to the recycling, landfilling or incineration production processes. Stock changes (S_{inv}) are also included in the investment account:

$$F_{inv}' \cdot i_\alpha - W_{inv}' \cdot i_\gamma - S_{inv}' \cdot i_\delta = 0 \qquad (4.7)$$

Unwanted materials, which have no technological function in the production process, can enter or leave a production process. The best example of an input that has no technological function is the packaging layer that accompanies all structural, auxiliary and investment inputs. This layer is only useful in the transportation and storage phase, but has no role to play in the production process itself.

Consumption also adheres to mass balance, as is shown in Equation 4.8:

$$C' \cdot i_\alpha + D_{cons}' \cdot i_\beta + R_{cons}' \cdot i_\gamma$$
$$-W_{cons}' \cdot i_\gamma - E_{cons}' \cdot i_\gamma - S_{cons}' \cdot i_\delta = 0 \qquad (4.8)$$

Consumers buy packaged products from production processes (*C*). Some of these products, such as fossil fuel-powered cars, require raw materials such as oxygen (D_{cons}). Small amounts of the residuals may also be used (R_{cons}) by consumers. The outputs of consumption are residuals that are supplied to other economic categories (W_{cons}) or emitted to the environment (E_{cons}), and stock changes (S_{cons}). Stocks of non-durable goods will be small.

The mass balance for the entire economy is defined in Equation 4.9. The raw material input of the economy $(d' \cdot i_\beta)$ is matched to the output: emissions $(e' \cdot i_\gamma)$ and stock change $(s' \cdot i_\delta)$:

$$d' \cdot i_\beta = e' \cdot i_\gamma + s' \cdot i_\delta$$

where:

$$d = D_{str} \cdot i_\beta + D_{aux} \cdot i_\beta + D_{cons} \cdot i_\beta$$

$$r = R_{str} \cdot i_\gamma + R_{aux} \cdot i_\gamma + R_{cons} \cdot i_\gamma \tag{4.9}$$

$$w = W_{str} \cdot i_\gamma + W_{aux} \cdot i_\gamma + W_{inv} \cdot i_\gamma + W_{cons} \cdot i_\gamma$$

$$e = E_{str} \cdot i_\gamma + E_{aux} \cdot i_\gamma + E_{cons} \cdot i_\gamma$$

$$s = S_{str} \cdot i_\delta + S_{aux} \cdot i_\delta + S_{inv} \cdot i_\delta + S_{cons} \cdot i_\delta$$

The waste processing flows of Table 4.4 require further clarification. Residuals are generated by production processes and consumers. One portion of these wastes is emitted to the environment (E_{str}, E_{aux}, E_{inv} and E_{cons}), while the other part is supplied to the economic sectors (W_{str}, W_{aux}, W_{inv} and W_{cons}). The latter residual flows are used by production processes as structural inputs (R_{str}) or auxiliary inputs (R_{aux}), while a small portion may be used by consumers (R_{cons}). The supply of residuals by the economy is therefore equal to the use of residuals, as shown in Equation 4.10:

$$w = r \tag{4.10}$$

The residuals that are used as structural inputs (R_{str}) are recycling flows. They are used to be embodied in physical goods. The recycling of residuals can occur in one of two ways. They can be used directly in production processes, for example scrap metal used to produce primary metal. Alternatively, they can be supplied to a recycling sector that treats the residual flow so that it may be reused, for example cars may be supplied to shredder companies. The auxiliary input of residuals (R_{aux}) is the use of residuals from the auxiliary production process. These flows include the input of residuals in the landfilling and incineration production processes.[14] In the case of landfilling, the output is a change in the stock of materials. For the incineration sector, the residuals are converted into emissions to nature and perhaps some residual ash. The latter would then be an input for the landfilling sector.[15]

4.6 THE FULL PIOT: A NUMERICAL EXAMPLE

A numerical example of a full PIOT is shown in Table 4.5. The corresponding MIOT, HIOT and price information is provided in Appendix 4.A. The technological and demand relationships are hypothetical. Ten production processes make physical products (mined metal, mined fossil fuel, basic metal, basic plastics, metal packaging, plastic packaging, recycled metal, recycled plastic, machines and objects). Three types of services are provided: landfilling, incineration and business services. Each of the 10 structural production processes of physical goods is discussed briefly.

1. *Mined Metal (MM)* is produced by extracting unmined metal ore from nature. The structural input is unmined ore. Structural outputs are mined metal and mining debris.
2.. *Mined Fossil Fuel (MFF)* is produced by extracting unmined fossil fuel from nature. The mined fossil fuel is packaged in metal packaging. Structural inputs are unmined fossil fuel and metal packaging. Structural outputs are mined fossil fuel and mining debris.
3. *Basic Metal (BM)* is produced by using mined metal and recycled metal. Structural inputs are mined metal and recycled metal. Structural outputs are basic metal and waste metal.
4. *Basic Plastic (BP)* is produced by using mined fossil fuel and recycled plastic. It is packaged in metal. Structural inputs are mined fossil fuels, recycled plastics and plastic packaging. Structural outputs are basic plastic, waste plastic and waste metal packaging.
5. *Metal Packaging (MP)* is produced using basic metal. The structural input is basic metal. The structural output is metal packaging.
6. *Plastic Packaging (PP)* is produced using basic plastic. The structural input is basic plastic. The structural output is plastic packaging.
7. *Machines (Mch)* are produced using basic metal and plastics. They are packaged in metal and plastic. Structural inputs are basic metal and basic plastics. Structural outputs are machines, waste metal, waste plastic and waste metal packaging (from the basic plastic inputs).
8. *Objects (Obj)* are produced using basic metal and plastics. They are packaged in metal and plastic. Structural inputs are basic metal and basic plastics. Structural outputs are objects, waste metal, waste plastic and waste metal packaging (from the basic plastic inputs).
9. *Recycled Metal (RM)* is produced using waste metal and waste metal packaging. Structural inputs are waste metal and waste metal packaging. The structural output is recycled metal.
10. *Recycled Plastic (RP)* is produced using waste plastic. The structural input is waste plastic. The structural output is recycled plastic.

The auxiliary production process is similar for most production processes: fossil fuels are used for energy. This combustion process requires oxygen and emits water and carbon dioxide. The landfilling and incineration sectors are different. For the landfilling sector, waste metal packaging, waste machines and objects are landfilled in storage sites, as indicated by the changes in

Table 4.5 A numerical example of a full PIOT (including packaging)

Full PIOT	Structural Production Process												
	MM	MFF	BM	BP	MP	PP	Mch	Obj	RM	RP	LF	IN	BS
Mined Metal (MM)			1843										
Mined Fossil Fuel (MFF)				1073									
Basic Metal (BM)					704		900	700					
Basic Plastics (BP)						220	550	660					
Metal Packaging (MP)		474		130			50	50					
Plastic Packaging (PP)							100	100					
Machines (Mch)													
Objects (Obj)													
Recycled Metal (RM)			691										
Recycled Plastic (RP)				390									
Landfilling (LF)													
Incineration (IN)													
Business Services (BS)													
Raw materials													
Unmined Metal (UM)	3686												
Unmined Fossil Fuel (UFF)		11850											
Oxygen (O₂)													
Use of residuals													
Waste Metal (WM)									410				
Waste Plastis (WP)										390			
Waste Metal Pack. (WMP)									281				
Waste Plastic Pack. (WPP)													
Waste Machines (WMch)													
Waste Objects (WObj)													
Supply of residuals													
Waste Metal (WM)			-230				-100	-80					
Waste Plastis (WP)				-65			-300	-220					
Waste Metal Pack. (WMP)				-98		-20	-50	-60					
Waste Plastic Pack. (WPP)													
Waste Machines (WMch)													
Waste Objects (WObj)													
Emissions to nature													
Mining debris (MD)	-1843	-7110											
Carbon dioxide (CO₂)													
Water (H₂O)													
Stock changes													
Waste Metal (WM)													
Waste Plastis (WP)													
Waste Metal Pack. (WMP)													
Waste Plastic Pack. (WPP)													
(Waste) Machines (WMch)													
(Waste) Objects (WObj)													
Total	1843	5214	2304	1430	704	200	1150	1150	691	390	0	0	0

Note: Pack. – Packaging; Cons. – Consumption; n.d. – Non-Durables; d. – Durables.

Table 4.5 (continued)

	Auxiliary Production Process												
	MM	MFF	BM	BP	MP	PP	Mch	Obj	RM	RP	LF	IN	BS
MM													
MFF	406	1043	507	286	39	11	220	220	38	21			251
BM													
BP													
MP													
PP													
Mch													
Obj													
RM													
RP													
LF													
IN													
BS													
Raw materials													
UM													
UFF													
O_2	1261	3244	1577	890	120	34	684	684	118	67		1352	781
Use of residuals													
WM													
WP													195	
WMP												423		
WPP													200	
WMch												727		
WObj												739		
Supply of residuals													
WM													
WP													
WMP	-37	-95	-46	-26	-4	-1	-20	-20	-3	-2			-23
WPP													
WMch													
WObj													
Emissions to nature													
MD													
CO_2	-1157	-2974	-1446	-816	-110	-31	-628	-628	-108	-61		-1239	-716
H_2O	-473	-1218	-592	-334	-45	-13	-257	-257	-44	-25		-507	-293
Stock changes													
WM													
WP													
WMP												-423		
WPP													
WMch												-727		
WObj												-739		
Total	0	0	0	0	0	0	0	0	0	0	0	0	0

Table 4.5 (continued)

	Investment													Cons.		Output
	MM	MFF	BM	BP	MP	PP	Mch	Obj	RM	RP	LF	IN	BS	n.d.	d.	
MM																1843
MFF														1100		5214
BM																2304
BP																1430
MP																704
PP																200
Mch	74	191	93	52	3	1	40	40	3	2	2	2	230		417	1150
Obj	37	95	46	26	1	0	20	20	1	1	2	2	115		781	1150
RM																691
RP																390
LF																0
IN																0
BS																0
Raw materials																
UM																3686
UFF																11850
O_2														3422		14235
Use of residuals																
WM																410
WP																585
WMP																704
WPP																200
WMch																727
WObj																739
Supply of residuals																
WM																-410
WP																-585
WMP	-5	-12	-6	-3	0	0	-3	-3	0	0	0	0	-15	-100	-52	-704
WPP	-10	-25	-12	-7	0	0	-5	-5	0	0	0	0	-30		-104	-200
WMch	-46	-119	-58	-33	-2	-1	-25	-25	-2	-1	-2	-2	-143		-272	-727
WObj	-23	-59	-29	-16	-1	0	-13	-13	-1	0	-2	-2	-71		-510	-739
Emissions to nature																
MD																-8953
CO_2														-3138		-13053
H_2O														-1284		-5343
Stock changes																
WM																0
WP																0
WMP																-423
WPP																0
WMch	-18	-47	-23	-13	-1	0	-10	-10	-1	0	-1	-1	-57		-91	-1000
WObj	-9	-24	-12	-7	0	0	-5	-5	0	0	-1	-1	-29		-170	-1000
Total	0	0	0	0	0	0	0	0	0	0	0	0	0	0	0	0

the auxiliary stocks shown in Table 4.5.[16] For the incineration sector, waste plastics and waste plastic packaging are burned in the presence of oxygen to produce water and carbon dioxide. Machines and objects are used as investment goods and consumer products. A distinction is made between non-durable consumption, such as fossil fuels on the one hand and machines and objects (durable commodities) on the other.

4.7 ENVIRONMENTAL INFORMATION FROM A PIOT

The full PIOT contains a wide variety of environmental information. A number of examples, based on the information in Table 4.5 and Appendix 4.A are provided in this section. Full PIOTs can provide a number of different types of information such as environmental pressure, chemical composition of products, element cycles in the economy, dematerialization indicators, and international indicators.

Environmental Pressure Indicators

The environmental inputs required by the economy are represented by the resource use vector d in Table 4.4. In Table 4.5, the extraction of metal and fossil fuel are environmental problems because of the depletion of these resources. Emissions to nature are recorded in vector e in Table 4.4. The numerical example of Table 4.5 includes carbon dioxide (CO_2) emissions, which lead to global warming. Mining debris can cause local environmental problems. The stock changes in Table 4.5, vector s in Table 4.4, are also of interest to environmental policy. For example, the increase in the wastes that are stored in landfills is recorded as changes in stocks. Furthermore, the other stocks in the economy will at some stage in the future, end up in landfills or be emitted to nature. Table 4.6 provides a number of examples of physical flows that are of interest to environmental policy such as CO_2 emissions and waste.

Table 4.6 Environmental pressure indicators

Environmental theme	ktons
Metal depletion	1843
Fossil fuel depletion	4740
CO_2 emissions	13053
Landfilled waste	1889
Incinerated waste	395
Mining debris	8953

Note that the full PIOT is useful for policy analysis because it can calculate these indicators separately for the structural production processes, auxiliary production process, investment goods account or consumers.

Composition of Products

Assuming that the chemical composition of the raw materials and residuals are known, the chemical composition of the product can be derived. Multiplying the mass of the inputs and outputs of the structural production process by the chemical composition yields a remainder, which is embodied in the product. The chemical compositions of materials and the derived composition of products are shown in Appendix 4.A (tables 4.A.4 and 4.A.5, respectively). The chemical composition (of Iron-Fe, Carbon-C, and Hydrogen-H) of products and their packaging layer (which is present for 4 of the 10 commodities) is provided in Figure 4.2.

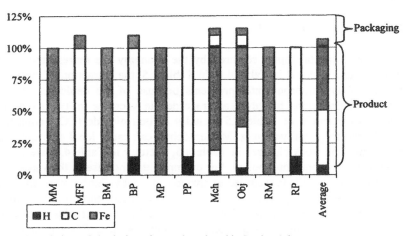

Note: Abbreviations of physical goods were introduced in Section 4.6.

Figure 4.2 Composition of products and packaging layers

This information indicator of product composition illustrates that a PIOT can provide a link between macroeconomic material flows and microeconomic concepts such as products. The product composition found by the PIOT can be compared with studies that have estimated the composition of products through direct means (Hansen, 1995). Knowledge about the composition of products is interesting between different time periods because the substitution of inputs becomes apparent. Note that relatively few of the elements of the periodic table are used in significant quantities in physical goods.

Element Cycles in the Economy

Environmental scientists construct element cycles, such as the carbon or nitrogen cycle, which provide insights into the sources, sinks and flows of certain elements.[17] Element cycles can also be produced for the economic system. Figure 4.3 depicts the economic carbon cycle for the numerical example. The full PIOT material and product flows of Table 4.5 are multiplied by the chemical composition data for carbon from Appendix 4.A. However, in the case of mined fossil fuel the composition should be corrected for a 10 percent metal packaging layer. In the case of machines and objects there a 5 percent metal packaging layer and a 10 percent plastic packaging layer. A PIOT for nitrogen already exists (Gravgård-Pedersen, 1999).

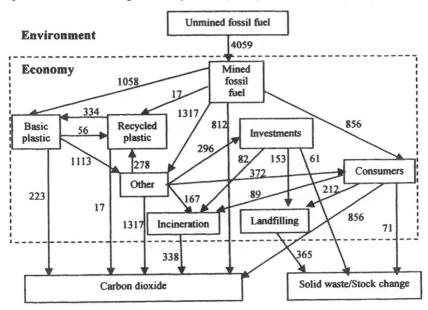

Figure 4.3 Carbon cycle in the economy (ktons)

Dematerialization Indicators

Environmental flows can be related to monetary indicators. For example, the environmental problems that were noted in Table 4.6 can be evaluated per unit of value added, for each individual production process. Figure 4.4 illustrates this by calculation of the CO_2 per unit of value added (labor payments plus capital depreciation), which are taken from Table 4.A.2, in

Appendix 4.A. In the numerical example, the mined metal, mined fossil fuel, basic metal, basic plastic and incineration exhibit high values for CO_2 emissions per unit of value added. For the latter production process this is not surprising: it incinerates carbon-containing plastics.

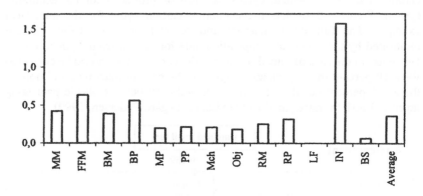

Note: Abbreviations of physical goods were introduced in Section 4.6.

Figure 4.4 CO_2 emissions per unit value added (ton per euro)

International Indicators

In the basic, extended and full PIOT presented in this chapter, a closed economy has been assumed. The frameworks can easily expanded to include imports and exports. Indicators of the physical trade balances can be constructed by adding information about trade (Giljum and Hubacek, 2001).

4.8 PIOT MODELING

A number of publications have discussed and applied PIOT models so far (Konijn et al., 1995; Konijn et al., 1997; Hubacek and Giljum, 2003; Giljum and Hubacek, 2004; Suh, 2004a, Dietzenbacher, 2005; Dietzenbacher et al., 2005). This section focuses on two IO modeling applications: impact analysis and imputation of primary inputs (see Box 2.2). These are applied to a hybrid model to illustrate the uses of the full PIOT. Equation 4.11 presents the hybrid IO model (see Section 2.5).

$$q^* = \left(I - A^*\right)^{-1} \cdot y^*$$

(4.11)

The data for this model are provided in Appendix 4.A (Table 4.A.1). The natural unit of fossil fuels is GJ (gigajoules), because it is used for energy purposes. However, in the production of basic plastic, the natural unit of fossil fuels is ktons, because they are used as a structural input. Theoretically, these two functions of fossil fuels should be represented on separate rows of the hybrid table. However, since the GJ/kg ratio is constant for this example, the result is the same.[18]

Impact Analysis

Impact analysis is a projection method in IO which is usually used to assess the influence of final demand changes on output (see Box 2.2). However, technological changes can also be analyzed in PIOT-based impact analyses. Table 4.7 presents five examples of impact analyses using the numerical example. The percentages presented are compared with those in the base case.

Table 4.7 Impact analysis on environmental indicators (%)

	Metal depletion	Fossil fuel depletion	CO_2 emissions	Addition to landfills	Incineration of waste	Mining debris	Value added
Consumption of machines	3.7	2.4	2.4	3.4	4.6	2.6	2.3
Consumption of services	0.2	1.1	1.3	0.2	0.0	0.9	5.9
Recycling	−19.0	−1.4	−1.6	−18.5	0.0	−5.1	−0.3
Substitution	−3.5	1.8	−0.4	1.8	−6.3	0.7	0.0
Miniaturization	−4.6	−2.4	−2.2	−4.1	−4.4	−2.8	−0.2

Note: In all these calculations, investment goods levels and prices are assumed constant.

The five impact analyses are:

1. *Consumption of machines*. The final consumption of machines increases by 20 percent. This demand increases all environmental indicators.
2. *Consumption of services*. The final consumption of business services increases by 20 percent. The environmental pressures do not increase as greatly as in the first impact analysis, while the value added increase is greater. The increases in wastes landfilled and incinerated are small.
3. *Recycling*. The use of recycled metal increases by 50 percent in the basic metals production process. These inputs replace mined metal in the production process, as is illustrated by the 19 percent decrease in metal depletion for basic metals. Furthermore, the increased demand for

residuals also decreases the quantity of landfilled waste by 18.5 percent.

4. *Substitution*. The plastic content of machines increases from 20 percent (see Figure 4.2) to 30 percent. The metal content therefore diminishes, while it is assumed that the weight of the machines remains the same. The results show how structural changes can shift environmental burdens. The depletion of metals, carbon dioxide emission and incineration decreases, but the other environmental indicators increase.

5. *Miniaturization*. Machines are assumed to become 10 percent lighter while maintaining their functionality. Again the environmental indicators decrease across the board.

Imputation to Final Demand

Box 2.2 discusses the imputation of labor and capital inputs to final demand. Similarly, raw material requirements and emissions can be imputed to final demand by using Equations 4.12.

$$
\begin{aligned}
\Phi &= \left(\left(D_{str} + D_{aux} \right) \cdot \hat{q}^{*-1} \right) \cdot (I - A^*)^{-1} \cdot Y^* \cdot i_\alpha \\
\Psi &= \left(\left(E_{str} + E_{aux} \right) \cdot \hat{q}^{*-1} \right) \cdot (I - A^*)^{-1} \cdot Y^* \cdot i_\alpha
\end{aligned}
\tag{4.12}
$$

where Φ is the set of direct and indirect raw material coefficients, and Ψ is the matrix for emission coefficients. Table 4.8 presents the results for the environmental indicators.

Table 4.8 Imputation of environmental indicators to final demand

	Natural units	Metal depletion	Fossil fuel depletion	CO_2 emissions	Landfilled waste	Incinerated waste	Mining debris
MM	ktons	1.02	0.50	0.84	0.02	-	1.42
MFF	GJ	-	0.02	0.01	-	-	0.02
BM	ktons	0.84	0.94	1.58	0.03	-	1.59
BP	ktons	0.19	2.51	1.90	0.08	0.02	2.20
MP	m²	0.01	0.01	0.02	-	-	0.02
PP	m²	-	0.03	0.02	-	-	0.02
Mch	units	0.01	0.03	0.04	-	-	0.03
Obi	units	0.01	0.03	0.04	-	-	0.03
RM	ktons	0.01	0.13	0.22	-	-	0.11
RP	ktons	0.01	0.13	0.22	-	-	0.11
LF	ktons landfilled	-	-	-	-	-	-
IN	ktons incinerated	-	-	3.14	-	-	-
BS	business service units	-	0.05	0.08	-	-	0.04
units		ktons	ktons	ktons	ktons	ktons	ktons

Note: Abbreviations of physical goods were introduced in Section 4.6.

The coefficients shown in Table 4.8 are ratios of two units. The units of the numerator are ktons, as indicated by the last row of the table. The denominator is measured in the natural units of the production processes, shown in the second column. For example, for the service unit production process, an increase in final demand of 1 *business service unit* leads to an increase of 0.04 *ktons* of mining debris. This is, of course, the effect of indirect demand, because there is no direct mining debris waste created in the production process of business services.

4.9 CONCLUSIONS

This chapter has discussed the physical input–output table (PIOT), which records all physical flows associated with economic activities. PIOT studies for five different countries and the EU were reviewed. It is argued that these studies should focus more on their role as a data source in environmental IO models. Three variations of the PIOT were presented. The *basic PIOT* uses a similar structure to the monetary input–output table (MIOT). The *extended PIOT* splits the production process into two distinct parts: the structural and the auxiliary production processes. Finally the *full PIOT*, which combines insights from the basic and extended PIOT was proposed in this chapter. It combines all aspects of material flows, such as residuals, packaging, recycling, landfilling and incineration, which are relevant to environmental accounting and policy. To illustrate the uses of the full PIOT structure, a numerical example was used. The example illustrates that the PIOT can yield environmental information and indicators. Furthermore, the full PIOT data is used in IO modeling applications, such as impact analysis and imputation to final demand.

APPENDIX 4.A DATA FOR NUMERICAL EXAMPLE

In this appendix, the hybrid table, the monetary table, price information, and the chemical composition of the numerical example are provided. The MIOT is shown in Table 4.A.1. Table 4.A.2 shows the HIOT, for which each row is measured in its own natural unit. The link between the two is provided by the prices provided in Table 4.A.3. The chemical composition of the raw materials and residuals are shown in Table 4.A.4. These values can be used, in combination with the full PIOT, to calculate the composition of the physical commodities shown in Table 4.A.5.

Table 4.A.1 Numerical example: the MIOT

MIOT		Production processes						
		MM	MFF	BM	BP	MP	PP	Mch
Production processes	Mined Metal (MM)			3686				
	Mined Fossil Fuel (MFF)	737	1896	922	2470	70	20	400
	Basic Metal (BM)					2816		3600
	Basic Plastics (BP)						800	2000
	Metal Packaging (MP)		2370		650			250
	Plastic Packaging (PP)							500
	Machines (Mch)							
	Objects (Obj)							
	Recycled Metal (RM)			691				
	Recycled Plastics (RP)				390			
	Landfilling (LF)	22	57	28	74	2	13	42
	Incineration (IN)				43			200
	Business Services (BS)	184	474	230	130	70	20	100
Primary inputs	Labor	2051	2906	2864	968	535	140	2623
	Capital costs machines	461	1185	576	325	18	5	250
	Capital costs objects	230	593	288	163	9	3	125
Use of residuals	Waste Metal							
	Waste Plastic							
	Waste Metal Packaging							
	Waste Plastic Packaging							
	Waste Machines							
	Waste Objects							
Supply of residuals	Waste Metal				−69			−30
	Waste Plastic					−13		−60
	Waste Metal Packaging							
	Waste Plastic Packaging							
	Waste Machines							
	Waste Objects							
	Total	3686	9480	9216	5200	3520	1000	10000

Table 4.A.2 Numerical example: the HIOT

HIOT		Production processes						
		MM	MFF	BM	BP	MP	PP	Mch
Production Processes	Mined Metal (MM)			1843				
	Mined Fossil Fuel (MFF)	36864	94801	46080	123500	3520	1000	20000
	Basic Metal (BM)					704		900
	Basic Plastics (BP)						200	500
	Metal Packaging (MP)		47401		13000			5000
	Plastic Packaging (PP)							10000
	Machines (Mch)							
	Objects (Obj)							
	Recycled Metal (RM)			691				
	Recycled Plastics (RP)			390				
	Landfilling (LF)	22	57	28	74	2	13	42
	Incineration (IN)				22			100
	Business Services (BS)	184	474	230	130	70	20	100

Table 4.A.1 (continued)

Obj	RM	RP	LF	IN	BS	Inv.	Consumption n.d.	d.	Output	Units (1000 euro)
									3686	
400	69	39			457			2000	9480	
2800									9216	
2400									5200	
250									3520	
500									1000	
						6373		3627	10000	
						3207		6793	10000	
									691	
									390	
48	2	1			14	713	60	813	1889	
147						192		208	790	
100	69	39						10000	11417	
3048	402	179	1535	716	8806					
250	17	10	236	49	1427				26773	
125	9	5	118	25	714				4809	
	123								2405	
		117								
									123	
									117	
−24										
−44										
									−123	
									−117	
10000	691	390	1889	790	11417					

Table 4.A.2 (continued)

Obj	RM	RP	LF	IN	BS	Inv.	Consumption n.d.	d.	Output	Units
									1843	ktons
20000	3456	1950			22834		100000		474006	GJ
700									2304	ktons
600									1300	ktons
5000									70401	m²
10000									20000	m²
						63730		36270	100000	units
						32065		67935	100000	units
									691	ktons
									390	ktons
48	2	1			14	713	60	813	1889	ktons landfilled
73						96		104	395	ktons incinerated
100	69	39					10000		11417	service units

Note: Inv. – Investment, n.d. – Non-Durables, d. – Durables

Table 4.A.3 Commodity prices

Commodity/material	Price per kton (1000 euro per kton)	Price per natural unit (1000 euro per natural unit)	Natural unit
Mined Metal (MM)	2.00	2.00	ktons
Mined Fossil Fuel (MFF)	2.00	0.02	GJ
Basic Metal (BM)	4.00	4.00	ktons
Basic Plastics (BP)	4.00	4.00	ktons
Metal Packaging (MP)	5.00	0.05	m2
Plastic Packaging (PP)	5.00	0.05	m2
Machines (Mch)	10.00	0.10	units
Objects (Obj)	10.00	0.10	units
Recycled Metal (RM)	1.00	1.00	ktons
Recycled Plastics (RP)	1.00	1.00	ktons
Landfilling (LF)	N/A	1.00	ktons landfilled
Incineration (IN)	N/A	2.00	ktons incinerated
Business Services (BS)	N/A	1.00	service units
Waste Metal (WM)	0.50	0.50	ktons
Waste Plastic (WP)	0.50	0.50	ktons
Waste Metal Pack. (WMP)	0.50	0.50	ktons
Waste Plastic Pack. (WPP)	0.50	0.50	ktons

Table 4.A.4 Composition of raw materials and wastes

Materials	Si (%)	H (%)	C (%)	O (%)	Fe (%)	Chemical composition
Unmined Metal (UM)	32			18	50	SiO_2(50%) and Fe(50%)
Unmined Fossil Fuel (UFF)	60	6	34			SiO_2(50%) and C_2H_4(50%)
Oxygen (O_2)				100		O_2
Waste Metal (WM)					100	Fe
Waste Plastic (WP)		14	86			C_2H_4
Waste Metal Pack. (WMP)					100	Fe
Waste Plastic Pack. (WPP)		14	86			C_2H_4
Waste Machines (WMch)		3	17		80	Mixed composition
Waste Objects (WObj)		5	33		62	Mixed composition

Note: Si: Silicon; H: Hydrogen; C: Carbon; O: Oxygen; and Fe: Iron.

Table 4.A.5 Composition of commodities (without packaging)

Commodity	Si (%)	H (%)	C (%)	O (%)	Fe (%)	Chemical composition
Mined Metal (MM)					100	Fe
Mined Fossil Fuel (MFF)		14	86			C_2H_4
Basic Metal (BM)					100	Fe
Basic Plastics (BP)		14	86			C_2H_4
Metal Packaging (MP)					100	Fe
Plastic Packaging (PP)		14	86			C_2H_4
Machines (Mch)		3	17		80	Mixed composition
Objects (Obj)		5	33		62	Mixed composition
Recycled Metal (RM)					100	Fe
Recycled Plastics (RP)		14	86			C_2H_4

NOTES

1. As in the monetary accounts, the accounting function is performed better in the supply and use framework than the IO set up.
2. An Austrian PIOT is currently being constructed at the Department for Social Ecology, Institute of Interdisciplinary Studies of Austrian Universities (IFF), Vienna, Austria.
3. The extended PIOT by Konijn et al. (1995) was proposed before the basic PIOTs reviewed here. This study is often overlooked or mentioned separately. Note that earlier work on PIOTs for Austria for 1983 is reported in Kratterl and Kratena (1990).
4. A separate physical account for emissions to air is also presented in the German study.
5. An example is the Finnish PIOT (Mäenpää and Muukkonen, 2001; Mäenpää, 2002). It features an impressive analysis of 21 different foodstuffs to evaluate the 'human metabolic balance'. Although these are intellectually interesting exercises, one wonders whether it would not be better to focus on other aspects of the material throughput of society. Given the limited resources that are available to statistical bureaus, it seems logical to focus time and resources on physical flows that cause more urgent environmental problems.
6. Note that current PIOTs could provide a more complete picture of environmental pressures, if micro-emissions were recorded as well.
7. The basic PIOT presented in this section differs slightly from those of the studies reviewed in Table 4.1. In our PIOT the supply of residuals are recorded as negative inputs.
8. The term 'residual' is adopted because it is used in the SEEA. It is used synonymously with the terms 'emissions' and 'wastes', which indicate any solid, liquid or gas by-product of production processes. These may be recycled, landfilled, incinerated or emitted to nature.
9. In the rest of the chapter, it is assumed that services do not produce any physical products.
10. The SEEA distinguishes two types of raw materials: natural resources and ecosystem inputs. 'Natural resources' cover mineral and energy resources, and biological resources. 'Ecosystem inputs' cover air and gases necessary for combustion and the water to sustain life. (SEEA, 2002: pp. 2-5, 2-6). The distinction is not of interest in this chapter.
11. Matrices D and E are quadrants (3) and (1), respectively, of Table 1.1.
12. The 'final destination' of value or mass is different. For example, goods and services are supplied to consumers. (Final) consumption of the goods and services leads to loss of value. In the MIOT, this is therefore the final destination of value. However, 'physical consumption' does not exist. Physical goods are used for the services that they provide. However, when they lose their value, they do not lose their mass. The final destination of physical flows is, therefore, the disposal of product waste (Ayres et al., 2005). In the case of recycled flows there is no source and destination for the accounting period in question.
13. Some of the raw material inputs associated with capital goods are recorded as auxiliary inputs. For example, if machines use fossil fuels for energy, this process requires a certain amount of oxygen. These are registered as auxiliary inputs, just as the fossil fuels are, because they are used within the accounting period.
14. Landfilling and incineration are regarded as services. The recycling sector produces a good because it makes a physical product that is supplied to the market.
15. The description of waste and recycling flows could be elaborated even further than is done in Table 4.4, since the 'use of residuals' rows of the PIOT do not specify the origin of the residuals that are used. Similarly, the 'supply of residuals' does not specify to whom the residuals are supplied. This information can easily be incorporated in the rows of the PIOT or in separate satellite accounts for recycling.
16. Negative values indicate increases in stocks.
17. The mystery of the missing CO_2 sink, which was an issue in the initial stages of global warming research, is an example where constructing these cycles was very important.
18. For this numerical example, uniform prices are assumed. The monetary and hybrid models will therefore yield equivalent results. An IO model based only on the physical data of the PIOT would yield incorrect results, because the services are not measured in ktons.

5. Hybrid Input–Output Tables for Iron and Steel and Plastics

5.1 INTRODUCTION

In Chapter 3, the theoretical aspects of constructing monetary, physical and hybrid IO tables (MIOTs, PIOTs and HIOTs respectively) were discussed. This chapter describes, step by step, the construction of a HIOT for the Netherlands for two years, 1990 and 1997.[1] The material flows examined are iron and steel and plastics for which physical supply and use tables (SUT) are constructed. Part of the work, discussed in Section 5.4, was done in cooperation with Statistics Netherlands (CBS).[2] This chapter can serve as a guideline for similar exercises later on, for different countries, materials or time periods.

The study focuses on iron and steel and plastics, because most economies use these materials in large amounts, in a variety of products. They are prime examples of how materials permeate the production and consumption processes of societies. Furthermore, the production of iron and steel and plastic products gives rise to a range of environmental problems, such as fossil fuel depletion, CO_2 emissions, chemical pollution and various wastes.

The IO data are constructed for 1990 and 1997. This will enable a structural decomposition analysis in Chapter 8, and the construction of forecasting and backcasting scenarios in Chapter 9. The year 1990 is chosen because the CBS had previously undertaken a project in which physical supply, use and IO tables for a wide variety of materials were constructed for 1990 (see Konijn et al., 1995). That project included material balances for iron and steel and plastics data, which served as the basis for the 1990 data constructed in this book. The terminal year, 1997, has been chosen because it was the most recent year for which the CBS could provide the raw data required.

An important problem concerns the fact that the National Accounts for 1990 and 1997 are based on different classification schemes. The CBS implemented a thorough revision of goods, services and industry classifications in 1995. In this study, the 1990 data was therefore converted into the 1997 scheme. This conversion process created problems, the solutions to which required a great deal of effort. With hindsight, an important additional criterion for selecting the base and terminal years should be the homogeneity of the classification schemes.

The organization of this chapter is as follows. Section 5.2 provides a summary of the data construction process. Sections 5.3 to 5.8 discuss in detail each of the six steps in this process. Section 5.9 concludes.

5.2 SUMMARY OF STEPS

This section summarizes the steps taken to produce the hybrid commodity-by-commodity IO tables that are used in the SDA of Chapter 8. It is beyond the scope of this book to produce an activity-by-activity IO table, as described in Chapter 3, because the additional information requirement is very time-consuming. Furthermore, detailed technological expertise of production processes is required. Instead, a commodity-by-commodity IO table is produced using the commodity technology assumption. The negative elements that occur in these types of tables will be analyzed and appropriate manual adjustments will be made to produce non-negative IO tables.

Table 5.1 A hybrid commodity-by-commodity IO table

	Other commodities	Iron and steel and plastic commodities	Final demand	Total output
Other commodities				
Iron and steel and plastic commodities				
Primary inputs				

Table 5.1 shows the goal of the exercise: a hybrid table in which the products of iron and steel and plastics are measured in mass units (1000 million kg), while the rest of the commodities are measured in monetary units (millions of euros, in 1997 prices). The tables for 1990 and 1997 are both measured in

1997 prices because SDA usually looks at volume changes, which necessitates the elimination of price effects. The primary inputs, also measured in monetary value, are added to the hybrid table as well, because they play a part in some of the SDAs of Chapter 8. The steps in the construction process are as follows.

Step 1. Constructing monetary SUT in 1997 prices
Tables 5.2 and 5.3 show the monetary SUT that are produced in the first step. The CBS produces these tables annually, in current prices, as well as in prices of the previous year. For 1997 the current price tables are used, while the 1990 SUT are inflated to 1997 prices.

Table 5.2 A monetary supply table

	Other industries	Iron and steel and plastic industries	Total output
Other commodities			
Iron and steel and plastic commodities			

Table 5.3 A monetary use table

	Other industries	Iron and steel and plastic industries	Final demand	Total output
Other commodities				
Iron and steel and plastic commodities				
Primary inputs				

Step 2. Constructing physical SUT
The areas with diagonal stripes in Tables 5.4 and 5.5 are the physical SUT for iron and steel and plastics. These contain physical data from several sources, such as international trade statistics, waste statistics and production statistics.

However, if physical data are not available, the data from the monetary SUT may be divided by appropriate price information. By using all this information, an initial estimate of the physical SUT is obtained.

Table 5.4 A physical supply table

	Other industries	Iron and steel and plastic industries	Total output
Other commodities		//////	
Iron and steel and plastic commodities	//////		//////
Supply of residuals		//////	
Emissions to nature		//////	

Table 5.5 A physical use table

	Other industries	Iron and steel and plastic industries	Final demand	Total output
Other commodities		//////		
Iron and steel and plastic commodities	//////		//////	//////
Raw materials		//////		
Use of residuals		//////		

The mass balance (MB) principle holds for both the commodity and industry dimensions of the physical SUT. Starting from the initial data, an iterative balancing process is applied to produce the definitive SUT. First, the initial data are adjusted so that the supply of each commodity is equal to its use. Individual entries in the initial physical SUT are adjusted, based on expert opinion of the quality of the data sources. Second, the industry-level MB is assessed. Again, the elements of the physical SUT are adjusted. The latter corrections disturb the commodity MBs, which were completed in the first adjustment. These commodity totals are therefore corrected, which in turn disturbs the industry balance. This iterative process continues until both dimensions are balanced. This procedure is similar to the production of monetary SUT that are used by many National Accounts departments.

Table 5.6 A hybrid supply table

	Other industries	Iron and steel and plastic industries	Total output
Other commodities			
Iron and steel and plastic commodities			

Table 5.7 A hybrid use table

	Other industries	Iron and steel and plastic industries	Final demand	Total output
Other commodities				
Iron and steel and plastic commodities				
Primary inputs				

Step 3. Constructing hybrid SUT
Table 5.6, the hybrid supply table, uses the monetary data for 'Other commodities' (from Table 5.2) and the physical data for 'Iron and steel and plastic commodities' (from Table 5.4). Table 5.7, the hybrid use table, uses the monetary data for 'Other commodities' and 'Primary inputs' (from Table 5.3) and the physical data for 'Iron and steel and plastic commodities' (from Table 5.5).

Step 4. Constructing 'square' hybrid SUT
The SUT are made 'square' by making the number of industries equal to the number of commodities. This is done by assigning each commodity to the

industry of which it is the principal product.

Step 5. Constructing hybrid commodity-by-commodity IO tables

The commodity-by-commodity IO table is produced using the commodity technology assumption. As discussed in Section 3.3, this assumption requires a square and invertible supply matrix. Furthermore, the use table has to be made square so that the resulting IO table is square. Application of the commodity technology assumption to the square SUT from Step 4 results in hybrid commodity-by-commodity IO tables.

Step 6. Constructing hybrid non-negative commodity-by-commodity IO tables

The commodity-by-commodity IO table from Step 5 will exhibit negative elements, as discussed in Sections 3.3 and 3.4. These elements are analyzed and adjustments are made to input structures, the classification of commodities, and the levels of aggregation, in order to yield a non-negative commodity-by-commodity IO table. Note that the table produced here is an IO table 'including imports', where imports are recorded as negative final demand. The difference between IO tables including imports and excluding imports is shown in Box 5.1.

Summary

Table 5.8 summarizes the data inputs and outputs of each of the six steps described. These are discussed in detail in Sections 5.3–5.9. The procedure uses a number of data sources, which are summarized in Table 5.9. Each data set is coded by a letter in square brackets throughout this chapter.

Table 5.8 Summary of the data construction process

Step	Inputs	Output
1	[A],[B],[C],[D] of Table 5.9	Monetary SUT (1990) in basic 1997 prices Monetary SUT (1997) in basic 1997 prices
2	[C],[E],[F],[E], [H],[I] of Table 5.9	Physical SUT (1990) for iron, steel and plastics Physical SUT (1997) for iron, steel and plastics
3	Output Steps 1 and 2	Hybrid SUT (1990) Hybrid SUT (1997)
4	Output Step 3	Square hybrid SUT (1990) Square hybrid SUT (1997)
5	Output Step 4	Hybrid IO table (1990) Hybrid IO table (1997)
6	Output Step 5	Non-negative hybrid IO table (1990) Non-negative hybrid IO table (1997)

Box 5.1 IO tables 'excluding imports' and 'including imports'

These examples are based on Konijn (1994: p. 51). An IO table 'excluding imports', shown below, records the imports in a similar way to primary inputs. The use of domestic and imported inputs by production processes is recorded separately. IO coefficients therefore measure the domestic intermediate inputs per unit of output.

IO table excluding imports

	Materials	Services	Final demand	Total
Materials	10	80	60	150
Services	50	30	120	200
Import of materials	10	20		
Import of services	40	10		
Value added	40	60		
Total	150	200		

The IO table 'including imports', shown below, does not distinguish between domestic and imported intermediates. The total import of each commodity is subtracted in an additional column of final demand. The advantage of this type of table is that the IO coefficients are better reflections of the input requirements of production processes. A major disadvantage is that the IO models that are based on these tables assume that the imported commodities are produced in the same way as domestic commodities, that is they are all competitive imports.

IO table including imports

	Materials	Services	Final demand	Imports	Total
Materials	20	100	60	-30	150
Services	90	40	120	-50	200
Value added	40	60			
Total	150	200			

The two IO tables, and the IO models that are based on them, have different interpretations. However, a full comparison of the theoretical and empirical implications of both models is lacking in the literature (see Dietzenbacher and Hoekstra, 2002) for an example of the empirical differences between the models, in the case of structural decomposition analysis).

Table 5.9 Data sources

Code	Name (valuation) [CBS name]	Time period	Commodity classif. (number) [CBS name]	Industry classif. (number) [CBS name]	Source	Comment
[A]	Supply tables (BP) and Use table (PP) [WERKTABEL]	1990–1995	PRE-disaggregated (800) [GOEDGROEP]	PRE-disaggregated (200) [REGKOL]	CBS: National Accounts	Uses the detailed classification scheme of the 1995 revision.
[B]	Supply tables (Basic prices) and Use table (PP) [Tijdreeksen]	1990–1995	POST-aggregated (60) [GOEDGROEP]	POST-disaggregated (200) [REGKOL]	CBS: National Accounts	Produced by a project to convert data preceding 1995 into the post-revision classification scheme. Commodity detail is aggregated, while the industry scheme is disaggregated.
[C]	Supply tables (BP) and Use table (PP) [WERKTABEL]	1995–1997	POST-disaggregated (800) [GOEDGROEP]	POST-disaggregated (200) [REGKOL]	CBS: National Accounts	Standard National Accounts classification after 1995.
[D]	Use tables (BP and PP) [EINDBESTAND]	1995–1997	POST-fairly disaggregated (270) [GGIO]	POST-fairly disaggregated (120) [REGKOLVI]	CBS: National Accounts	All the valuation levels (including basic and purchaser prices) of the use tables are provided. The aggregation is less detailed than the standard National Accounts [C].

73

Table 5.9 (continued)

[E]	Physical Supply and Use tables [Materiaal balansen project]	1990	PRE-disaggregated (120 iron and steel, 23 plastic)	PRE-disaggregated (40 iron and steel, 6 plastics)	CBS: Material balances project, National Accounts	Produced by a project that produced a wide variety of physical supply, use and I/O tables for various materials (Konijn et al., 1995).
[F]	Trade statistics	1997	POST-disaggregated	POST-disaggregated	CBS: Trade statistics, National Accounts	Trade statistics are collected monthly and are considered to be a very reliable data source for the National Accounts.
[G]	Production statistics	1997	POST-disaggregated	POST-disaggregated	CBS: Production statistics	A sample of companies is sent a questionnaire annually.
[H]	Waste statistics	1990	N/A	PRE-disaggregated	CBS: Environmental Statistics (CBS, 1992)	Waste statistics are published every two years. Data is based on a sample of companies.
[I]	Waste statistics	1996 & 1998	N/A	POST- aggregated	CBS: Environmental Statistics CBS (1998, 2000)	Waste statistics are published every two years. Data is based on a sample of companies. Recycled flows are recorded.
[J]	Recycling statistics	1990 & 1997	N/A	Varying aggregated classification	Eurostat, RIVM, NFK, UN, IISI	References: Eurostat (1998), RIVM (1989), NFK (1997), UN (1997), IISI (1998).

Note: (PRE) Pre-revision refers to the classification scheme before 1995, while (POST) post-revision signifies the scheme after 1995, classif. – classification; BP – Basic prices; PP – purchaser prices.

5.3 CONSTRUCTING MONETARY SUT

Aim and Data

The aim here is to construct four tables:

- A monetary supply table for 1990 in basic 1997 prices.
- A monetary use table for 1990 in basic 1997 prices.
- A monetary supply table for 1997 in current basic prices.
- A monetary use table for 1997 in current basic prices.

All tables are constructed using the commodity and industry classification adopted after the 1995 revision.

Constructing Monetary SUT for 1990–1997

In order to inflate the 1990 SUT to 1997 price levels, a consistent time series of tables for the period 1990–1997, in current prices and prices of the previous year, is required. Time series [B], of Table 5.9, is used as a data source for the period 1990–1995, while [C] provides supply and tables for 1996 and 1997. However, the time series distinguishes only aggregated commodity groups (60). The data for the period 1995–1997 are therefore aggregated from 800 to 60 commodities. Both [B] and [C] are reported in the detailed industry classification (200). Therefore, the resulting SUT distinguish 200 industries and 60 commodities groups. Commodities that were introduced after 1995, and these only appear in [C], were assigned a commodity group in [B]. Exports and imports, which distinguish EU and non-EU components, are aggregated into one export and import column.[3] The different types of stocks in the National Accounts were aggregated.

Converting the Use Tables from Purchaser Prices to Basic Prices

In the data sets [B] and [C], the supply table is provided in basic prices while the use table values are in purchaser prices. IO analysis requires basic prices data, which means that the use table has to be converted.

To calculate the basic price use table, the taxes, subsidies, trade and transport margins have to be subtracted from the purchaser price. Data set [D] provides information about the taxes, margins and subsidies. However, the classification scheme that is used for the 1990-1995 period [D] is more aggregated, which makes it necessary to convert [B] and [C] to this classification scheme. For the period 1995–1997, the use table in basic prices is obtained directly from [D].

For the period 1990–1995, the total amount of product-related taxes, product-related subsidies and trade and transport margins per commodity group are provided in [B]. An estimate of these values is required for each element of the use table. Since basic price and purchaser price data are available for 1995, an estimate for 1994 was made by taking the ratio from 1995 and multiplying this by the equivalent element of the use table of 1994. This initial estimate did not equal the 1994 commodity totals of taxes, subsidies and margins reported in the supply tables of [B]. To adjust the elements to match the 1994 use table row and column totals, a Lagrangian optimization procedure is used which balances row and column totals (van Dalen and Sluis, 2002). This procedure uses the absolute magnitude of each element as the weight in the optimization.

Once the estimate of the 1994 use table in basic prices is calculated, the procedure is repeated for 1993, and then iteratively to 1990. This approach is superior to applying the 1995 ratios to all years between 1990–1994, since the elements are adjusted using specific information from each year. The method does, however, have its limitations. Taxes, subsidies or margins that, in reality, existed in 1994, but not in 1995, will not show up in the estimated 1994 table. The error could become worse as the process works back to 1990.

Producing SUT for 1990 in 1997 Prices

To inflate the 1990 SUT to 1997 prices, a price index is required. This is possible because of the availability of SUT, in current as well as in prices of the previous year for all years of the period 1990–1997. The index is found for each element of the SUT using Equation 5.1.

$$\frac{price^{97}}{price^{90}} = \frac{volume^{97} \cdot price^{97}}{volume^{97} \cdot price^{96}} \cdot \cdots\cdots \cdot \frac{volume^{91} \cdot price^{91}}{volume^{91} \cdot price^{90}} \qquad (5.1)$$

Where *volume^t* and *price^t* are, respectively, the volume and price in year *t*. Since the SUT only provide the product of these two, the chain shown in Equation 5.1 has to be used. *volume^t·price^t* is the value taken from a current price table, while *volume^t·price^{t-1}* signifies the values from a SUT in prices for the previous year. The SUT for 1990 and 1997 prices are found by using the price index found in Equation 5.1 and multiplying it by the current price table of 1990 (*volume^{90}·price^{90}*):

$$volume^{90} \cdot price^{97} = volume^{90} \cdot price^{90} \cdot \frac{price^{97}}{price^{90}} \qquad (5.2)$$

If the chain is incomplete, that is one of the elements of the supply or use table is zero for a certain year, it is not possible to find the price index. In this case, more aggregate price indices, such as a price index for intermediate use or the average price index, are used.

The resulting SUT in constant prices generally do not balance, that is the commodity and industry totals of the SUT are not the same. For example, the total use of a commodity in 1990, expressed in 1997 prices, is not exactly equal to the total supply of the respective commodity in 1990, expressed in 1997 prices. This discrepancy could be caused by errors in the data. In addition, Appendix 5.A shows that there is also a theoretical reason for the imbalance: where price discrimination and different volume growth amongst the users occurs simultaneously, differences in the commodity and industry totals of the constant price tables may occur. There is no theoretical reason to prefer the supply or use totals as the real value. Nevertheless, the commodity totals of the supply table are selected because the underlying data sources are deemed to be more reliable. The commodity totals of the use tables of 1990, in 1997 prices, are therefore balanced using the column and row balancing procedure discussed above.

The procedure followed in the case of the industry totals is different. The operating surplus (profits) of companies cannot be deflated because there is no real price and volume component. The operating surplus in constant prices can be defined as the difference in the supply in constant prices and the use of all inputs in constant prices. This assumption is normal practice at CBS where current prices tables are constructed simultaneously with the tables in prices of the previous year (de Boer et al., 1999).

The differences between the commodity and industry totals in the SUT are not large. Overall, the commodity totals are similar, with the exception of tobacco products (the use total is 12.1 percent higher than the supply total), coal (3.71 percent higher), transport over land (2.87 percent higher) and water (2.51 percent higher). The following differences are present in the industry totals: forestry sector (25.72 percent lower), the fuels sector (8.81 percent higher), the food sector (6.37 percent higher), air transport (5.21 percent higher). However, the sum total of the commodities is only 0.03 percent higher for the supply table, compared with the use tables total. The industry totals are only 0.66 percent higher. Considering the fact that a seven-year period is inflated, the problems of changing volume and price discrimination do not seem to be very serious for this time period, except for a few specific commodities and industries.

Other Adjustments

Some additional small adjustments were made to the data:

- The sale of second-hand military goods is included in the supply table, even if it is not the result of a production process. Since the military does not make profits, the income from the sales of these goods cannot be simply subtracted from the operating surplus. The revenues of the sales of these goods are therefore added to the value of the output of military services.

- Banks pay interest on the money in their accounts. However, they receive higher rates for money lent than they pay for money borrowed. This premium is known as the interest margin. The SNA recommends recording this in a dummy column. From an IO perspective, the premium is regarded as the reward for 'banking services'. For this study, the interest margin is divided among the industries and final consumers, relative to the amount of bank services that are listed in the use table. In other words, industries with a high demand for bank services were assigned a large portion of the interest margins. The intermediate costs of these industries therefore rise, and the operating surplus in the use table is adjusted downwards. Without more detailed knowledge of the banking sector, this procedure is the only feasible solution (see, for example Konijn, 1994).

- Nearly all industries produce services on a contract basis as a by-product. For example, a clothing firm may send its textiles to another firm to be cut and sewn. The goods do not, therefore, change ownership. However, in the National Accounts these services are recorded on a gross basis in the SUT, that is the value of the incoming goods that are being worked on are recorded in the use table, while the value of the products on the way out are also recorded on the supply side. For IO analysis, a net measure is better, and this data was obtained from the National Accounts department of the CBS.

- Services on a contract basis and investments on own account do not have a principal producer but are produced as by-products by nearly all industries in the economy. Services on a contract basis are explained in the comment above, while investment on own account encompasses investment goods that are produced by companies for internal use. Two new industries are added to the SUT to act as principal producers of these goods. Each of these industries is assumed to produce the entire output of the two commodities in question. Therefore, the production of services on a contract basis and investments on own account are set to zero for all other industries. The decrease in the output of these industries is matched by a decrease in the inputs that are required to produce the services and investments. Input requirements are estimated from the inputs structure in Konijn et al. (1995), and subtracted from the industry columns of the use table. If this subtraction leads to negative elements, less of the input in question is subtracted, while the other input requirements are adjusted upwards. The input structure for services on a contract basis and investments on own account are thereby created for each industry. The total input requirements for both these production processes are inserted into the corresponding columns of the use table. Similarly, a new industry for both production processes is inserted into the supply table, which supplies the total production of these goods in the economy.

● Intermediate consumption entails a number of basic goods that are used by all industries in the economy in small quantities, for example, plastic cups and coffee. The National Accounts register the total quantity of intermediate consumption of these goods so as not to clutter the intermediate input matrix of the use matrix with small values. For this study, an industry is added to the SUT which is assumed to be the sole producer of this commodity group. The input structure of the use table is maintained.

5.4 CONSTRUCTING PHYSICAL SUT[4]

Aim and Data

The aim here is to produce four tables:

● A physical supply table for 1990 for iron and steel and plastics.
● A physical use table for 1990 for iron and steel and plastics.
● A physical supply table for 1997 for iron and steel and plastics.
● A physical use table for 1997 for iron and steel and plastics.

All tables should use the detailed post-revision commodity and industry classification, with respect to iron and steel and plastics. For the 1990 data the material balances project [E] is used, which is in the pre-revision classification scheme. In some cases the physical data for 1990 was more detailed and was therefore aggregated to the 1997 classification scheme.

The final classification scheme distinguishes 23 basic plastics or plastic products and 120 raw materials and products of iron and steel. Six industries produce or process basic plastics or plastic products, while 40 industries are involved in the production of iron and steel products. The four tables were produced in collaboration with the National Accounts of the CBS.[5]

Creating an Initial Estimate of the Physical SUT for 1997

The 1997 tables were produced first. The first step in the procedure is to produce an initial estimate of the 1997 physical SUT. This estimate is based on the monetary SUT for 1997 [C], the elements of which are divided by price information. However, physical data are available in production [G], trade [F], waste [I] and recycling statistics [J].

Data of iron and steel and plastic products supplied and used are recorded in the production statistics [G] of large companies (>50 workers). Most inputs and outputs are reported in monetary units, but sometimes physical quantities are provided. Whenever this data are available, they are used in the physical SUT. The implicit price, which the combination of monetary and physical data provides, is used as a proxy for smaller non-surveyed companies. The international trade statistics are a valuable source of physical data. The mass, as well as the value, of all physical goods is reported.

For those elements of the SUT for which no physical data are available, the monetary value is divided by an appropriate price. These prices are derived either from trade or production statistics. For example, if an element of the supply table only has a monetary value, then an appropriate price from the production statistics was sought. If none existed, the monetary value of the supply table is divided by the export price. Since there is always price data from the international trade statistics, this procedure ensures an outcome is obtained.

Physical data are also obtained from industrial waste statistics [I]. These are collected every two years by the Environmental Statistics Department of the CBS (1998, 2000). For this study, an average of the 1996 and 1998 data are calculated, because no data were available for 1997. The waste statistics [I] are based on surveys of companies and are reported at a highly aggregated industry level. Since the physical SUT are more disaggregated with respect to the industry classification scheme, the waste statistics were divided amongst the industries in proportion to their labor volume. The waste statistics distinguish different types of materials and report the amount that is recycled, burned or landfilled as well as distinguishing between process-dependent and process-independent wastes. The former can be interpreted as the waste from the structural production processes, while the latter is from the auxiliary production processes, investment goods and packaging.

In this study, only the process-dependent waste materials were included because the structural production process material balance is required to provide a good estimate of the mass of iron and steel and plastic commodities. Balancing the auxiliary production process would not improve the estimates of the commodities under investigation. However, it would be important in a PSUT for typical auxiliary inputs such as fossil fuels.

Conversion of the Initial Estimates to Definitive Physical SUT for 1997

The data from the different sources are entered into the supply and use frameworks to produce an initial estimate. The commodity and industry totals of these initial tables were not balanced. In other words, the commodity total of the supply table does not correspond to the commodity total of the use table. For the industry level, the mass of structural inputs used by an industry does not equal the mass of products and structural wastes. Therefore, an iterative balancing process is carried out to construct the definitive SUT.

In this iterative process, first the mass balance of commodities for iron and steel and plastic products is adjusted. If the total supply of a commodity does not equal the total mass of the commodity used, alterations are made to either the elements of the supply or use table to ensure mass balance (MB). The modifications are based on expert opinions on the reliability of the data. For example, trade statistics were rarely altered because they are deemed to be relatively reliable. However, less reliable elements of the SUT, such as stocks or industries with many heterogeneous firms, were adjusted more easily.

Once all the MBs at the level of commodities were achieved, the second phase of the balancing process could begin. In this phase, MB at the level of industries was investigated. As noted in the previous step, only the structural production process was balanced. The structural inputs were added up and compared with the mass of the products and process-dependent wastes produced by the industry. A number of structural inputs and products that are not made of iron and steel and plastics had to be estimated using monetary and price information. The elements of the SUT were adjusted, in order to achieve mass balance at the industry level. Again, the quality of the underlying data sources was the guiding principle for adjustments.

Unfortunately, it was beyond the scope of this project to balance the structural production process of the primary metal and plastic industries. In these industries, iron ore is transformed into basic iron and steel, and chemical monomers are converted to basic plastics. These are complex conversion processes, which require specialized technology. Furthermore, the basic chemical sector is characterized by many products, for which it is difficult to match the input to output. However, the quality of the resulting physical supply and use values is good because these sectors contain large companies, which are all surveyed in production statistics.

In the process of balancing industry totals, the supply and use totals of commodities may alter, thereby disturbing the MB. The third phase is, therefore, to analyze and restore the commodity balances. These alterations lead to an imbalance in the structural production processes of industries, requiring another alteration. This iterative process continues until the MB holds for the both dimensions. The result is the physical SUT for 1997.

Constructing the Physical SUT for 1990

The physical SUT for 1990 are constructed in a different way. The data from the materials project [E] are converted into the post-revision classification. In the transformation process, the results are checked with the data from [C]. Special attention is paid to 'metal sheets and wiring', which represents a large part of the iron and steel industries. After the 1995 revision of the classification schemes, this commodity group was split into five separate commodities. The 1990 data of sheets and wiring are therefore disaggregated into these five commodities, using [F] and [G].

Waste statistics for 1990 are available from [H]. The waste types are harmonized with those used for the 1997 table. The pre-revision industry classification is converted to the post-revision scheme. The waste data are reported at a two-digit level of aggregation, which is converted into the disaggregated industry classification using labor volume data. The iterative process of balancing each commodity's SUT, as described for 1997, is repeated for 1990. Based on expert opinion within the CBS, the plausibility and consistency with other data sources of all these steps were checked and corrected.

5.5 CONSTRUCTING HYBRID SUT

Aim and Data

The aim here is to produce four tables:

- A hybrid supply table for 1990, monetary data in 1997 prices.
- A hybrid use table for 1990, monetary data in 1997 prices.
- A hybrid supply table for 1997.
- A hybrid use table for 1997.

To produce hybrid SUT, the monetary data described in Section 5.3 is combined with the physical data discussed in Section 5.4.

Harmonizing the Classification Schemes

The classification scheme of the monetary and physical data are not the same. The monetary data of Section 5.3 use the classification scheme of [D]. The physical data of Section 5.4 use the detailed National Accounts [C] classification for iron and steel and plastic commodities and industries. The scheme is similar for the iron and steel and plastic industries. However, the aggregation of the physical data leads to a reduction from 143 to 10 commodities. This is unfortunate, but inevitable, given the aggregation.

Replacing the Monetary by Physical Data

To produce hybrid SUT, the monetary rows for iron and steel and plastic products of the monetary tables produced in Section 5.3 were replaced by the rows of the physical tables produced in Section 5.4. For seven of the 10 physical commodities this does not pose a problem. However, three commodity groups in the monetary tables: namely, 'chemicals', 'rubber and plastic products' and 'basic metals', include products that are not made of iron and steel, or plastics. This means that the physical data cannot replace the monetary data directly. For example, the commodity group basic metals encompasses both non-ferrous and ferrous metals. Only the ferrous metals are included in the physical SUT. The monetary data of these three commodity groups was split into six commodity groups: three that remain monetary commodities in the hybrid tables ('chemicals', 'rubber products' and 'non-ferrous basic metals'), and three that are replaced by the physical data ('basic plastics', 'plastic products' and 'basic iron and steel'). Splitting the commodity groups into subgroups for 1997 was achieved by using the detailed information about the underlying commodities from the National Accounts [C]. The 1990 data uses the 1997 proportions scaled to 1990 totals.

5.6 CONSTRUCTING SQUARE HYBRID SUT

Aim and Data

The aim here is to produce four tables:

- A square hybrid supply table for 1990.
- A square hybrid use table for 1990.
- A square hybrid supply table for 1997.
- A square hybrid use table for 1997.

The hybrid SUT from Section 5.5 are the basis for these square tables.

Assigning Commodities to Industries

The number of industries exceeds the number of commodity groups in the hybrid SUT of Section 5.5. The industries were therefore aggregated. This is done by looking at the most prominent product of each industry and assigning the industry to that principal product. The result is 45 monetary rows (1997 prices) and 10 physical rows (mass).

Splitting the Rubber and Plastics Sector

The classification of the data obtained in Section 5.5 distinguishes only one industry that produces both rubber and plastics products. Rubber is not included in the physical SUT. Since the commodity group rubber products is measured in monetary units and plastic products in physical units, two separate industries were distinguished. For 1997, detailed monetary and physical data are available from [C] and Section 5.4 respectively. For 1990, the 1997 structure is used but is adjusted to 1990 totals, that is the 1997 relative values for 1997 are use to scale the absolute values of 1990.

5.7 CONSTRUCTING HYBRID COMMODITY-BY-COMMODITY INPUT–OUTPUT TABLES

Aim and Data

The aim here is to produce two tables:

- A hybrid commodity-by-commodity IO table for 1990.
- A hybrid commodity-by-commodity IO table for 1997.

The square hybrid SUT produced in Section 5.6 are used.

Applying the Commodity Technology Assumption

The commodity technology assumption, discussed in Section 3.3, is applied to the square SUT. The resulting commodity-by-commodity IO table included negative elements in the intermediate input matrix. The sources of these negative elements were discussed in a numerical example in Section 3.4. Table 5.10 summarizes the characteristics of negative elements that result after the first application of the commodity technology assumption.[6]

Note that the IO table contains 2475 monetary and 550 physical elements. Many of these exhibit negative values: for 1990, 42 percent and 41 percent of the monetary and physical elements, respectively. For 1997, these proportions are 36 percent and 41 percent, respectively. However, the overall impression is that the magnitudes are not very significant. The values of negative elements constitute only −1.33 percent and −3.14 percent of the total intermediate monetary and physical use, respectively.

Table 5.10 First application of the commodity technology assumption

Monetary (million 1997 guilders)						Physical (10 million kg)					
1990			1997			1990			1997		
<0	<-10	<-100	<0	<-10	<-100	<0	<-1	<-10	<0	<-1	<-10
698	110	13	593	116	21	189	32	8	189	50	9

5.8 CONSTRUCTING HYBRID NON-NEGATIVE COMMODITY-BY-COMMODITY INPUT–OUTPUT TABLES

Aim and Data

The aim here is to produce two tables:

- A non-negative hybrid commodity-by-commodity IO table for 1990.
- A non-negative hybrid commodity-by-commodity IO table for 1997.

The negative elements of the hybrid commodity-by-commodity IO tables produced in Section 5.7 are analyzed, and subsequently the SUT are adjusted in such a way that these problems are resolved. The commodity technology assumption is then applied to the adjusted data. This procedure is repeated until the negative elements are largely resolved.

Eliminating the Negative Elements

Table 5.10 summarized the negative elements from the first application of the commodity technology assumption. The smallest negative elements, and the actions undertaken to resolve them, are summarized in Table 5.11.

In Section 3.4, four reasons for the occurrence of negative elements were summarized: measurement errors, heterogeneous production processes, aggregation and non-uniform prices. Since the occurrence of measurement errors is difficult to assess, it is assumed that these are negligible. However, the issue of non-uniform prices is solved because hybrid units are used to construct the IO table. This leaves two sources of negative elements: heterogeneous production processes and commodity aggregation. To assess which of these reasons is relevant for each element, the by-products of the industries are analyzed. The problematic by-products are summarized in Table 5.11. The table also summarizes the procedures followed to solve the negative elements.

Table 5.11 Solutions to problems in the first application of the commodity technology assumption

Industry	Problematic by-product	Adjustment	Commodities with negative element	[P]	Before		After	
					1990	1997	1990	1997
Fisheries	Food	Food supplied by fisheries is reclassified as fishery products.	Agricultural		-263	-209	0	0
			Food		-147	-139	0	0
Other products	Government services	An input structure for government services is derived.	Construction		-185	-184	8	12
			Environmental services			-143		3
			VAT		-148	-172	-2	-2
Car repair	Trade and transport margins	Trade and transport supplied by the car repair industry is reclassified as car repair.	Banking services		-139	-128	99	132
Education	Research	Research by the education industry is reclassified as education.	Research		-1218	-1294	40	57
			Import of travel services			-119		5
			Subsidies			438		-42
			Product subsidies		409		-26	
			Primary plastics	[P]	-104	-164	-1	-1
			Crude oil and natural gas		-148	-190	-1	0
			Textiles			-118		313
Trade and transport margins	Clothing, Fuels, Non-ferrous basic metals, Real estate services, Iron and steel products, Machines	An input structure for the by-products is derived.	Non-ferrous basic metals		-462	-635	-11	-5
			VAT			-115		0
			Primary iron and steel	[P]	-347	-309	-63	95
			Iron and steel products	[P]	-132	-263	-70	

Industry	Source industries	Description
Life insurance and pensions	Real estate services	An input structure for the real estate services is derived.
Other business services	Construction, iron and steel products	An input structure for the by-products is derived.
Primary plastics	Chemicals	An input structure for chemicals is derived.
Office equipment & computers	Real estate services	An input structure for the real estate services is derived.
Electronics	Machines, Instruments, Research, Other business services, Electronics, Trade and transport margins	Machines supplied by the electronics industry are reclassified as electronics. An input structure for the problematic by-products is derived.
Publishing	Paper	Paper supplied by the publishing industry is reclassified as publishing.
Non-ferrous basic metals	Iron and steel products	An input structure for the iron and steel products is derived.
Primary iron and steel	Iron and steel products, Non-ferrous basic metals	An input structure for the by-products is derived.
Iron and steel products	Basic iron and steel, Machines, Cars and engines	An input structure for the by-products is derived.

Construction		-315	-319	66	95
Primary iron and steel	[P]	-1342	-2235	-45	-52
Construction products			-121		55
Fuels			-158		193
Product subsidies		120		94	
Electrical appliances	[P]				-104
Iron ore	[P]	-2240	-6161	0	3
Other income		-140	-120		-139
Real estate services			-120		13
Wages			-236		739
Social charges and pensions			-138		62
Other income		-132	-202	221	298
Machines	[P]		-171		13
Primary plastics	[P]	-124	-188	-49	-47
Primary iron and steel	[P]	-198	-410	10	39
Iron and steel products	[P]	-116		29	
Cars and engines	[P]	-214			1

Note: [P] – Physical element of hybrid-unit IO table. Empty entries denote elements that are not smaller than –100 million guilders or –10 million kg.

In case of heterogeneous production processes, an input structure for the by-product is estimated. It is then assumed that the input requirements of the by-product differ from the industry where this by-product is the principal product. An input structure is estimated by selecting the IO coefficients of the initial application of the commodity technology assumption. The negative elements are set to zero, and the other inputs adjusted, so that when the by-product is subtracted from the input structure of the industry no negative elements occur. The supply of the by-product is added to the industry where the by-product is the principal product. Furthermore, the inputs required for this by-product are subtracted from the industry where it was a by-product and added to the industry where it is the principal product.

In case of aggregation, it is assumed that it is better to reclassify the by-product as the principal product of the industry. This is done in cases where the by-product is made by a similar production process as the principal product. The supply of the by-product is adjusted downward, and the output of the principal product is increased. The use tables are adjusted accordingly.

After these adjustments are made to the hybrid SUT, the commodity technology assumption is applied again. Table 5.12 summarizes the resulting negatives, and shows that most large negative elements have disappeared. The remaining negative values are set to zero. The IO table is completed by using the same row and column balancing procedure discussed in Section 5.3. This resulting hybrid non-negative commodity-by-commodity IO tables for 1990 and 1997 are shown in Tables 5.13 and 5.14.

Table 5.12 Second application of the commodity technology assumption

Monetary (million 1997 guilders)						Physical (million kg)					
1990			1997			1990			1997		
<0	<−10	<−100	<0	<−10	<−100	<0	<−1	<−10	<0	<−1	<−10
617	39	1	537	41	0	160	21	0	176	36	1

5.9 CONCLUSIONS

This chapter has described the six steps that are required to produce non-negative commodity-by-commodity IO tables in hybrid units. The procedure was applied to iron and steel and plastics products in the Netherlands years 1990 and 1997. The resulting tables distinguish ten iron and steel and plastic commodities in kilograms and 46 commodities in 1997 prices. Furthermore, they include nine primary input categories and export, consumption, government consumption, investment, stock changes and import.

Table 5.13 Hybrid input–output table for 1990

	1	2	3	4	5	6	7	8	9	10	11	12	13	14	15	16
1	3263	0	3	0	12709	351	13	3	7	89	18	4	4	0	14	3
2	0	7	0	0	119	0	0	0	0	0	0	0	0	0	0	0
3	0	0	188	3	87	0	4	0	0	0	59	0	6265	350	2	41
4	60	1	0	120	27	0	1	0	0	0	16	0	0	127	0	351
5	3275	0	0	0	7039	0	0	0	63	0	50	1	0	260	0	0
6	0	0	0	0	0	0	17	0	0	0	0	0	0	0	0	0
7	11	17	1	1	7	24	637	472	4	1	37	6	0	23	31	16
8	6	2	1	0	6	0	3	17	0	0	4	1	4	2	0	1
9	3	3	0	1	4	1	0	11	68	2	0	4	1	0	0	0
10	37	0	0	3	27	3	2	0	0	496	32	8	4	31	0	32
11	17	0	0	2	659	126	25	5	3	7	1283	1044	3	127	5	44
12	0	0	0	3	168	43	13	9	3	8	86	1719	19	84	4	30
13	169	60	0	27	22	1	0	0	0	3	2	7	656	1255	1	56
14	565	2	56	4	184	14	256	1	12	22	121	184	81	3259	50	35
15	0	0	0	0	4	0	14	0	0	0	0	2	1	1	40	1
16	19	0	0	0	197	0	0	0	0	0	3	7	0	11	0	596
17	0	0	0	0	0	0	2	0	0	0	15	6	0	26	0	13
18	0	4	0	0	0	0	0	0	0	0	0	0	0	0	0	0
19	0	0	0	0	0	0	0	0	17	0	0	0	0	0	0	0
20	0	0	0	0	0	0	0	0	0	0	0	0	0	0	0	2
21	744	4	12	11	410	10	53	5	4	19	64	64	38	266	11	124
22	74	0	1	3	20	0	1	1	1	1	12	7	4	31	0	6
23	69	4	0	3	35	1	5	6	0	3	9	6	25	21	1	15
24	120	0	20	18	290	17	20	8	0	30	25	61	22	124	0	60
25	3	0	5	0	53	5	7	5	1	6	12	40	3	41	3	18
26	61	3	17	4	55	3	8	6	1	7	12	337	14	49	2	14
27	271	0	2	13	100	9	21	2	0	8	11	73	1	0	3	6
28	46	9	0	3	52	3	12	3	1	4	9	13	13	30	2	10
29	3	0	2	0	46	1	2	2	0	6	8	8	4	24	0	7
30	0	0	0	14	92	9	23	4	3	17	27	129	61	9	3	29
31	59	0	118	13	98	1	5	6	6	3	21	60	32	25	4	22
32	4	0	40	0	54	2	5	2	0	3	7	17	4	37	2	10
33	24	0	40	4	132	9	15	10	1	2	12	14	23	336	6	13
34	609	9	246	27	1122	306	107	43	11	61	159	944	125	887	37	198
35	6	0	4	1	39	4	3	1	0	1	9	32	5	52	1	10
36	187	0	0	2	14	1	1	1	1	0	1	8	1	0	0	2
37	76	1	12	6	52	4	8	1	4	8	29	13	13	85	4	29
38	39	0	12	3	21	1	2	3	1	3	5	18	1	3	1	5
39	0	0	0	0	2	0	0	3	0	0	0	5	0	0	0	0
40	0	0	0	0	0	0	0	0	0	0	0	0	0	0	0	0
41	0	0	0	0	0	0	0	0	0	0	0	0	0	0	0	0
42	647	25	154	30	1830	138	142	91	31	196	175	244	132	1124	15	360
43	13	2	2	3	22	1	7	2	2	7	11	8	4	12	2	10
44	0	0	0	0	0	0	0	0	0	0	0	0	0	0	0	0
45	136	0	0	14	190	18	125	228	12	109	51	361	119	134	8	144
46	1	1	8	0	52	10	6	2	2	2	8	25	14	37	2	9
100	0	0	0	0	2	14	49	0	3	2	39	0	0	70	1	35
101	20	0	1	3	145	5	11	2	6	7	31	30	1	111	4	29
102	0	0	0	12	96	0	0	0	0	0	0	0	0	0	50	172
103	1	0	2	13	192	5	0	4	1	14	5	7	3	73	0	11
104	59	0	16	2	25	0	6	0	0	2	5	8	7	20	3	9
105	0	0	0	0	2	0	1	0	0	1	1	1	1	3	2	1
106	0	0	0	3	7	0	0	0	0	0	3	2	2	8	0	3
107	0	0	0	0	0	0	0	0	0	0	0	0	0	0	0	0
108	0	0	0	0	0	0	0	0	0	0	0	0	0	0	0	0
109	0	0	2	0	0	0	0	0	0	0	0	0	0	0	0	0
1000	1274	118	171	93	3286	162	384	255	102	429	746	2423	100	1660	151	955
1001	6334	156	6928	219	2029	764	194	101	39	65	461	1028	741	3270	58	792
1002	0	0	0	0	0	0	0	0	0	0	0	0	0	0	0	0
1003	408	2	6	8	183	0	9	1	1	3	17	6	73	55	0	17
1004	-129	0	0	0	-210	-3	-4	-2	-1	0	-2	-2	-1	-7	-1	0
1005	181	9	28	19	592	34	64	39	14	49	87	317	29	192	18	117
1006	157	2	11	17	267	22	11	10	0	13	18	26	36	77	4	17
1007	-290	-2	0	0	-552	0	0	0	0	-9	-1	-3	0	0	0	0
1008	8	0	0	1	40	3	11	11	1	2	11	26	43	34	2	13
Total	19132	479	8271	790	32873	2173	2370	1415	429	1751	3981	9480	8842	14756	586	4551

Note: *Coding is provided in Appendix 5.B. Rows with codes 1–46 and 1000–1008 are in million euros (in 1997 prices) and rows with codes 100–109 are in million kg.*

Table 5.13 (continued)

	17	18	19	20	21	22	23	24	25	26	27	28	29	30	31	32
1	2	2	0	0	42	1	44	6	131	5	2	2	2	46	1	1
2	0	0	0	0	0	0	0	0	26	0	0	0	0	0	0	0
3	8	0	1	0	3197	0	0	0	0	0	0	0	0	0	0	0
4	1	0	1	0	0	0	251	0	0	0	0	0	0	0	0	0
5	0	0	3	0	1	0	12	1	1968	2	1	3	0	2	2	6
6	0	0	0	0	0	0	0	0	1	0	0	0	0	0	0	0
7	0	0	98	0	0	0	6	0	22	8	0	1	1	0	0	0
8	0	2	4	0	4	0	16	6	15	11	1	1	0	1	0	1
9	1	1	106	0	1	0	7	1	5	1	0	0	0	1	0	0
10	11	1	206	0	0	2	1104	1	6	0	0	1	0	126	0	0
11	12	15	48	0	6	8	21	3	58	23	26	18	13	13	1	11
12	8	14	18	0	16	8	16	128	63	30	206	83	48	36	8	21
13	10	0	14	1	54	4	116	22	7	19	26	8	6	10	100	3
14	21	5	62	0	9	20	296	26	3	0	1	0	1	3	0	25
15	2	2	6	1	4	7	53	88	0	16	0	0	0	0	0	0
16	0	44	7	0	0	0	3180	19	30	0	0	0	0	141	0	0
17	739	56	13	5	3	2	281	0	0	0	0	0	0	0	0	0
18	0	156	0	0	0	0	21	0	0	0	0	0	0	0	0	0
19	0	0	195	0	0	1	251	0	9	0	3	3	2	120	0	0
20	3	0	0	0	0	0	2	0	0	0	0	0	0	0	0	0
21	165	7	27	0	2788	42	48	81	228	39	31	13	13	25	5	6
22	6	2	0	0	20	113	0	6	12	3	4	1	1	6	0	6
23	2	2	4	0	166	17	9939	26	47	41	69	30	30	2800	4	0
24	12	23	41	0	4	6	511	257	67	45	57	16	22	44	300	28
25	5	18	0	0	5	4	13	29	44	30	92	42	22	35	2	39
26	6	14	0	0	22	15	122	68	70	518	592	88	115	205	14	50
27	13	0	5	0	23	5	344	45	70	45	683	521	158	44	0	12
28	6	5	6	0	9	1	73	66	35	11	17	291	0	121	119	6
29	2	6	8	0	6	2	43	24	13	6	422	2215	80	6	8	8
30	2	18	29	0	11	7	210	280	497	96	121	70	37	313	38	88
31	8	14	13	0	8	3	467	21	18	58	33	34	32	23	50	191
32	1	0	2	0	3	9	14	12	8	56	209	63	24	25	5	262
33	8	114	0	0	0	9	35	0	0	43	0	0	4	2	0	5
34	66	254	90	1	114	40	1473	667	549	672	486	291	166	415	278	296
35	4	24	2	0	1	0	28	18	13	0	11	4	5	14	2	22
36	1	0	7	0	2	1	10	11	6	19	25	21	18	4	0	6
37	10	6	5	0	7	1	149	13	2	2	1	0	3	29	3	0
38	3	3	4	0	4	8	200	16	35	3	15	8	7	30	5	8
39	0	0	0	0	0	0	0	0	50	0	0	0	0	2	0	0
40	0	0	0	0	0	0	21	13	88	14	2	1	0	0	3	0
41	0	0	0	0	0	0	0	0	0	0	0	0	0	0	0	0
42	104	213	213	1	52	18	2416	366	451	132	78	4	20	169	0	51
43	3	11	2	0	6	2	26	6	8	3	1	43	2	5	5	0
44	0	0	0	0	0	0	0	0	0	0	0	0	0	0	0	0
45	23	34	146	0	172	30	19	5	0	9	0	0	0	0	0	0
46	5	6	8	0	14	4	82	28	44	11	9	0	0	118	16	41
100	6	2	91	0	0	0	51	0	0	0	0	0	0	2	0	0
101	11	15	49	0	8	5	231	3	3	0	1	0	1	9	0	3
102	1	41	101	0	1	0	342	0	0	0	0	0	0	0	0	0
103	19	6	21	0	1	0	707	0	1	0	0	0	0	0	0	0
104	8	6	4	1	6	2	137	1	3	10	1	0	0	13	12	3
105	0	1	0	0	0	0	2	0	0	0	0	0	0	0	0	0
106	2	14	0	0	9	1	108	7	2	15	0	0	0	0	0	1
107	0	28	0	0	0	0	31	2	0	27	0	0	0	0	0	0
108	0	0	0	0	0	0	3	213	0	0	0	0	0	0	0	0
109	0	0	0	0	0	0	4	0	0	0	0	0	0	0	0	0
1000	281	706	1491	1	616	281	9588	2286	2178	2145	4094	1319	1346	1149	149	1456
1001	290	197	-40	1	2533	616	5665	1351	2301	2431	465	707	861	22407	2151	591
1002	0	0	0	0	0	0	0	0	0	162	307	80	85	595	0	0
1003	2	2	0	0	10	13	58	89	82	16	29	30	6	1015	125	2
1004	-6	-3	-1	0	0	0	-33	-1	-4	0	-18	0	0	-1	-4	-3
1005	33	89	35	1	101	39	1733	260	244	330	902	300	239	199	17	110
1006	16	14	4	0	323	13	137	48	199	20	33	10	8	41	110	7
1007	-2	0	0	0	0	0	-11	-5	-9	0	-5	-1	-2	-8	0	0
1008	132	20	8	0	183	1	253	29	17	0	0	0	0	15	0	28
Total	2148	2996	3345	15	10699	1421	44086	7488	9787	7280	9048	6326	3384	30458	3588	3427

Table 5.13 (continued)

	33	34	35	36	37	38	39	40	41	42	43	44	45	46	100	101
1	0	3	4	69	16	11	20	6	0	0	97	0	10	63	12	0
2	0	0	0	8	0	0	0	0	0	0	1	0	0	0	0	0
3	0	0	0	0	0	0	0	0	0	0	0	3	0	0	92	2
4	2	0	0	0	0	0	0	0	0	2	31	1	0	0	4	0
5	1	28	8	394	2	7	166	0	0	30	70	0	0	298	14	1
6	0	0	0	0	0	0	0	0	0	0	0	0	0	27	0	0
7	0	8	2	55	4	0	4	5	0	0	26	0	0	5	0	13
8	0	20	0	27	11	0	2	1	0	45	56	0	0	2	3	0
9	0	4	0	8	1	0	0	0	0	11	13	0	0	4	0	0
10	1	53	7	3	9	0	3	55	0	85	0	3	0	30	37	15
11	0	77	23	134	1	3	0	5	0	320	58	0	0	5	50	75
12	6	1370	235	131	33	17	1	13	0	1157	311	0	3	23	10	20
13	22	52	18	9	19	8	21	2	0	878	132	0	0	0	70	4
14	137	71	27	555	0	1	28	90	0	52	54	8	0	4	1937	146
15	5	14	2	43	0	0	0	0	0	90	2	0	0	1	0	3
16	44	2	11	21	6	0	14	26	0	6	0	4	0	0	23	26
17	0	0	2	0	0	0	0	0	0	0	7	23	0	0	12	2
18	2	77	20	316	0	0	0	0	0	16	246	0	0	18	0	0
19	0	21	22	23	4	10	15	6	0	67	17	0	0	24	0	0
20	0	0	0	0	0	0	0	0	0	0	0	0	0	0	0	1
21	64	98	122	268	173	32	108	37	0	674	66	30	53	0	124	68
22	6	8	8	33	6	2	6	8	0	68	32	0	0	0	7	2
23	3	592	181	274	110	36	113	4	0	239	1709	0	12	0	16	7
24	35	205	42	94	66	18	29	18	0	1345	85	0	0	0	53	39
25	3	252	44	141	14	47	57	3	0	1058	242	0	30	0	9	12
26	41	382	99	217	33	52	373	10	0	1009	435	0	36	0	18	12
27	14	353	0	18	21	205	150	9	0	2079	460	0	29	0	24	16
28	20	97	51	39	22	18	25	7	0	460	13	0	5	0	13	12
29	5	90	0	24	8	5	6	4	0	57	0	0	0	0	2	1
30	39	828	203	539	103	23	73	115	0	2744	264	0	41	0	13	23
31	11	199	33	41	50	27	101	21	0	884	0	0	5	0	21	25
32	5	59	30	17	17	16	8	0	0	199	418	0	0	0	14	9
33	1648	58	18	0	18	0	0	0	0	4	273	0	42	0	250	19
34	97	6666	540	475	300	238	942	132	0	6261	1492	0	195	3	132	205
35	106	112	43	87	3	1	0	6	0	154	220	0	0	0	33	8
36	3	43	66	409	6	4	8	2	0	124	83	0	0	0	9	2
37	5	6	4	94	794	8	27	0	0	92	832	0	0	0	33	11
38	0	103	10	119	7	11	8	6	0	111	53	0	6	0	5	4
39	0	1425	26	18	1	0	2063	0	0	0	0	0	0	0	0	0
40	11	22	10	216	4	13	23	97	0	33	33	0	0	0	0	0
41	0	0	0	0	0	0	0	0	0	0	0	0	0	0	0	0
42	78	386	115	567	55	32	62	94	0	4568	374	156	96	383	304	238
43	4	40	608	5	1	3	6	1	0	58	650	0	0	0	0	0
44	0	0	0	0	0	0	0	0	0	0	0	0	0	0	0	0
45	0	7	0	0	5	0	0	0	0	48	6	59	84	0	29	62
46	1	47	0	14	0	17	0	5	0	309	0	0	0	0	7	7
100	26	0	0	0	0	0	0	0	0	0	0	0	0	0	197	954
101	4	16	1	8	4	1	3	1	0	37	0	9	4	6	6	120
102	1	0	3	0	9	0	0	0	0	0	0	26	0	0	0	7
103	1	113	7	2	36	0	0	1	0	0	43	44	19	3	6	7
104	0	6	1	2	15	0	0	1	0	47	40	10	7	0	10	5
105	0	1	1	0	1	0	0	0	0	3	2	0	0	0	0	0
106	4	3	1	0	5	0	0	0	0	5	5	7	3	1	3	1
107	0	0	0	0	0	0	0	0	0	3	2	0	0	1	0	0
108	0	0	0	0	0	0	0	0	0	0	5	0	0	0	0	0
109	0	0	0	0	0	0	0	0	0	24	38	0	0	0	0	0
1000	1766	13317	8999	11923	654	1238	931	606	18	22027	13035	1374	2907	0	499	749
1001	647	4641	1507	5706	824	72	1474	694	1010	13181	5665	49	1029	0	127	369
1002	0	0	175	594	99	115	157	31	0	1	1186	0	0	12	0	0
1003	14	52	106	50	113	7	23	2	0	259	131	0	0	0	15	3
1004	-38	-38	-3	-51	0	-2	-18	-4	0	-118	0	0	0	0	-8	-1
1005	230	1488	1975	1752	126	158	149	87	3	2575	4138	359	610	0	104	100
1006	36	110	37	47	55	27	68	12	0	826	142	9	2	65	28	26
1007	-465	-81	-11	-5	-7	-1	-112	0	0	-37	-35	0	0	0	0	0
1008	134	124	3	0	0	15	6	4	0	1490	138	0	0	0	32	10
Total	4810	33842	15495	25599	3989	2603	7159	2250	1030	66919	34121	2400	5343	1028	3676	1210

Table 5.13 (continued)

	102	103	104	105	106	107	108	109	900	901	902	903	904	905	Total
1	0	1	9	0	2	1	2	1	5360	1215	0	211	10	-4757	19132
2	0	0	0	0	0	0	0	0	194	176	0	0	0	-51	479
3	13	0	0	0	3	1	1	1	3325	0	0	309	251	-5934	8271
4	10	0	0	0	0	0	0	0	319	24	0	0	63	-622	790
5	0	1	2	0	0	0	0	0	12828	12373	0	0	173	-6217	32873
6	0	0	0	0	0	0	0	0	1195	1102	0	0	17	-185	2173
7	0	1	0	0	0	0	0	0	1174	1524	0	149	11	-2035	2370
8	0	2	2	0	1	0	2	3	419	2432	0	17	79	-1822	1415
9	1	2	6	0	0	0	1	0	140	792	0	0	8	-786	429
10	5	23	13	2	5	1	15	9	330	265	0	74	-6	-1420	1751
11	7	37	14	2	11	5	7	3	2161	270	0	0	34	-2946	3981
12	3	31	66	4	10	9	12	14	1044	2821	0	0	18	-778	9480
13	2	10	14	0	7	0	7	13	5834	1230	0	0	-208	-1961	8842
14	16	89	33	0	19	9	92	45	10785	1790	0	0	93	-6639	14756
15	3	2	31	2	3	0	124	43	295	123	0	0	20	-473	586
16	18	40	0	1	78	9	16	13	1037	183	0	44	414	-1740	4551
17	57	277	78	0	262	70	14	35	1462	0	0	0	124	-1435	2148
18	0	0	41	0	12	4	4	177	1796	746	0	1134	26	-1819	2996
19	0	0	0	0	0	0	11	19	767	2198	0	1443	116	-2019	3345
20	3	0	2	0	0	0	0	0	2	0	0	0	0	0	15
21	95	52	67	3	33	13	17	19	10	3200	0	66	4	-152	10699
22	5	6	10	0	0	0	5	5	0	860	0	0	0	0	1421
23	1	12	17	0	6	11	2	1	324	570	0	26613	0	-143	44086
24	20	94	95	14	16	15	67	35	0	2858	0	0	0	-5	7488
25	6	23	80	7	9	11	13	23	0	7118	0	0	0	0	9787
26	7	19	55	2	6	6	5	17	303	2044	0	0	0	-394	7280
27	14	12	85	31	0	3	4	2	556	2660	0	83	0	-266	9048
28	1	9	15	5	2	1	4	15	162	4846	0	0	0	-493	6326
29	4	12	18	1	10	2	8	5	61	133	0	0	0	-34	3384
30	6	68	110	16	9	5	19	36	0	22084	0	759	0	0	30458
31	34	39	50	6	15	1	13	27	328	459	0	0	0	-248	3588
32	10	13	2	1	1	0	0	3	511	52	0	1706	0	-546	3427
33	23	0	141	26	31	605	54	62	627	0	976	0	0	-926	4810
34	55	379	446	68	131	79	122	220	5809	1078	0	2825	-9	-5784	33842
35	2	17	34	5	7	92	9	30	0	1872	12340	0	0	0	15495
36	0	5	12	0	2	0	1	8	0	22568	1896	0	0	0	25599
37	9	25	21	5	7	0	10	19	0	734	677	0	0	0	3989
38	3	32	45	2	8	6	8	7	4	1304	277	0	0	0	2603
39	0	1	0	0	0	1	0	0	614	2755	621	0	7	-435	7159
40	0	0	0	0	0	0	0	0	0	1646	0	0	0	0	2250
41	0	0	0	0	0	0	0	0	0	1030	0	0	0	0	1030
42	133	283	771	83	173	75	543	272	16434	28425	0	3485	27	-912	66919
43	7	9	13	1	8	0	6	8	206	412	31656	207	0	-25	34121
44	0	0	0	0	0	0	0	0	0	0	0	2400	0	0	2400
45	97	1083	341	0	147	138	90	442	1966	0	0	0	0	-1346	5343
46	5	17	16	3	5	3	2	3	0	0	0	0	0	0	1028
100	0	0	2	0	26	1	28	0	3137	0	0	0	15	-1084	3676
101	8	35	44	7	13	9	24	9	623	63	0	87	9	-688	1210
102	658	2434	719	3	75	100	281	184	4383	2	0	0	130	-4234	5599
103	3	438	341	24	37	17	133	97	1022	78	0	439	14	-778	3235
104	11	7	245	0	5	0	17	13	524	102	0	585	10	-827	1209
105	1	1	0	1	0	0	0	0	57	3	0	53	-1	-71	69
106	2	0	31	15	70	5	28	16	129	27	0	38	2	-257	335
107	0	0	26	9	7	105	0	5	132	37	0	26	-2	-144	295
108	0	0	15	0	0	0	211	0	492	257	0	548	49	-1025	767
109	0	0	0	0	0	0	0	30	144	60	0	297	9	-166	443
1000	725	1121	2446	135	592	313	672	427							
1001	364	759	532	-63	263	100	182	-23							
1002	0	0	0	0	0	0	0	0							
1003	13	19	6	0	2	1	2	6							
1004	-1	-4	-36	-3	-4	0	-5	-42							
1005	125	71	315	9	80	5	99	31							
1006	36	29	38	3	13	5	16	16							
1007	0	-1	0	0	-3	-16	0	0							
1008	250	20	64	5	8	23	4	19							
Total	5599	3235	1209	69	335	295	767	443							

Table 5.14 Hybrid input–output table for 1997

	1	2	3	4	5	6	7	8	9	10	11	12	13	14	15	16
1	2869	0	3	0	12786	419	7	10	12	134	13	3	2	0	18	5
2	0	5	0	0	121	0	0	0	0	0	0	0	0	0	0	0
3	0	0	364	17	102	3	6	0	0	0	63	1	8302	293	1	61
4	57	1	0	141	19	0	1	0	0	0	9	0	0	159	0	357
5	2982	0	0	0	8433	0	1	0	48	0	44	0	0	316	0	1
6	0	0	0	0	0	0	23	0	0	0	0	0	0	0	0	0
7	15	18	2	1	9	27	666	296	3	1	45	3	0	21	29	24
8	5	1	1	0	6	0	1	14	0	0	2	1	2	3	0	3
9	5	1	1	0	5	0	0	12	69	3	1	4	0	1	0	1
10	36	0	0	7	43	4	2	1	1	539	40	10	4	21	0	34
11	18	1	0	4	755	163	27	8	3	9	1399	1172	6	175	2	55
12	0	0	0	0	216	50	16	14	3	8	109	1788	11	102	4	25
13	124	64	2	26	26	1	1	0	5	8	9	672	1898	0	0	58
14	453	1	76	4	270	22	276	5	13	31	152	220	105	4410	53	90
15	0	0	0	0	2	0	17	0	0	0	3	1	1	12	36	0
16	24	0	0	0	243	0	5	0	0	9	5	0	0	29	0	631
17	0	0	0	0	0	0	1	0	0	0	7	4	0	31	0	19
18	0	2	0	0	0	0	0	0	0	0	0	0	0	0	0	0
19	0	0	0	0	5	0	0	15	1	1	1	0	0	1	0	0
20	0	0	0	0	0	0	6	0	0	0	0	0	0	0	14	24
21	868	4	14	27	417	10	49	5	3	28	95	75	8	299	10	119
22	88	0	3	2	21	0	1	0	0	0	5	4	4	16	0	9
23	79	4	9	2	51	2	6	5	1	4	10	6	12	26	1	13
24	111	0	30	7	297	18	22	6	3	30	26	67	22	153	0	63
25	6	0	4	1	59	3	8	5	2	4	12	37	2	43	3	16
26	81	4	19	1	59	3	7	7	1	5	9	287	12	44	2	15
27	254	1	5	3	78	2	9	10	3	7	24	67	0	16	2	19
28	109	7	3	3	40	2	7	5	2	7	12	22	9	27	2	15
29	9	0	2	0	38	2	1	2	0	1	5	6	2	19	0	6
30	0	0	0	3	99	0	22	10	2	26	21	145	57	15	2	31
31	52	0	159	28	113	2	8	10	2	11	22	87	35	45	3	24
32	16	1	53	5	135	5	11	6	1	5	38	54	61	155	3	33
33	30	0	56	4	174	8	15	6	0	1	15	16	8	459	6	19
34	650	8	260	26	1626	434	110	52	16	86	211	983	222	1230	33	269
35	8	0	6	1	47	3	5	1	1	0	11	23	7	67	1	8
36	220	0	1	0	16	1	1	1	0	2	5	12	0	9	0	5
37	159	0	17	2	61	3	7	2	4	9	31	16	19	118	4	30
38	45	0	11	2	31	2	4	3	0	4	6	18	2	18	1	8
39	0	0	0	0	5	0	0	2	0	0	2	24	0	0	0	1
40	4	0	1	0	8	0	1	0	0	1	0	8	1	4	0	1
41	0	0	0	0	0	0	0	0	0	0	0	0	0	0	0	0
42	595	26	213	39	2045	156	156	85	25	206	208	307	149	1462	4	402
43	13	1	4	2	18	1	4	3	1	6	13	6	3	15	1	11
44	0	0	0	0	0	0	0	0	0	0	0	0	0	0	0	0
45	113	0	0	0	215	28	139	264	12	145	70	397	155	333	7	158
46	2	1	7	0	49	8	17	3	2	6	11	26	9	38	2	16
100	0	0	0	0	1	2	70	2	5	2	65	0	0	31	0	46
101	30	0	2	3	190	8	5	3	3	12	45	39	3	90	1	29
102	0	0	0	10	60	0	0	0	0	0	0	0	0	2	47	432
103	0	0	0	17	224	21	0	6	1	20	7	9	4	69	0	17
104	76	2	16	4	28	1	3	0	0	7	9	8	11	23	1	11
105	0	0	0	1	4	0	0	0	0	0	2	1	1	4	1	1
106	0	0	3	1	11	1	2	1	0	1	4	2	3	8	0	3
107	0	0	0	0	0	0	0	0	0	0	0	0	0	0	0	0
108	0	0	0	0	0	0	0	0	0	0	0	0	0	0	0	0
109	0	0	2	0	0	0	0	0	0	0	0	0	0	0	0	0
1000	1343	88	83	55	3155	161	356	259	63	420	708	2437	138	1574	121	901
1001	8256	166	7912	330	3897	1016	274	101	36	190	558	1836	534	3269	67	835
1002	0	0	0	0	0	0	0	0	0	0	0	0	0	0	0	0
1003	376	2	7	7	166	1	10	4	1	1	19	7	114	51	0	21
1004	-1291	0	0	0	-90	0	-1	-1	-1	-3	-1	-6	-8	0	0	-3
1005	172	8	7	14	546	31	48	33	8	43	83	360	33	261	14	112
1006	164	1	29	20	764	41	12	9	2	18	21	33	42	107	3	25
1007	-108	-2	0	0	-349	0	-1	-3	-1	-8	-4	-1	-2	-34	0	-1
1008	9	0	0	1	34	2	9	13	1	2	10	26	36	52	1	16
Total	19594	447	9585	876	37792	2748	2515	1318	360	2105	4468	10823	10935	18112	499	5004

Note: Coding is provided in Appendix 5.B. Rows with codes 1–46 and 1000–1008 are in million euros (in 1997 prices) and rows with codes 100–109 are in million kg.

Table 5.14 (continued)

	17	18	19	20	21	22	23	24	25	26	27	28	29	30	31	32
1	2	3	0	0	40	1	52	10	233	7	3	2	4	55	1	1
2	0	0	0	0	0	0	0	0	35	0	0	0	0	0	0	0
3	11	1	1	0	4391	0	0	0	0	0	0	0	0	0	0	0
4	0	5	8	0	0	0	318	0	0	0	0	0	0	0	0	0
5	0	0	0	0	0	0	14	0	2357	1	2	0	0	4	3	10
6	0	0	0	0	0	0	0	0	0	0	0	0	0	0	0	0
7	0	0	121	0	0	0	7	0	22	6	1	1	1	0	0	0
8	1	2	4	0	4	0	17	8	13	15	1	1	1	1	1	2
9	1	5	121	0	1	0	4	1	2	2	0	0	0	1	0	0
10	14	1	215	0	0	0	1329	0	8	0	0	2	0	217	0	0
11	14	12	57	0	11	3	30	6	89	20	38	25	21	15	0	10
12	7	22	19	0	5	7	35	150	73	55	242	108	58	54	15	41
13	16	0	30	0	47	2	131	32	7	18	20	8	5	15	115	5
14	20	22	85	32	30	18	319	43	1	0	0	0	0	5	0	94
15	2	2	5	4	6	2	58	121	0	15	0	0	0	0	0	0
16	0	30	8	15	0	0	3501	18	42	0	0	0	0	259	0	0
17	855	67	14	101	1	1	358	0	0	0	0	0	0	0	0	0
18	0	178	0	0	0	0	18	0	0	0	0	0	0	0	0	0
19	0	0	161	0	0	0	352	0	17	0	5	6	3	202	0	0
20	36	0	0	0	0	0	50	0	0	0	0	0	0	0	0	0
21	201	13	21	4	4128	34	63	112	334	26	44	20	12	34	7	10
22	6	2	0	0	13	82	0	2	4	2	4	1	0	9	0	3
23	6	10	5	24	139	20	10977	23	57	102	57	43	42	3515	4	0
24	13	27	39	6	5	3	565	521	63	57	77	29	25	59	555	39
25	7	18	2	0	12	4	21	38	40	56	110	68	34	51	2	71
26	8	14	8	0	31	14	162	92	74	940	806	134	136	347	23	97
27	3	4	1	1	40	8	354	60	94	66	911	855	246	38	8	37
28	5	5	9	1	11	2	111	79	57	10	11	322	0	167	137	10
29	3	7	5	0	6	2	32	18	8	4	643	3160	74	6	7	8
30	3	10	27	4	7	3	255	380	661	138	148	103	53	385	50	130
31	10	12	21	5	28	6	694	45	65	92	41	45	41	35	131	280
32	18	21	7	1	53	21	83	48	18	82	566	136	36	45	18	587
33	23	179	0	0	0	9	55	0	0	60	0	0	5	4	0	2
34	97	464	136	17	240	70	2095	809	793	1449	902	611	227	614	503	804
35	5	29	2	0	1	2	32	16	13	0	13	2	5	16	3	51
36	3	3	6	0	7	1	20	14	10	35	30	35	19	9	0	26
37	17	7	1	4	13	3	181	23	13	6	3	0	0	30	4	3
38	2	6	1	0	7	4	264	26	54	8	20	11	11	44	11	23
39	1	0	0	0	0	0	1	0	35	0	0	0	0	1	0	0
40	1	3	8	0	3	1	3	14	112	7	3	1	0	0	5	0
41	0	0	0	0	0	0	0	0	0	0	0	0	0	0	0	0
42	119	221	221	26	86	7	2781	471	570	221	126	0	30	279	0	126
43	3	9	0	1	6	1	25	7	7	3	1	52	1	6	6	0
44	0	0	0	0	0	0	0	0	7	3	0	0	0	0	0	0
45	41	95	121	1	169	18	25	4	0	9	0	0	0	0	0	0
46	3	2	14	0	15	2	110	37	43	12	14	0	0	141	16	42
100	0	4	181	0	0	0	52	0	0	0	0	0	0	2	0	0
101	3	16	81	0	10	2	250	2	3	0	0	0	1	12	0	2
102	0	30	127	0	1	0	248	0	0	0	0	0	0	2	0	0
103	26	7	33	0	1	1	1038	0	0	0	0	0	0	0	0	0
104	8	5	4	2	11	2	167	2	4	8	1	0	1	14	15	3
105	0	2	0	0	1	0	3	0	0	0	1	1	0	0	0	0
106	0	33	0	0	12	1	131	7	3	28	0	0	0	1	0	0
107	0	40	0	0	0	0	33	2	0	40	0	0	0	0	0	0
108	0	0	0	0	0	0	4	232	0	0	0	0	0	0	0	0
109	0	0	0	0	0	0	6	0	0	0	0	0	0	0	0	0
1000	356	758	1530	22	671	213	9745	2443	2792	2060	4258	1423	1636	1450	249	2443
1001	265	431	-36	14	2723	767	4653	1638	2435	4319	2254	1068	1409	26457	2676	1538
1002	0	0	0	0	0	0	0	0	0	137	502	180	122	845	0	0
1003	4	5	0	0	38	19	66	113	112	12	51	37	9	1143	172	2
1004	-4	0	0	-1	-1	-1	-118	-15	-37	0	-30	0	0	0	0	-3
1005	51	88	51	0	100	23	1944	296	303	281	778	319	271	301	30	196
1006	21	10	8	4	544	14	204	52	272	27	45	22	20	66	191	19
1007	-2	0	-1	0	-1	-1	-15	-1	-5	-2	-5	-1	-2	-5	0	-2
1008	50	17	7	0	303	2	302	28	27	0	0	0	0	23	6	51
Total	2484	3955	3646	304	14190	1420	48088	9188	12017	10676	12712	8841	4571	37100	5065	6801

Table 5.14 *(continued)*

	33	34	35	36	37	38	39	40	41	42	43	44	45	46	100	101
1	0	6	6	86	25	14	16	7	0	0	120	0	0	86	11	0
2	0	0	0	9	0	0	0	0	0	0	2	0	0	0	0	0
3	0	0	0	0	0	0	0	0	0	0	0	3	0	0	113	1
4	1	0	1	0	0	0	0	0	0	4	43	1	0	0	4	0
5	1	48	6	465	3	10	195	0	0	46	69	0	0	334	14	2
6	0	0	0	0	0	0	0	0	0	0	0	0	0	17	0	0
7	0	7	3	75	6	1	6	6	0	141	28	0	0	6	1	12
8	0	32	0	30	15	0	3	1	0	55	72	0	0	1	1	1
9	0	3	0	7	2	0	0	0	0	14	9	0	0	3	1	0
10	0	90	7	5	19	0	1	63	0	117	0	4	0	37	26	16
11	2	139	31	164	1	7	0	4	0	400	80	0	4	31	42	72
12	13	1820	256	179	47	15	7	17	0	1366	358	0	4	31	9	25
13	17	69	12	9	38	9	15	2	0	1271	88	0	0	0	72	1
14	174	69	35	685	0	1	30	106	0	56	51	9	0	3	2381	185
15	5	13	2	56	0	0	0	0	0	124	1	0	0	1	0	4
16	62	25	13	26	7	0	16	29	0	9	0	4	0	0	16	23
17	0	0	2	0	0	0	0	0	0	0	4	15	0	0	9	2
18	3	140	19	361	0	0	0	0	0	20	150	0	0	17	0	1
19	2	22	27	22	5	19	14	11	0	69	21	0	0	22	0	1
20	0	0	0	0	0	0	0	0	0	0	0	0	0	0	12	24
21	91	138	165	325	152	45	136	40	0	805	189	31	57	0	128	87
22	5	7	6	27	2	2	5	5	0	63	26	0	0	0	8	2
23	9	874	179	284	198	42	119	1	0	319	1922	0	13	0	17	9
24	36	256	45	112	111	21	44	15	0	1723	85	0	0	0	51	40
25	3	388	43	178	20	61	74	5	0	1310	272	0	33	0	15	13
26	68	581	97	294	40	73	417	11	0	1485	461	0	39	0	8	17
27	17	399	15	75	8	234	186	8	0	2574	510	0	31	0	9	13
28	17	143	39	60	27	15	20	6	0	488	11	0	5	0	23	13
29	5	80	1	22	7	14	7	3	0	48	0	0	0	0	4	2
30	38	1276	76	608	68	154	67	114	0	3830	321	0	45	0	0	37
31	15	457	35	55	89	37	123	29	0	1143	3	0	6	0	23	29
32	11	176	50	59	43	32	34	4	0	446	537	0	0	1	76	18
33	1559	77	26	0	18	0	2	0	0	34	279	0	45	0	347	24
34	201	10458	606	634	361	289	1225	146	0	8347	1527	0	211	2	226	249
35	115	165	37	70	7	1	0	3	0	157	205	0	0	0	50	8
36	4	103	73	580	9	3	14	3	0	173	129	0	0	0	4	4
37	10	30	6	110	1162	6	33	0	0	130	1395	0	0	0	39	14
38	0	157	11	145	6	14	7	10	0	152	54	0	7	0	5	5
39	1	1037	6	15	2	0	2390	0	0	0	0	0	0	0	0	1
40	13	29	3	161	6	13	17	71	0	37	13	0	0	0	0	2
41	0	0	0	0	0	0	0	0	0	0	0	0	0	0	0	0
42	94	551	129	755	110	37	79	98	0	6471	369	202	103	459	287	263
43	4	47	759	3	1	3	7	1	0	49	586	0	0	0	6	2
44	0	0	0	0	0	0	0	0	0	0	0	0	0	0	0	0
45	0	20	1	0	8	0	0	0	0	88	6	61	92	0	29	83
46	1	66	0	17	0	22	2	6	0	363	0	0	0	0	7	7
100	36	2	0	0	0	0	3	0	0	0	0	0	0	0	423	1213
101	7	20	2	5	4	2	2	2	0	76	0	12	5	2	15	112
102	0	0	4	0	7	0	0	0	0	9	0	19	0	0	6	3
103	1	160	8	2	42	0	0	2	0	0	72	50	25	0	20	5
104	1	8	1	2	18	0	0	1	0	62	33	13	8	0	17	5
105	0	2	1	1	1	0	0	0	0	6	4	0	0	0	2	0
106	11	21	2	1	8	0	0	0	0	9	0	19	4	1	4	1
107	25	59	0	0	0	0	0	0	0	18	1	0	0	1	0	0
108	0	0	0	0	0	0	0	0	0	0	7	0	0	0	0	0
109	0	0	0	0	0	0	0	0	0	38	15	0	0	0	0	0
1000	1788	19184	9819	13584	786	1465	980	659	22	25202	13168	1693	3148	0	476	780
1001	802	7545	1325	6316	1202	42	1931	700	1199	18781	6239	57	1307	0	818	585
1002	0	0	205	732	210	139	143	33	0	0	1481	0	0	18	19	4
1003	15	45	116	63	112	7	33	2	0	270	145	0	0	1	0	3
1004	-440	-181	-19	-335	0	-5	-37	-15	0	-299	-160	0	0	0	0	-1
1005	260	2128	2296	2120	143	226	164	79	2	3292	3849	448	661	0	90	103
1006	41	174	37	76	88	34	93	11	0	1256	161	12	3	81	25	24
1007	-157	-61	-13	-3	-3	-2	-133	0	0	-33	-63	0	0	0	54	9
1008	151	181	2	0	0	0	17	7	4	1693	166	0	0	0	54	9
Total	5315	49916	16699	29419	5453	3127	8519	2324	1223	86088	35941	2946	5981	1204	5529	1532

Table 5.14 (continued)

	102	103	104	105	106	107	108	109	900	901	902	903	904	905	Total
1	2	0	8	0	2	2	1	1	7223	1747	0	220	-239	-6457	19594
2	0	0	0	0	0	0	0	0	200	176	0	0	0	-101	447
3	0	0	0	0	6	1	2	0	3799	0	0	345	-102	-8201	9585
4	12	1	0	0	0	0	0	0	362	42	0	0	49	-718	876
5	0	1	1	0	0	0	0	0	20394	11611	0	0	-56	-9571	37792
6	0	0	0	0	0	0	0	0	2164	675	0	0	0	-132	2748
7	0	0	0	0	0	0	10	7	1374	1340	0	185	32	-2045	2515
8	2	3	3	0	2	1	1	3	430	2362	0	11	32	-1851	1318
9	1	5	9	0	0	0	1	0	145	865	0	0	9	-957	360
10	8	33	14	3	11	1	7	9	402	380	0	127	62	-1868	2105
11	15	53	24	4	16	24	7	2	2652	316	0	0	35	-3772	4468
12	5	37	67	5	16	15	19	13	1202	3000	0	0	3	-945	10823
13	3	15	9	0	27	0	6	4	6692	1444	0	0	-30	-2185	10935
14	29	92	32	0	34	40	100	13	13218	2620	0	0	188	-8888	18112
15	4	3	38	2	3	0	149	38	371	144	0	0	17	-760	499
16	15	21	2	0	123	14	26	23	1189	312	0	88	-6	-1854	5004
17	149	289	51	1	292	144	18	21	1971	0	0	0	73	-2016	2484
18	0	10	166	0	25	6	8	154	3027	808	0	1330	-20	-2468	3955
19	0	0	3	0	0	0	22	22	922	2689	0	1557	203	-2779	3646
20	51	0	37	0	0	0	0	0	34	0	0	0	14	0	304
21	109	80	71	5	40	18	26	31	9	4465	0	65	0	-209	14190
22	8	6	8	0	3	0	5	6	0	944	0	0	0	0	1420
23	5	17	12	0	6	9	9	3	846	700	0	27476	0	-236	48088
24	22	91	118	12	24	11	74	23	0	3345	0	0	0	-8	9188
25	9	17	59	3	11	17	16	6	0	8724	0	0	0	0	12017
26	10	22	61	4	12	8	10	6	537	3531	0	0	0	-558	10676
27	15	29	43	3	8	8	4	8	1129	4336	0	136	0	-311	12712
28	6	25	33	1	6	2	6	9	194	6846	0	0	0	-361	8841
29	4	9	15	2	11	1	7	5	87	200	0	0	0	-40	4571
30	1	121	116	6	11	6	19	44	0	26346	0	1005	0	0	37100
31	24	72	68	4	17	2	9	15	451	659	0	0	0	-452	5065
32	44	34	41	18	49	229	24	28	1046	153	0	2322	0	-991	6801
33	35	4	135	34	55	1072	84	66	811	0	767	0	0	-1313	5315
34	96	480	581	73	198	217	307	195	8943	2061	947	3744	-3	-8453	49916
35	4	16	35	8	12	148	15	13	0	1549	13702	0	0	0	16699
36	2	9	11	1	3	1	5	3	0	25569	2224	0	0	0	29419
37	14	28	27	4	14	2	11	12	0	901	717	0	0	0	5453
38	4	34	49	4	11	12	5	4	2	1480	301	0	0	0	3127
39	1	1	0	0	0	1	0	0	737	4162	620	0	12	-537	8519
40	1	7	7	1	0	1	1	1	0	1749	0	0	0	0	2324
41	0	0	0	0	0	0	0	0	0	1223	0	0	0	0	1223
42	179	329	1048	101	234	146	654	210	22349	33147	0	4589	11	1722	86088
43	7	12	12	1	7	2	6	7	306	479	33173	261	0	-29	35941
44	0	0	0	0	0	0	0	0	0	0	0	2946	0	0	2946
45	165	937	481	29	153	254	86	633	1416	0	0	0	0	-1088	5981
46	5	18	20	1	5	9	2	5	0	0	0	0	0	0	1204
100	1	1	4	1	41	0	20	1	4701	0	0	0	8	-1391	5529
101	8	33	43	21	40	8	37	3	898	75	0	90	8	-845	1532
102	744	3865	732	2	111	159	311	134	5081	2	0	0	87	-5161	7070
103	4	767	385	39	53	33	181	72	1511	105	0	635	19	-1011	4687
104	18	0	283	0	7	1	20	16	561	125	0	661	-46	-798	1459
105	2	2	0	11	0	0	0	0	87	5	0	100	0	-89	163
106	3	0	36	84	132	17	38	16	281	26	0	32	3	-366	641
107	0	0	28	11	25	43	0	4	279	46	0	40	0	-141	556
108	0	0	15	0	0	0	330	1	707	290	0	629	0	-1253	965
109	0	0	0	0	0	0	0	27	105	66	0	189	7	-135	321
1000	692	1463	2264	206	566	345	733	408							
1001	520	711	1090	31	263	139	555	33							
1002	0	0	0	0	0	0	0	0							
1003	12	12	5	0	5	2	5	3							
1004	0	-28	-31	-11	-5	-1	-21	-38							
1005	105	101	290	19	70	29	95	19							
1006	48	32	54	6	12	6	18	13							
1007	0	0	-16	0	-3	-81	-6	0							
1008	306	21	55	5	8	24	6	7							
Total	7070	4687	1459	163	641	556	965	321							

APPENDIX 5.A MONETARY BALANCE IN SUT

Section 5.3 discusses the fact that the commodity and industry totals for constant price SUT do not necessarily balance. In this section, the conditions under which this occurs are illustrated using the following example. Assume that there is one supplier of a particular commodity (industry A), and that there are two users (industries B and C). The development of the prices and volumes of the commodities may vary. Three possibilities exist:

1. No price discrimination, that is, both B and C pay the same price and the price indices for both users (for the 1990–1997 period) are the same.
2. Constant price discrimination, that is, B and C pay different prices and the associated price indices are the same for both users (for 1990–1997).
3. Changing price discrimination, that is, B and C pay different prices and the associated price indices (for the 1990–1997 period) are different.

For the volumes there are two possibilities:

a) Constant volume growth: the same volume indices for users B and C.
b) Changing volume growth: different volume indices for users B and C.

In total there are, therefore, six possibilities to consider:

1a) No price discrimination, constant volume growth
1b) No price discrimination, changing volume growth
2a) Constant price discrimination, constant volume growth
2b) Constant price discrimination, changing volume growth
3a) Changing price discrimination, constant volume growth
3b) Changing price discrimination, changing volume growth

These six options are illustrated in the schemes below. The schemes show the volumes and prices of the SUT for the years 1990 and 1997. The current and constant price values and the volume and price indices are shown.

The results illustrate that current price tables are always balanced. However, situation 2b (Constant price discrimination, changing volume growth) and situation 3b (Changing price discrimination, changing volume growth) lead to unbalanced commodity totals for the constant price tables (for 2b the constant price values are unequal: 300 is not equal to 327, and for 3b this is also the case: 400 is not equal to 367). The conclusion follows that, in a situation with one supplier and two users, the commodity totals of the constant price SUT are unequal. The inequality arises only if price discrimination (either changing or constant) occurs simultaneously with changes in the volume index. More generally, industries have many producers and their products are purchased by many other industries at different prices. The lack of balance will therefore occur in larger SUT as well. This contradicts the standard practice of the statistical bureaus, which make balanced constant price tables.

1a) No price discrimination, constant volume growth

Supply 1990	Ind. A
Volume	100
Price	2.00
Cur. Price	200
1997 Price	300

Use 1990	Ind. B	Ind. C	Total
Volume	40	60	100
Price	2.00	2.00	
Cur. Price	80	120	200
1997 Price	120	180	300

Supply 1997	Ind. A
Volume	200
Price	3.00
Cur. Price	600
1990 Price	400

Use 1997	Ind. B	Ind. C	Total
Volume	80	120	200
Price	3.00	3.00	
Cur. Price	240	360	600
1990 Price	160	240	400

Indices	Supply	Use	
	Ind. A	Ind. B	Ind. C
Price index	1.50	1.50	1.50
Volume index	2.00	2.00	2.00

1b) No price discrimination, changing volume growth

Supply 1990	Ind. A
Volume	100
Price	2.00
Cur. Price	200
1997 Price	300

Use 1990	Ind. B	Ind. C	Total
Volume	40	60	100
Price	2.00	2.00	
Cur. Price	80	120	200
1997 Price	120	180	300

Supply 1997	Ind. A
Volume	200
Price	3.00
Cur. Price	600
1990 Price	400

Use 1997	Ind. B	Ind. C	
Volume	60	140	200
Price	3.00	3.00	
Cur. Price	180	420	600
1990 Price	120	280	400

Indices	Supply	Use	
	Ind. A	Ind. B	Ind. C
Price index	1.50	1.50	1.50
Volume index	2.00	1.50	2.33

2a) Constant price discrimination, constant volume growth

Supply 1990	Ind. A
Volume	100
Price	2.00
Cur. Price	200
1997 Price	300

Use 1990	Ind. B	Ind. C	Total
Volume	40	60	100
Price	3.00	1.33	
Cur. Price	120	80	200
1997 Price	180	120	300

Supply 1997	Ind. A
Volume	200
Price	3.00
Cur. Price	600
1990 Price	400

Use 1997	Ind. B	Ind. C	Total
Volume	80	120	200
Price	4.50	2.00	
Cur. Price	360	240	600
1990 Price	240	160	400

	Supply	Use	Use
Indices	Ind. A	Ind.	Ind. C
Price index	1.50	1.50	1.50
Volume index	2.00	2.00	2.00

2b) Constant price discrimination, changing volume growth

Supply 1990	Ind. A
Volume	100
Price	2.00
Cur. Price	200
1997 Price	300

Use 1990	Ind. B	Ind. C	Total
Volume	40	60	100
Price	3.00	1.33	
Cur. Price	120	80	200
1997 Price	196	131	327

Supply 1997	Ind. A
Volume	200
Price	3.00
Cur. Price	600
1990 Price	400

Use 1997	Ind. B	Ind. C	Total
Volume	60	140	200
Price	4.91	2.18	
Cur. Price	295	305	600
1990 Price	180	187	367

Indices	Supply	Use	Use
	Ind. A	Ind.	Ind. C
Price index	1.50	1.64	1.64
Volume index	2.00	1.50	2.33

3a) Changing price discrimination, constant volume growth

Supply 1990	Ind. A
Volume	100
Price	2.00
Cur. Price	200
1997 Price	300

Use 1990	Ind. B	Ind. C	Total
Volume	40	60	100
Price	3.00	1.33	
Cur. Price	120	80	200
1997 Price	160	140	300

Supply 1997	Ind. A
Volume	200
Price	3.00
Cur. Price	600
1990 Price	400

Use 1997	Ind. B	Ind. C	Total
Volume	80	120	200
Price	4.00	2.33	
Cur. Price	320	280	600
1990 Price	240	160	400

Indices	Supply	Use	
	Ind. A	Ind.	Ind. C
Price index	1.50	1.33	1.75
Volume index	2.00	2.00	2.00

3b) Changing price discrimination, changing volume growth

Supply 1990	Ind. A
Volume	100
Price	2.00
Cur. Price	200
1997 Price	300

Use 1990	Ind. B	Ind. C	Total
Volume	40	60	100
Price	3.00	1.33	
Cur. Price	120	80	200
1997 Price	160	154	314

Supply 1997	Ind. A
Volume	200
Price	3.00
Cur. Price	600
1990 Price	400

Use 1997	Ind. B	Ind. C	Total
Volume	60	140	200
Price	4.00	2.57	
Cur. Price	240	360	600
1990 Price	180	187	367

	Supply	Use	Use
Indices	Ind. A	Ind.	Ind. C
Price index	1.50	1.33	1.93
Volume index	2.00	1.50	2.33

APPENDIX 5.B CODING USED IN TABLES 5.13 AND 5.14

1	Agriculture and forestry	37	Environmental services
2	Fishery	38	Worker and organization services
3	Crude oil and natural gas	39	Culture and recreation
4	Quarrying products	40	Personal services
5	Food	41	Household services
6	Tobacco	42	Trade and transport
7	Textiles	43	Government services
8	Clothing	44	Investment on own account
9	Leather products	45	Services on a contract basis
10	Wood	46	Other products and services
11	Paper	100	Basic plastics
12	Publishing	101	Plastic products
13	Fuels	102	Basic iron and steel
14	Chemicals	103	Iron and steel products
15	Rubber	104	Machines
16	Construction products	105	Office equipment & computers
17	Non-ferrous basic metals	106	Electrical appliances
18	Instruments	107	Electronics
19	Other products	108	Cars and engines
20	Recycling products	109	Transportation equipment
21	Energy	900	Export
22	Water	901	Consumption households
23	Construction	902	Consumption government
24	Car repair	903	Investment
25	Catering and lodging	904	Stocks
26	Post and telecommunications	905	Imports
27	Bank services	1000	Wages
28	Life insurance and pensions	1001	Other income
29	Insurance	1002	VAT
30	Real estate services	1003	Taxes
31	Renting of movables	1004	Subsidies
32	Computer services	1005	Pension payments
33	Research	1006	Product taxes
34	Other business services	1007	Product subsidies
35	Education	1008	Non-competitive imports
36	Health services		

NOTES

1. The approach used here can be described best as an application of the commodity technology assumption, discussed in Section 3.3. The resulting negative elements, as presented in Section 3.4, are analyzed and corrections are made so that a non-negative IO table results. The approach is therefore similar to the construction of an activity-by-activity IO table, because of the iterative and detailed analysis of the negative elements, but it does not fully apply the activity technology model since production processes are not separated.
2. See Bos (2003) for an overview of the history and policy applications of National Accounts from a Dutch perspective
3. There are several types of imports. Firstly there are the imports that are destined for the Dutch market. Secondly, there are imports that are repackaged or processed before they are re-exported. Thirdly, there are imports that enter a port and are re-exported after some cargo handling procedures. The first and second types of imports are included in the data for Statistics Netherlands. However, since the analysis in this book wants to focus on the actual imports (the first type), the second type of imports were subtracted from the import data and from the export data.
4. See Joosten (2001) for the 'STREAMS' approach to constructing SUT for plastics, which is similar to the approach described here. The STREAMS approach does not employ the iterative balancing procedure described here.
5. A full description of the construction method is available in Dutch (CBS, 2001).
6. In the case of subsidies, positive elements are targeted. For subsidies, the elements are counted if they have a value larger than 0, 10 and 100 million guilders.

6. Environmental Structural Decomposition Analysis

6.1 INTRODUCTION[1]

In Chapters 6 to 9 various aspects of environmental structural decomposition analysis (SDA) are discussed. SDA uses historical IO data from two or more years. Using comparative static analysis, the influence of structural changes on environmental variables can be determined. Determinant effects, such as the technological changes and changes in final demand, can be distinguished. This chapter provides a general introduction to this method, which includes a review of the environmental SDA literature. Applications include studies of energy use, carbon dioxide emissions, acidifying emissions, material flows and nitrogen loading.

The organization of this chapter is as follows. Section 6.2 discusses the theoretical background of decomposition analysis. Additional theoretical and methodological features that are specific to SDA are examined in Section 6.3. Section 6.4 describes specific methods that have been used to decompose physical flows data. Section 6.5 presents a survey of empirical SDA applied to physical indicators. Section 6.6 suggests further topics for research. Section 6.7 concludes.

6.2 DECOMPOSITION: THEORETICAL BACKGROUND

Mathematical and Graphical Derivation

Decomposition analysis covers a variety of comparative static methods. The common feature of these methods is that they help to understand the underlying determinant effects that influence the development of a variable. When decomposition analysis makes use of the IO model it is called structural decomposition analysis (SDA). The other main decomposition approach is index decomposition analysis (IDA),[2] which uses sector-level or country-level data (Ang, 1999). IDA has been applied to environmental issues more extensively than SDA (Ang and Zhang, 2000, present an overview).

IDA has the advantage of requiring less data. This allows, for instance, decompositions of annual data. SDA, however, is capable of detailed decompositions of technology and demand changes because of its use of IO data. But first the general theoretical aspects of decomposition are discussed.

Assume a functional relationship $u'=f(v'_1,...,v'_n)$. To derive the effects of the changes in determinants $v_1,...,v_n$ on variable u total differentiation is used:

$$du = \frac{\partial u}{\partial v_1} dv_1 + ... + \frac{\partial u}{\partial v_n} dv_n \qquad (6.1)$$

In order to approximate this relationship in discrete time, du and $dv_1 ... dv_n$ are replaced by Δu, $\Delta v_1 ... \Delta v_n$, where Δ denotes the change in the variable over a discrete period of time. For example, the relationship $u = v_1 \cdot v_2$ can be decomposed in the following way:

$$\Delta u \approx v_2 \cdot \Delta v_1 + v_1 \cdot \Delta v_2 \qquad (6.2)$$

Equation 6.2 shows that the change in u can be decomposed into parts that depend on the changes in v_1 and v_2. Similarly the equation $u = v_1/v_2$ can be decomposed using the quotient rule of differentiation as:

$$\Delta u \approx \frac{1}{v_2} \cdot \Delta v_1 - \frac{v_1}{(v_2)^2} \cdot \Delta v_2 \qquad (6.3)$$

The conversion from continuous to discrete time is rarely discussed in the SDA literature because the decomposition equations are often derived in discrete terms. In general, the IDA literature approaches decomposition from a continuous time perspective. The first step is the summation of infinitesimal changes between time periods $t - 1$ and t.

$$\Delta u = \int_{t-1}^{t} \left(\frac{du}{dt} \right) dt =$$
$$\int_{t-1}^{t} \left(\frac{\partial f(v_1,...,v_n)}{\partial v_1} \cdot \frac{dv_1}{dt} \right) dt + ... + \int_{t-1}^{t} \left(\frac{\partial f(v_1,...,v_n)}{\partial v_n} \cdot \frac{dv_n}{dt} \right) dt \qquad (6.4)$$

Liu et al. (1992) show that, under certain conditions, the discrete approximation of this integral function is the following parametric equation:

$$\Delta u \approx \left(w_1^{t-1} + \alpha_1 \cdot \Delta w_1 \right) \cdot \Delta v_1 + ... + \left(w_n^{t-1} + \alpha_n \cdot \Delta w_n \right) \cdot \Delta v_n \qquad (6.5)$$

The superscripts denote the time periods. The $dv_1 \ldots dv_n$ terms are integrated separately from the partial derivatives. Note that this continuous approach leads to a result similar to the discrete decomposition in Equation 6.2. Equation 6.5 shows that the integral of the partial derivative is estimated by weights w_1 to w_n. The value of these weights is determined by their value in period $t - 1$ and t and a parameter α. The choice of an α-parameter corresponds to a choice in index. For example, α-values of 0, 0.5 and 1 lead to Laspeyres, Marshall-Edgeworth and Paasche indices, respectively. These and other indices, not represented by the parametric specification in Equation 6.5, are discussed later in this section and in detail in Chapter 7.

The above mathematical derivation is one of four possible ways of decomposing variable u (Ang, 1994). They are shown for equation $u = v_1 \cdot v_2$ in Table 6.1.

Table 6.1 Multiplicative and additive decomposition of $u = v_1 \cdot v_2$

	Determinants (v_1 and v_2)	
Var. u	Absolute change (Abs. Δ)	Relative change (Rel. Δ)
Abs. Δ	$\Delta u \approx v_2 \cdot \Delta v_1 + v_1 \cdot \Delta v_2$ [a]	$\Delta u \approx v_1 \cdot v_2 \cdot \ln\left(\dfrac{v_1^t}{v_1^{t-1}}\right) + v_1 \cdot v_2 \cdot \ln\left(\dfrac{v_2^t}{v_2^{t-1}}\right)$ [b]
Rel. Δ	$\dfrac{u^t}{u^{t-1}} \approx e^{\frac{1}{v_1}\cdot\Delta v_1} \cdot e^{\frac{1}{v_2}\cdot\Delta v_2}$ [c]	$\dfrac{u^t}{u^{t-1}} = \dfrac{v_1^t}{v_1^{t-1}} \cdot \dfrac{v_2^t}{v_2^{t-1}}$ [d]

The reason that there are four options is because both sides of the equation may be expressed in absolute or relative changes. Expressing the left-hand side variable in change terms (du), as was done in Equation 6.4, leads to additive decompositions [a] and [b] (where the right-hand side determinants are expressed in absolute and relative growth terms, respectively). If both sides of Equation 6.4 are divided by u, the variable is expressed in relative change terms (du/u). Integration of this type of variable leads to multiplicative equations [c] (determinants in absolute change terms) and [d] (determinants in relative change terms) that decompose the ratio of the terminal and base year.[3] Equation 6.4 is an example of a decomposition type [a]. To illustrate, Equation 6.6 shows decomposition of type [d].

$$\frac{u^t}{u^{t-1}} = \int_{t-1}^{t} \left(\frac{\left(\dfrac{du}{dt} \right)}{u} \right) dt =$$

$$\int_{t-1}^{t} \left(\frac{\dfrac{\partial f(v_1,...,v_n)}{\partial v_1} \cdot v_1 \cdot \left(\dfrac{dv_1}{dt} \right)}{u} \cdot \frac{1}{v_1} \right) dt + ... + \int_{t-1}^{t} \left(\frac{\dfrac{\partial f(v_1,...,v_n)}{\partial v_n} \cdot v_n \cdot \left(\dfrac{dv_n}{dt} \right)}{u} \cdot \frac{1}{v_n} \right) dt \qquad (6.6)$$

To derive this equation, both sides of Equation 6.4 are divided by u and the determinant effects are expressed in relative growth terms. As Table 6.1 shows, Equation 6.6 simplifies to a simple decomposition formula for the two determinant multiplicative case.

The specification of the decomposition relationship depends on the objective of the analysis. For example, when assessing growth in energy use, it is logical to focus on actual changes in the absolute quantities of energy used. However, when doing inter-country comparisons of energy use or intensities, it is more insightful to decompose the relative growth. The choice of the determinant specification is, however, less evident, because the absolute and relative growth rates are mathematically equivalent representations that give empirical differences because of discrete approximation. Nevertheless, when there are zero values in the data, as is likely in IO tables, it is necessary to express the determinants in absolute change terms (either type [a] or [c]). Most SDA studies use the additive decomposition type [a].[4] The IDA literature is more diverse and uses all of the above decomposition types.

It is helpful to show graphically what decomposition entails. Figure 6.1 visualizes the additive decomposition of type [a] for equation $u = v_1 \cdot v_2$. It is assumed that the function of variable u and determinants v_1 and v_2 is continuous and given by the non-linear curve from point a to c. The total change in u due to the changes in determinants v_1 and v_2 is equal to the sum of the area with dots and diagonal stripes, respectively.

Indices

As Equation 6.5 shows, each determinant effect is given a weight, which is referred to as an index. Indices are best known in economics from the literature on price and volume changes, which has resulted in a wide range of possible indices (Vogt and Barta, 1997). Fisher (1922), probably the most influential publication in this field, compared the results and properties of a large number of indices. This study helped to found the axiomatic approach to index numbers, in which the mathematical properties of indices are evaluated. The most important conclusion of this line of research is that an ideal index, that has all the desirable properties, is mathematically impossible (Balk, 1995). An index should therefore be selected on the basis of the properties that are regarded as important to the analysis.[5] The discussion of the properties of indices is continued in Section 7.2.

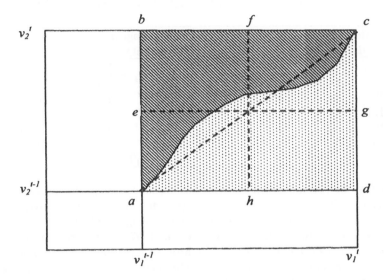

Figure 6.1 Graphical representation of additive decomposition of $u = v_1 \cdot v_2$

Vogt (1978) notes that, if it is assumed that the relationship that is being decomposed is continuous, then each index represents a time path between two discrete points. Since measurements are usually only taken at discrete points in time, the solid curve in Figure 6.1 is unknown leaving an infinite number of paths from a to c and therefore an infinite amount of possible indices.[6] Table 6.2 below summarizes the graphical decomposition results and paths of the three very common indices: Laspeyres (L), Paasche (P) and Marshall-Edgeworth (M-E) indices, which use, respectively, the base year, terminal year and average of the two years, as weights.

The residual in Table 6.2 indicates the degree to which the sum of the determinant effects overestimate or underestimate the total variable change. As shown in Figure 6.1, these effects, also known as 'interactions terms' or 'joint effects', can be substantial. The size of the residual is dependent on the sizes of the determinant effects and is zero if either effect is zero. If there is no residual the decomposition is said to be 'complete'. Table 6.2 shows that if both determinants are given Laspeyres or Paasche weights, then the total change is not estimated correctly. Marshall-Edgeworth weights for both determinants result in a complete decomposition, but this only holds for the two determinant case. Note that the paths of the L-L, P-P and ME-ME index combinations are mutually inconsistent.

Table 6.2 Laspeyres, Paasche and Marshall-Edgeworth indices (Figure 6.1)

Effect of change of determinant v_1			Effect of change of determinant v_2			Residual
Index	Size	Path	Index	Size	Path	
L	$\Delta v_1 \cdot v_2^{t-1}$	adc	L	$\Delta v_2 \cdot v_1^{t-1}$	abc	$\Delta v_1 \cdot \Delta v_2$
P	$\Delta v_1 \cdot v_2^{t}$	abc	P	$\Delta v_2 \cdot v_1^{t}$	adc	$-\Delta v_1 \cdot \Delta v_2$
L	$\Delta v_1 \cdot v_2^{t-1}$	adc	P	$\Delta v_2 \cdot v_1^{t}$	adc	None
P	$\Delta v_1 \cdot v_2^{t}$	abc	L	$\Delta v_2 \cdot v_1^{t-1}$	abc	None
M-E	$\frac{1}{2} \Delta v_1 \cdot (v_2^{t-1} + v_2^{t})$	aegc	M-E	$\frac{1}{2} \Delta v_2 \cdot (v_1^{t-1} + v_1^{t})$	ahfc	None

Recently, the decomposition literature has introduced many alternatives to the Laspeyres, Paasche and Marshall-Edgeworth indices: the conventional Divisia (Boyd et al., 1987), the refined Divisia (Ang and Choi, 1997), and the adaptive weighting Divisia index (Liu et al., 1992), Dietzenbacher and Los (1998), Sun (1998) and Casler (2001). Most of these have been proposed in the IDA literature. In Chapter 7, the IDA and SDA index approaches are compared. The IDA approaches will be transferred to SDA, and Dietzenbacher and Los (1998), the only approach that is unique to SDA, is translated to the IDA setting.

The bottom line of the index discussion is that the ideal index does not exist. Any choice of index will have drawbacks that will have to be accepted. The most important properties that are required of an index should first be defined in order to choose an appropriate index. The choice of index should always be motivated by the research.

6.3 STRUCTURAL DECOMPOSITION ANALYSIS

Basic Specification

If the function that is decomposed is based on the IO model, then it is referred to as structural decomposition analysis (SDA). Rose and Casler (1996, pp. 34) define SDA as an 'analysis of economic change by means of a set of comparative static changes in key parameters in an IO table'. The strength of SDA is that it analyses the effect of changes in the economic structure. Since it is based on the IO model, it is capable of distinguishing the direct and indirect influence of final demand and input technology changes.[7] Assuming that the matrix of IO coefficients, A, defines the intermediate input requirements per unit output of each sector, the IO model is (see Chapter 2):

$$q = L \cdot y \qquad (6.7)$$

where q is output, $L = (I\text{-}A)^{-1}$ is the Leontief inverse matrix, and y is the vector of final demand. Decomposing this equation results in an 'IO coefficients effect',[8] due to changes in the intermediate input structure, and a 'final demand effect', attributable to changes in y:

$$\Delta q = \Delta L \cdot y + L \cdot \Delta y \qquad (6.8)$$

Both effects can be further decomposed, as discussed below.

Decomposition of Changes in IO Coefficients

Changes in the intermediate input coefficient matrix A lead to changes in the Leontief inverse matrix L. The relationship may be decomposed additively (Equation 6.9) or multiplicatively (Equation 6.10) (Rose and Casler, 1996). Note that the results of these two methods have not been compared, either theoretically or empirically.

$$\Delta L = (I - \Delta A)^{-1} \qquad (6.9)$$

$$\Delta L = L \cdot \Delta A \cdot L \qquad (6.10)$$

The next tier of decomposition is to attribute the changes in the IO coefficient matrix to more detailed underlying changes in the input structure. This may be done in two ways: by splitting the matrix into its individual coefficients (Equation 6.11), or by using the 'RAS' approach (Equation 6.12):

$$\Delta A = \Delta A_{11} + \Delta A_{12} + ... + \Delta A_{ij} + ... + \Delta A_{nn} \qquad (6.11)$$

$$\Delta A = \Delta r \cdot A^{t-1} \cdot s + r \cdot A^{t-1} \cdot \Delta s + \varepsilon \qquad (6.12)$$

Equation 6.11 illustrates the first method in which the total change in the IO coefficient matrix is equal to the changes in the $\beta \cdot \beta$ individual coefficients of the matrix, where β is the number of sectors and A_{ij} is a zero matrix with an entry at in row i and column j. The studies that use this decomposition method usually group the IO coefficients. Rose and Chen (1991a) and Casler and Rose (1998) use a closed IO model, which groups the coefficients into capital, labor, energy and materials (KLEM). This specification of technology allows for detailed decompositions of technology.

Technological changes may occur due to technical input substitution, that is, shifts between inputs, or productivity changes, that is, changes in the efficiency with which an input is used. These effects can be distinguished at the aggregate level (capital, labor, energy and materials in the KLEM framework) or at the sub-aggregate level (for example, coal, natural gas and oil for the aggregate energy). Among others, Han and Lakshmanan (1994), Lin and Polenske (1995) and Mukhopadhyay and Chakraborty (1999) group the IO coefficients into energy and non-energy inputs.

The underlying forces that cause input substitution or productivity effects are explored in Rose and Chen (1991b). The energy conservation literature usually distinguishes between autonomous changes in energy productivity, on the one hand, and the price-induced changes stemming from ordinary price changes or taxation, on the other (see Rose and Lin, 1995). SDA can assess the influence of regulation on energy use, for example, using a 'regulation index' as an indicator of policy stringency (Rose and Chen, 1991b).

The second method of decomposing IO coefficients is based on the RAS procedure. This method is used in IO analysis to update the IO coefficients matrix using projected row and column totals of the intermediate input matrix (Stone, 1961) as shown in Equation 6.12. Van der Linden and Dietzenbacher (1995) develop Stone's economic interpretations of the multipliers. These technology effects were pursued in the SDA context in Dietzenbacher and Hoekstra (2002). The method identifies the average change in the rows and columns of the IO coefficients. A substitution effect and intermediate input intensity effect is calculated for each sector. The former identifies the average shifts toward an input, while the latter is a measure of the productivity changes in the use of an input. The decomposition takes the following form.

The first two terms of Equation 6.12 are substitution and intermediate input intensity effect (where r and s are the RAS multipliers). The third term, ε, represents cell-specific changes that are not captured by the two other effects.

Decomposition of Changes in Final Demand

Final demand is the term used for economic demand categories, such as private consumption, exports, government purchases and investments. The final demand matrix has dimensions i by j, where j is the number of final demand categories and i the number of sectors (or products) distinguished in the IO table. Changes of the final demand can be decomposed into the following determinant effects (Lin and Polenske, 1995):

$$\Delta Y =$$
$$\Delta Y^{bridge} \cdot y^{cat} \cdot y^{lev} + Y^{bridge} \cdot \Delta y^{cat} \cdot y^{lev} + Y^{bridge} \cdot y^{cat} \cdot \Delta y^{lev} \qquad (6.13)$$

The elements of matrix Y^{bridge} are known as the bridge coefficients and are equal to the final demand matrix elements divided by their equivalent column sums. The coefficients y^{cat} indicate the share of each final demand category in the total final demand. Scalar y^{lev} represents total level of final demand. Changes in these determinants yield three types of effects: the product mix effect, that is, shifts in the mix of the i products consumed; the category effect, that is, shifts between the j final demand categories; and the final demand level effect, that is, the effect of total level of final demand change.

Variations on this specification are common. The last two effects of Equation 6.13 are sometimes combined into a single 'level effect'. Another possibility is to calculate the (product) mix and level effects for each final demand category separately. The specification of the final demand decomposition is dependent on the goals of the analysis. Assuming enough information is available, decomposition of final demand is capable of establishing the impact of changes in domestic consumption or trade patterns on environmental indicators.

6.4 SDA OF PHYSICAL FLOWS

Methods

This section discusses the methods used by studies that have applied SDA to environmentally-relevant physical flows. Environmental indicators come in three types: changes in absolute quantities, intensities (physical units per unit output) and output elasticities (relative change in physical units per relative change in monetary output). Environmental SDA studies usually decompose absolute changes, and to a lesser extent changes in physical intensity. The decomposition of output elasticity has only been applied in the IDA literature (Ang and Lee, 1996). There are two ways to link the IO model to physical flows: through the monetary or hybrid method. These methods have already been discussed in Section 2.5. In the former approach the monetary IO model is multiplied by the sector-level intensity n (physical flow per unit output) to calculate the total physical flow m:

$$m = n \cdot L \cdot y \tag{6.14}$$

Using additive decomposition [a] of this absolute quantity indicator gives:

$$\Delta m = \Delta n \cdot L \cdot y + n \cdot \Delta L \cdot y + n \cdot L \cdot \Delta y \tag{6.15}$$

The second and third effects of Equation 6.15 are the IO coefficient and final demand effects, which were discussed in Section 6.3. The first term, the intensity effect, measures the influence of changing physical flow per unit of monetary output. This effect is also caused by technological changes, but is different to the IO coefficients effect.

Note that the decomposition in Equation 6.15 can be decomposed into more than three determinant effects. For example, industrial CO_2 emissions can be studied by linking a vector of fuel type use per unit output and a vector for CO_2 emissions per fuel type to the IO model. This decomposition makes it possible to analyze the influence of changes in the fuel mix. Linking an intensity coefficient vector to the monetary IO model is common in non-environmental SDA studies, such as value added and labor productivity.

The hybrid model is very similar to the monetary IO model. However, the IO coefficients are better descriptors of technology. Furthermore, the hybrid model adheres to the mass balance (MB) principle under non-uniform prices, while the monetary IO models do not (see Box 2.3). The decomposition equations for hybrid model are similar to the monetary model equations, and are therefore not shown. Note that the model for 'supply of physical goods', in Table 2.2, differs for the monetary and hybrid models. The monetary model distinguishes an IO coefficients effect and an intensity effect, while the hybrid model only distinguishes an IO coefficients effect, because the intensity vector does not change.

Important Decisions in SDA

The following decisions are made in an environmental SDA study:

- Historic SDA or intercountry SDA. The majority of studies investigate changes in environmental indicators over time (historic SDA). However, it is also possible to investigate the influence of the economic structures between countries by using intercountry SDA.
- Hybrid model or monetary model. The hybrid method is better under

non-uniform prices, but requires more data (see Section 2.5). Mass balance is preserved in the hybrid IO model (see Box 2.3).

- Absolute quantity, physical intensity or output elasticity. The variable chosen for decomposition is dependent on the research question. For example, studies that investigate changes in CO_2 emissions are most informative if absolute quantity decomposition is used. Studies that deal with relative performance of environmental and economic indicators or intercountry SDA should use the intensity or elasticity approaches.
- Time period. This is usually restricted by the availability of IO data. Few countries produce annual IO tables. Moreover, the technological and final demand effects that SDA investigates will only be revealed over longer periods. Proops et al. (1993) argue that an added benefit of SDA studies for longer periods is that they diminish the presence of a time-independent zero-mean error term. The stage of the business cycle that the first and terminal years are in is important. Comparing a boom year with a recession year could lead to biased outcomes, which do not reflect the long-term structural change in the economy.
- Index. The choice of index is arbitrary. Different indices can give distinct results and residual terms. Discussions of the most appropriate indices for decomposition purposes are inconclusive. Many studies fail to report the index they use, despite the fact that results are affected significantly.
- Multiplicative or additive decomposition. This choice will affect the ease of interpretation of the results. Additive decompositions are generally easier for non-specialists to interpret.
- Imports. Imports can be registered in an IO model 'including imports' or 'excluding imports' (see Box 5.1). In the first case, it is assumed that imports have the same input requirements as the domestic products. The ideal, but laborious, solution would be to identify the input structure of imported products by studying the IO tables of the source countries. The IO table excluding imports leads to the 'IO coefficients effect', which reflects a shift in the domestic intermediate input structure only.
- IO coefficients effect. The change in the input requirements of sectors can be decomposed using individual or groups of IO coefficients. It is possible to group the inputs using a KLEM specification, so that technological effects within and between these aggregates can be studied. Non-energy and energy coefficients are distinguished in many SDA applications. Another way of decomposing the changes in the IO coefficients is by using a method that is based on the RAS procedure.
- Final demand. The shifts in final demand can be decomposed into product mix, category and level effects. Variations of these decompositions are possible. Individual final demand categories, such as exports and private consumption, are often decomposed separately.

6.5 SURVEY OF ENVIRONMENTAL SDA

Methods Used

This section reviews the literature since the first application of SDA to an environmental issue (Leontief and Ford, 1972). Table 6.3 summarizes the methodological characteristics of 34 studies.[9] As the reference list shows, the majority of publications appeared in the 1990s. From Table 6.3 a number of observations may be made about environmental SDA studies. Nearly all countries or regions under investigation are developed countries or newly industrialized Asian economies, such as China and Taiwan. The only developing country that is studied is India. Most publications analyze energy use or energy-related emission. Sector disaggregation varies from 15 to 117.

About a third of the studies use the hybrid method. Furthermore, most publications decompose the absolute indicator changes using additive decomposition techniques. Table 6.3 indicates that many different index approaches are used. Few studies perform sensitivity analysis of the use of indices. In fact, the majority of studies do not report the index that is used.[10]

The change in IO coefficients is decomposed in many different ways. The simplest specifications distinguish the changes in the IO and intensity coefficients. However, Rose and Chen (1991a), and a number of subsequent articles, divide the sectors according to the neoclassical KLEM classification system to investigate the input substitution and productivity effects of core production factors. Several studies distinguish between the influence of energy and non-energy input coefficients. Fuel mix effects are decomposed in a few studies concerning CO_2 emissions.

The ways of decomposing final demand are less diverse. Most studies analyze the mix and level effects of final demand changes. Some studies assess the influence of separate final demand categories, such as exports.

Empirical Results

The empirical outcomes are difficult to compare because the countries, periods, environmental issues and decomposition methods vary significantly. An indication of the problems of comparing empirical results is provided by the results of Rose and Chen (1991a) and OTA (1990). Both studies investigate energy use in the United States for similar time periods (1972–1982 and 1972–1985, respectively). However, Rose and Chen (1991a) use a closed IO model, which includes labor and capital in the IO coefficient matrix. OTA (1990) uses the open IO model, which is used most frequently in SDA. Other differences are the energy carriers that are included in the study and the interaction terms. Furthermore, the technological effects that are distinguished for both studies are different. This illustrates that even if SDA investigates similar problems the variation in methodologies is still so large that meaningful comparison of the results is difficult.

Despite the problems of comparing SDA results, this section attempts to summarize insights about the relationship between the economy, technology and environmentally-relevant physical flows. Nearly all the studies report the influence of changes in the final demand level, final demand mix, and technology effects, such as the intensity effect and IO coefficients effects. The final demand level effect is generally the most important long-term determinant of increased physical flows. The final demand mix effect, that is, the changes in product mix of the final demand categories, is mostly responsible for modest reductions in physical flows. Changes in technology, either through changes in input–output or intensity coefficients, are generally the most important source of downward pressure on material throughput. However, the relative magnitude and sign of these three effects vary significantly, depending on the variable, environmental issue, time period or country under investigation. Furthermore, the country level outcomes may differ significantly from the results for individual sectors.

The tentative results from the SDA literature suggest the following current developments. Final demand effects generally exceed the environmental improvements due to technological changes. Some policy implications follow. Firstly, policies that target technological developments, such as increasing renewable energy in the fuel mix or enhancing energy efficiency, would be required at a much faster rate than that observed in the past two or three decades. Secondly, policies can be implemented that affect the level and mix of final demand. Finally, a combination of technology and demand-related policies could be implemented. Decision makers are generally averse to measures that reduce the final demand level. Altering the product mix of final demand is a socially and politically more feasible policy. The advantage of SDA and input–output studies is that they allow assessment of direct and indirect emissions. Thus, it can aid policy makers in shifting final demand towards a more environmentally-acceptable consumption package.

Some of the SDA studies attempt comparisons of different economies using intercountry SDA. Rather than a comparative static analysis between two time periods, these studies decompose the differences between two countries. For instance, Proops et al. (1993) show that the German economy was more fuel-efficient than the United Kingdom at the beginning of the 1980s. Similarly, Chung (1998) concludes that in 1990 Japanese technology was less CO_2 intensive than the Chinese technology. South Korea exhibited the most CO_2-intensive input structure. Kagawa and Inamura (2004) present an SDA in which the influence of Japanese demand is analysed for China and vice versa, in an historical SDA.

Table 6.3 Summary of environmental SDA studies

Study	Physical flow indicator	Period	Region (number of sectors)	Multiplicative or additive (index used)
Leontief and Ford (1972)	Particulates, SO_x, HC, CO, NO_x	58-80	United States (90)	Additive (Laspeyres)
Pløger (1984)	Primary energy use	66-70-73-75-78-80	Denmark (117)	Additive (unknown)
Gould and Kulshreshtha (1986)	Natural gas, electricity, liquid fuels and coal	74-79	Saskatchewan, Canada (20)	Additive (mixed)
Gowdy and Miller (1987)	Energy use	63-67-72-77	United States (25)	Additive (mixed)
Chen and Rose (1990)	Coal & coal products, refined petroleum, natural gas and electricity	71-76-81-84	Taiwan (37)	Additive (mixed)
OTA (1990)	Coal, crude oil & gas, refined petroleum, primary electricity and utility gas	72-77-80-82-85	United States (88)	Additive (Paasche)
Rose and Chen (1991a)	Coal, petroleum, natural gas and electricity	72-82	United States (80)	Additive (mixed)
Common and Salma (1992)	CO_2 emissions	74/75-79/80-82/83-86/87	Australia (27)	Additive (unknown)
Proops et al. (1993)	CO_2 emissions	78-80-82-84-86-88 (Germany) 68-74-79-84 (UK) and inter-country SDA	Germany and the UK (45)	Additive (Marshall-Edgeworth)

Table 6.3 (continued)

Technology (number of effects, excluding interactions terms)	Final demand (number of effects, excluding interactions terms)	Monetary model or hybrid model	Comments
IO coefficients effect (1)	Mix and level effects (results for the latter are not reported) (2)	Hybrid model	Leontief's augmented environmental IO model is used. The comparative static method aims to project future (1980) emissions.
IO coefficients and intensity effects (2)	Mix and level effects (2)	Monetary model	SDA and econometric estimations conclude that the output mix is important in explaining the energy coefficient.
IO coefficients and intensity effects (2)	Final demand effect (1)	Monetary model	The IO coefficients are derived from supply and use tables.
Direct and indirect effects, substitution of energy and non-energy inputs (4)	Mix and level effects (2)	Hybrid model	First example of hybrid unit use in SDA.
Various technological effects based on KLEM production factors (9)	Mix and level effects of exports and other final demand categories, import substitution effect (5)	Monetary model	KLEM (capital, labor, energy and materials) specification used to analyze energy. Based on Rose and Chen (1991a).
Energy and non-energy IO coefficients effects (2)	Mix and level effects (2) More detailed decompositions of final demand categories.	Hybrid model	Extensive analysis of the historical and future primary energy use of the United States.
Various technological effects based on KLEM production factors (9)	Mix and level effects (2)	Monetary model	Comparison of SDA with neoclassical (KLEM) approach. The results from this study are compared with those of Chen and Rose (1990) in Rose and Chen (1991b).
Fuel-mix changes of industries and households. Technological coefficient change (3)	Household consumption and other final demand effects (2)	Monetary model	Decomposes CO_2 emissions by households as well as by industries. Scenario analyses are included.
IO coefficients and intensity effects (2)	Mix and level effects (2)	Monetary model	Decomposes CO_2 emissions by households as well as by industries. Comprehensive study of CO_2 including IDA, SDA, scenario and optimization models.

Table 6.3 (continued)

Study	Physical flow indicator	Period	Region (number of sectors)	Multiplicative or additive (index used)
Chen and Wu (1994)	Electricity demand	76-81-84-86	Taiwan (15)	Additive (mixed)
Han and Lakshmanan (1994)	Primary energy use: coal, crude oil, natural gas, petrol products, coal products, electricity and utility gas	75-80-85	Japan (84)	Multiplicative and additive (Laspeyres)
Alcántara and Roca (1995)	Energy use and carbon dioxide	80-90	Spain (1)	Additive (Laspeyres)
Lin and Polenske (1995) and Lin (1996)	Coal, petroleum, gas and hydropower	81-87	China (18)	Additive (mixed)
Rose et al., (1996)	Plastics, rubber, glass, iron & steel, non-ferrous metals	72-82	United States (41 materials sectors, non-materials not specified)	Additive (mixed)
Casler and Rose (1998)	CO_2 emissions	72-82	United States (not specified)	Additive (mixed)
Chang and Lin (1998)	CO_2 emissions	81-91	Taiwan (34)	Additive (Laspeyres)
Chung (1998)	CO_2 emissions	Inter-country SDA	China, Japan, South Korea (45)	Additive (Marshall-Edgeworth)
Moll et al. (1998a,b)	Total material requirement (TMR)	80-90	West Germany (55)	Additive (Marshall-Edgeworth)
Wier (1998)	Energy use, CO_2, SO_2, NO_x emissions	66-70, 71-75, 76-80, 81-85, 85-88	Denmark (117)	Additive (Marshall-Edgeworth)
Garbaccio et al. (1999)	Energy-output ratio	87-92	China (29)	Additive (Conventional Divisia Index)

Table 6.3 (continued)

Technology (number of effects, excluding interactions terms)	Final demand (number of effects, excluding interactions terms)	Monetary model or hybrid model	Comments
Various technological effects based on KLEM production factors (9)	Mix and level effects of exports and other final demand, import substitution effect (5)	Monetary model	Uses decomposition of technology from Rose and Chen (1991a).
Energy and non-energy IO coefficients effects (2)	Mix and category effects including import (7)	Hybrid model	Uses 'double denominator' method to account for primary energy requirement of electricity production from fossil fuels.
Energy transformation effect, fuel mix effect (3)	Category effects, including industrial, residential and transport energy use (3)	Hybrid model	Deviates from normal SDA. Only distinguishes 1 sector. Nevertheless, the conversion matrix from primary to final use of energy is expressed as a Leontief inverse. Double counting discussed.
Energy and non-energy IO coefficients effects (2)	Mix, category and level effects (3), more detailed decompositions of final demand categories	Hybrid model	The effects of changes in rural and urban consumption are decomposed.
Various technological effects based on KLEMO production factors (11)	Mix and level effects (2)	Monetary model	The first decomposition of non-energy related physical flows.
Various technological effects based on KLEM production factors (7)	Mix and level effects (2)	Hybrid model	Investigates the same period as Rose and Chen (1991a), using a similar decomposition method.
IO coefficients, ratio of domestic intermediate input, intensity and inter-fuel substitution effect (4)	Mix and level effects of exports and other final demand effect (4)	Monetary model	
IO coefficients and energy mix effects (2)	Mix and level effects (2)	Monetary model	
IO coefficients, domestic and import intensity effects (3)	Final demand effect (1). More detailed decompositions of final demand categories	Monetary model	
IO coefficients, energy intensity, fuel-mix, and emissions-factor effects (4)	Mix and level effects (2)	Monetary model	
IO coefficients effect (1)	Domestic demand mix effect, mix and level effect of imports and level effect of exports (4)	Hybrid model	Includes sensitivity test for the price deflators and other errors in the data.

Table 6.3 (continued)

Study	Physical flow indicator	Period	Region (number of sectors)	Multiplicative or additive (index used)
van der Kruk (1999a, b)	Coal, combustible renewables, crude oil, electricity, natural gas, heat, hydroelectricity, nuclear, petroleum products and solar and wind energy	Periods are country-specific and range from 68-90	Australia, Canada, Denmark, France, Germany, Japan, the Netherlands, the United Kingdom, the United States (36)	Additive (variation of Dietzenbacher and Los, 1998)
Mukhopadhyay and Chakraborty (1999)	Coal, crude petroleum and electricity	73/74-83/84-91/92	India (22)	Additive (Laspeyres)
Wier and Hasler (1999)	Marine loading of nitrogen by agriculture and sewage	66-76-86-88	Denmark (117)	Additive (Marshall-Edgeworth)
Jacobsen (2000)	Energy use	66-75-80-85-92-92	Denmark (117)	Additive (Dietzenbacher and Los, 1998)
Kagawa and Inamura (2000, 2001)	Energy intensity and absolute use	85-90	Japan (94)	Additive (Dietzenbacher and Los, 1998)
Zheng (2000)	Coal, oil & gas, electricity, petroleum and coke	90-95	China (30)	Additive (unknown)
de Haan (2001)	CO_2 emissions, air pollutants and solid waste	Annual time steps 87-98	The Netherlands (32)	Additive (Dietzenbacher and Los, 1998)
de Nooij et al. (2003)	Energy use	Inter-country SDA	Australia, Canada, Denmark, France, Germany, Japan, the United Kingdom, and the United States (18)	Additive (Dietzenbacher and Los, 1998)
Seibel (2003)	CO_2 emissions	93-00	Germany (70)	Additive (Dietzenbacher and Los, 1998)
Kagawa and Inamura (2004)	Energy demand	85-90	China and Japan (32)	Additive (Marshall-Edgeworth)

Note: Alcántara and Roca (1995), Seibel (2003) and Kagawa and Inamura (2004) are not included in Hoekstra and van den Bergh (2002).

Table 6.3 (continued)

Technology (number of effects, excluding interactions terms)	Final demand (number of effects, excluding interactions terms)	Monetary model or hybrid model	Comments
IO coefficients effect (1)	Mix and level effects (2). More detailed decompositions of final demand categories.	Hybrid model	Decomposition of OECD data for 9 countries.
Energy and non-energy IO coefficients effects (2)	Mix effect of domestic demand. Level effect. Energy and non-energy imports, exports and stock changes (8)	Monetary model	
Emission factor and input-mix effects (2)	Mix and level effects (2)	Monetary model	
IO coefficients and intensity effect. Domestic share of intermediate input (3)	Level effect. Export and domestic share of final demand (3)	Monetary model	
Non-energy input and output coefficient and energy intensity effects (3)	Non-energy final demand effect (1)	Hybrid model	
Energy and non-energy IO coefficients effects (2)	Mix, category and level effects (3)	Hybrid model	
IO coefficients and intensity effects (2)	Mix and level effects (2)	Monetary model	
IO coefficients and intensity effects (2)	Mix, level and category effects (3)	Monetary model	
IO coefficients, intensity effects and fuelmix effects (3)	Mix and level effects (2)	Monetary model	Decomposes the emissions of households into number, size and living space effects.
Domestic IO coefficients and intensity effects (2)	Intermediate and final demand effect Japan or China. Many import and domestic final demand categories (8).	Monetary model	The influence of the Japan and China on each other's energy demand is examined.

6.6 CHALLENGES

This section discusses some promising directions for environmental SDA. A number of these suggestions have already been hinted at in the text.

Some articles link SDA to neoclassical economic theory (Rose and Chen, 1991a, b; Rose and Casler, 1996; Casler and Rose, 1999; Milana, 2000). Rose and Chen (1991a) suggest that SDA analysis is a substitute for production function modeling. It achieves results that would require a long time series if econometrically estimated. Linking SDA and neoclassical theory will facilitate interaction between the two approaches.

Dietzenbacher and Los (2000) introduced the notion of 'dependent determinants', which asserts that SDA implicitly violates IO model assumptions. It shows that the results of the traditional decomposition technique and another variant, which corrects dependency, differ significantly.

Assuming import and export data is broken down into country-specific data, the influence of shifting trade patterns can be analyzed (Oosterhaven and Hoen, 1998; Hoen, 1999). This could lead to 'carbon leakage' analysis, where the shifting of environmental burdens between countries can be assessed. Budget survey data and population data could lead to decomposition of consumption patterns and demographic characteristics on physical flows. Lin and Polenske (1995), for example, use demographic information to distinguish between rural, urban and social consumption. Related to this is the development of decomposition methods on data from Social Accounting Matrices (SAM). A comprehensive summary of the empirical results obtained in the SDA literature so far, as well as a comparison of methods, would benefit environmental economics and SDA.

6.7 CONCLUSIONS

This chapter shows that structural decomposition analysis (SDA) is a powerful method for studying the determinants that affect material flows in the economy. It is therefore a useful tool for analyzing the relationship between changes in the economic structure and environmental problems over time or between countries. The method allows the changes in the physical flow to be ascribed to IO coefficient (technological) and final demand effects. These aggregate effects can be further decomposed into sub-determinants. Technological effects can be split into substitution and productivity (or efficiency) effects, while the final demand effect can be divided into product mix, category and level effects. Furthermore, important final demand categories, such as exports and consumption, can be decomposed separately.

The review of the literature reveals that most of the 34 articles deal with energy or energy-related emissions such as CO_2. In general, the SDA literature studies apply additive decomposition on absolute changes in environmental indicators. Relatively few studies use multiplicative decomposition techniques for the physical intensities. The specific technological and final demand effects, sector aggregation, and index approach vary significantly among the studies (summarized in Table 6.3).

The empirical results of the SDA studies in this chapter are difficult to compare because of the differences in the environmental issues, time periods, countries and decomposition methods that are used. It would be desirable to have a comprehensive review of the results. However, tentative conclusions were drawn in this chapter. The final demand level effect seems to have been the most important underlying factor behind increases in physical flows. Changes in the input technology have generally reduced the physical flows. Nevertheless, this downward pressure rarely exceeds the upward pressure of the level effect.

NOTES

1. This chapter is based on Hoekstra and van den Bergh (2002). The discussion of the empirical results (Section 6.5) has been revised and three studies have been added to Table 6.3.
2. 'Structural decomposition analysis' (SDA) is the accepted name for decomposition studies that use the IO model for decomposition. It is also referred to as 'IO structural decomposition analysis' or 'IO decomposition analysis'. However, the term used to identify decomposition methods that do not use the IO model is less uniform. This chapter adopts the term 'index decomposition analysis' (IDA), because it is used by the extensive overview paper by Ang and Zhang (2000). IDA is also referred to as 'index number analysis', 'energy decomposition' or 'decomposition analysis'.
3. The integral of du/u evaluated from $t - 1$ to t, is equal to $ln(ut/ut - 1)$. Taking the exponential of both sides leaves the right-hand side as a product of several effects.
4. Dietzenbacher et al. (2000) and Han and Lakshmanan (1994) are exceptions.
5. The Laspeyres index, for instance, fails the time reversal test. This is easily shown: if a quantity goes from 80 units to 100 and back to 80 the Laspeyres index indicates a 25 percent growth followed by a 20 percent drop.
6. Intuitively, the straight dashed line *ac* in Figure 6.1 would seem like the best approximation of the path. This 'natural index' was proposed by in Vogt (1978) and Vogt and Barta (1997). However, it fails the linear homogeneity test, which states that, if a determinant is multiplied by a scalar, the determinant effect increases by the same relative magnitude.
7. SDA uses the IO model but is less restricted by the assumptions of constant IO coefficients than regular IO analysis. The constant coefficient assumption holds for a single year but, since SDA uses data from two or more years, the IO coefficients vary between years. These changes are used to explain changes in a variable under investigation.
8. Sometimes referred to simply as the 'technological effect'. The terms 'IO coefficients effect' or 'intermediate input effect' are more accurate, because the effect does not reflect changes in all inputs required for production.
9 For another recent survey, see Rose (1999). Although electricity is not a physical flow, it is included here because it is an integral part of energy demand.
10. The term 'mixed' in Table 6.3 refers to the alternate use of Laspeyres and Paasche weights.

7. Comparing Structural and Index Decomposition Analysis

7.1 INTRODUCTION[1]

To analyze and understand historical changes in economic, environmental, employment or other socio-economic indicators, it is useful to assess the driving forces or determinants that underlie these changes. Two techniques for decomposing indicator changes at the activity level are structural decomposition analysis (SDA) and index decomposition analysis (IDA). Both methods have been used to assess the influence of economic growth, sectoral shifts and technology changes on a variety of environmental and socio-economic indicators.

SDA uses the IO model and data to decompose changes in indicators while IDA uses only activity level data. These two fields of decomposition analysis have developed separately, which has resulted in different approaches and techniques being adopted. This chapter wishes to bring together the two strands of the literature. Generally speaking, the literature on IDA has extensively studied the implications of index theory and the specification of the decomposition. On the other hand the SDA literature has focused attention on distinguishing many different types of determinant changes, which the IO model makes possible.

This chapter has several aims. First, it summarizes the fundamental differences and similarities between SDA and IDA. Second, the decomposition techniques and indices are transferred, that is, the many methods used in IDA are transferred to the SDA setting and vice versa. Finally, the SDA and IDA techniques are compared using a numerical example.

The organization of this chapter is as follows. Section 7.2 presents a general overview of the differences and similarities between SDA and IDA. Section 7.3 discusses the transfer of IDA decomposition techniques to an SDA context. Section 7.4 explores the use of SDA techniques in the IDA setting. Section 7.5 illustrates the results of, and differences between, the various decomposition forms using a numerical example. Section 7.6 concludes.

7.2 SDA AND IDA COMPARED

Fundamental Differences

SDA and IDA are decomposition methods that are used to assess the effect of certain driving forces on a change in an indicator. Historical data is used, usually from two periods, to analyze which determinant changes have contributed most to a change in an indicator. For example, many studies use SDA or IDA to gauge the influence of technological and economic changes on energy use. In their review of SDA, Rose and Casler (1996) briefly discuss SDA and IDA. They note that if IO information were added to IDA, it 'might actually generalize to IO SDA' (pp.38). However, a comprehensive comparison of the two methods is lacking in the literature.

The main difference between the two decomposition methods is the model that is used. SDA uses the IO framework, while IDA uses an aggregate model of the economy. Table 7.1 shows a data for a two activity economy (materials and services activities) which could be used in either SDA or IDA analysis (see Appendix 7.A for the definitions of symbols). In the last column of Table 7.1 we have also added an environmental indicator, material use. Note that this could be any indicator that is related to the output. Possibilities include energy use, CO_2 emissions or labor requirements. The economic IO model in SDA is based on IO coefficients ($A_{ij} = Z_{ij}/q_j$) and final demand (y_j) per activity (Miller and Blair, 1985). IDA, however, uses the output per activity (q_i) for the economic decomposition. Both methods can analyze an intensity measure ($n_i = m_i/q_i$), that is, a measure of the sector's material use (m_i) per unit of output (q_i).

Table 7.1 Data used in IDA and SDA

	Materials	Services	Final demand	Output	Material use
Materials	Z_{11}	Z_{12}	y_1	q_1	m_1
Services	Z_{21}	Z_{22}	y_2	q_2	m_2

An advantage of IDA over SDA is a lower data requirement. However, this is clearly also a disadvantage, since IDA is capable of less detailed decompositions of the economic structure than SDA. SDA can distinguish between a range of technological effects and final demand effects that are not possible in the IDA framework.

Another advantage of SDA is that the IO model includes indirect demand effects. Indirect effects emerge when a direct demand increase in one activity leads to increases in the demand for inputs from other sectors. It is a spillover effect of demand that is captured by the Leontief inverse of the IO model (Miller and Blair, 1985). The IDA model is only capable of assessing the impact of the direct effects.

A number of determinant effects are distinguished in SDA and IDA decompositions. The *production effect* (IDA and SDA) measures the effect of total output (Δq_i) change on the material use. The *structure effect* (IDA only) assesses the effect of a shift in the production shares (Δh_i) of sectors in the economy. The *IO coefficients effect* (SDA only) indicates the effect of the changes in the Leontief inverse coefficients (ΔL_{ij}). This matrix is based on the IO coefficients matrix (A_{ij}), which is a description of the intermediate input requirements per unit of output. The IO coefficients effect is therefore interpretable as a technological effect of changes in the intermediate input structure. Another technological effect is the *intensity effect* (SDA and IDA), which assesses the effect of change in the material use per unit of output (Δn_i). Lastly, the *final demand effect* (SDA only) estimates the change in the material use that can be ascribed to the shift in the final demand for products from each activity (Δy_i).

In summary, some of the determinant effects that can be distinguished in SDA and IDA are different. SDA uses a greater amount of data and a more complex economic model, which allows for a more detailed analysis of technological[2] and final demand effects. However, IDA remains a popular tool precisely because the data that it requires are relatively abundant. As a result, the IDA literature is characterized by greater detail of time periods and countries investigated.

Differences in Applications

There are many different approaches that may be followed when performing a decomposition analysis. The SDA and IDA methods have developed independently of each other, which has led to few insights being transferred from one field to the other. This has resulted in differing approaches in the SDA and IDA applications. In the following paragraphs, the decisions that are made in a decomposition analysis are reviewed.

Indicator and Time Period

Decomposition starts by identifying the indicator as well as the time period for which its driving forces are to be investigated. For both SDA and IDA, a sizeable literature has emerged that investigates energy use and other environmentally-relevant indicators. Ang and Zhang (2000) summarize 109 IDA and 15 SDA articles in this field, while Table 6.3 reports 34 SDA publications.

Often the choice of time period will be dictated by the availability of data. SDA studies are often characterized by 3- to 10-year time periods because, for many countries, IO tables are not constructed annually. IDA studies are often highly detailed in terms of the time periods under investigation. Annual time steps are common, because the aggregate activity level data is often readily available.

Indicator Form

There are three types of indicator forms: absolute, intensity and elasticity. The choice of form depends on the aim of the analysis. For example, to analyze energy use it is possible to investigate the absolute change in energy use (that is, the change in Joules or BTUs required by the economy). However, decomposition analysis can also explain the change in the energy intensity (that is, the change in the Joules or BTUs required per unit of economic output or value added). Finally, the energy output elasticity could be decomposed into determinant effects (that is, the relative change in the indicator divided by the relative change in output). The intensity and elasticity indicator types are therefore ratios of the indicator and economic variables. While the IDA literature has developed all three indicator forms, the SDA literature generally restricts itself to investigation of absolute changes in variables (an exception being an investigation of labor productivity by Dietzenbacher et al., 2000). Since each indicator form leads to specific determinant effects, the choice of indicator form is also dependent on the effects that are of interest to a researcher.

Additive versus Multiplicative Forms

A decomposition approach can adopt either an additive or a multiplicative mathematical form. The additive form decomposes the difference of indicator form (I) between time t and $t - 1$, into determinant effects (Equation 7.1):

$$I^t - I^{t-1} = Determinant\ effect + ... + Determinant\ effect + Residual \quad (7.1)$$

The multiplicative decomposition form decomposes the relative growth of an indicator I into determinant effects, as in Equation 7.2:

$$\frac{I^t}{I^{t-1}} = Determinant\ effect \times ... \times Determinant\ effect \times Residual \quad (7.2)$$

The existence of a residual term will be discussed in the paragraph on indices.

The reason to choose the additive or multiplicative decomposition is generally a matter of presentation or interpretation. Non-experts interpret additive decompositions relatively easily. But, since determinant effects are normalized to 1 in a multiplicative decomposition, they can be easily presented graphically. SDA studies, however, rarely use multiplicative decomposition (a few exceptions include Han and Lakshmanan, 1994; Dietzenbacher et al., 2000), while both additive and multiplicative forms are commonly used in the IDA literature. Presenting the mathematical derivations in this chapter may make it easier to implement the different forms in SDA.

Indices

The issue of indices in decomposition analyses was introduced in Section 6.2. Many index approaches have been proposed in decomposition analysis, particularly in IDA. Both SDA and IDA use the Laspeyres (base-year weights), Paasche (terminal-year weights) and Marshall-Edgeworth (mean of base- and terminal-year weights). The IDA literature has developed their use of indices by differentiating and integrating under different assumptions (Liu et al., 1992). This derivation method has led to indices such as the 'conventional Divisia', 'refined Divisia' and the 'adaptive weighting Divisia index'.

A very different approach to weighting determinants in the IDA setting is introduced in Sun (1998). This article introduces the idea of a straight growth path between two discrete points in time. This idea was previously discussed in Vogt (1978), who noted that each index is the result of a discrete evaluation of a continuous function. Vogt coined the term 'natural index' as the straight line between the two points in time. Sun (1998) uses this idea to arrive at an index in which the residual term that exists when the Laspeyres weights are applied should be equally split amongst the determinant variables that created them. This method has only been developed for additive decomposition. The mathematical complexities of all the above IDA indices are revealed in Section 7.3 and the index approaches are transferred to the SDA setting.

The final index approach in decomposition that will be discussed is unique to the SDA setting (Dietzenbacher and Los, 1998). It is not a single index but rather a range of index combinations that produce decomposition formulae without residual terms (known as a 'complete' decomposition). The article cited shows that if there are β determinants, then there will be $\beta!$ different index combinations that lead to complete decompositions, assuming Laspeyres or Paasche weights for each determinant variable. This SDA method is discussed in Section 7.4 where the approach is translated to the IDA setting.[3]

Index Properties

Finally, this paragraph will take a closer look at the properties that the different decomposition index approaches have (see Table 7.2 which is based mostly on Ang, 1999). There are many tests, but the following are particularly relevant for decomposition:

• *Completeness.* A complete decomposition has no residual. In the additive case this means that the residual equals 0 (Equation 7.1), while it equals 1 in the multiplicative case (Equation 7.2). A residual indicates that the sum of the determinant effects has overestimated or underestimated the total indicator change.
• *Time reversal.* This test shows, whether, if the time period of the determinants were reversed, the decomposition would yield the reciprocal result. For example, if a quantity changes from 80 to 100 the Laspeyres index indicates that this is a 25 percent increase, while if the variable changes from 100 to 80 it gives a 20 percent decrease. The Laspeyres index therefore fails the time reversal test.
• *Zero value robustness.* Some indices use logarithms, which creates problems when there are zero values in the data set. This is therefore a particularly important property for SDA, since the IO coefficients matrix is characterized by zero coefficients. The normal procedure is to replace the zero value by a small number δ. Ang and Choi (1997) show that the refined Divisia index converges as δ approaches zero. This does not hold for the conventional Divisia Index.

Table 7.2 Index properties

Index	Complete	Time reversal	Zero-value robust
Laspeyres	No	No	Yes
Marshall-Edgeworth	For 2 determinants	Yes	Yes
Paasche	No	No	Yes
Conventional Divisia	Yes	Yes	No
Refined Divisia	Yes	Yes	Yes, converges as values approach zero
Adaptive weighting Divisia	No	No	No
Sun (1998)	Yes	Yes	Yes
Dietzenbacher and Los (1998)	Yes	Yes	Yes

7.3 IDA INDEX APPROACHES TRANSFERRED TO SDA

In this section, the indices from the IDA literature are transferred to SDA:

Multiplicative decomposition of the intensity indicator

1a) Parametric Method 1 (conventional Divisia index)
1b) Non-parametric Method 1 (refined Divisia index)
1c) Parametric Method 2 (Laspeyres, Marshall-Edgeworth, Paasche indices)
1d) Parametric Methods 1 and 2 combined (adaptive weighting Divisia index)

Additive decomposition of the absolute indicator

2a) Parametric Method 1 (conventional Divisia index)
2b) Non-parametric Method 1 (refined Divisia index)
2c) Parametric Method 2 (Laspeyres, Marshall-Edgeworth, Paasche indices)
2d) Parametric Methods 1 and 2 combined (adaptive weighting Divisia index)

Additive decomposition of the elasticity indicator

3a) Laspeyres, Marshall-Edgeworth, Paasche indices

Additive Decomposition of the absolute indicator, using Sun (1998)

The first three derivations are part of a generalized set of decomposition index approaches that are summarized in Ang (1999). The additive decomposition of the intensity indicator and the multiplicative decomposition of the absolute indicator are not discussed because the derivation is very similar. The last IDA approach that will be derived in the SDA setting is from Sun (1998). All the equivalent IDA decomposition equations can be found in Appendix 7.B and the symbols used are given in Appendix 7.A.

Multiplicative Decomposition of the Intensity Indicator

In an economy with β sectors, the material use intensity n of the economy is given by the following equation:

$$n = \frac{m}{q} = \frac{\sum_i x_i \cdot n_i}{q} = \frac{\sum_i \sum_j L_{ij} \cdot y_j \cdot n_i}{q} \tag{7.3}$$

where $q_i = L_{ij} \cdot y_j$ is the IO model, and $L_{ij} = (I - A_{ij})^{-1}$.

The variables without subscripts are economy-wide values, while subscripts i and j indicate activity level variables. The national material use intensity n is equal to the ratio of the total material use and total output of the country. The product of the Leontief inverse L_{ij} and the final demand y_j is the IO model specification for activity level output (q_i) (Miller and Blair, 1985). Differentiating with respect to time, and dividing both sides by n gives:

$$\hat{n} = \sum_i \sum_j \left(\frac{dL_{ij}}{dt}\right) \cdot \left(\frac{y_j \cdot n_i}{m}\right) +$$
$$\sum_i \sum_j \left(\frac{dy_j}{dt}\right) \cdot \left(\frac{L_{ij} \cdot n_i}{m}\right) + \sum_i \sum_j \left(\frac{dn_i}{dt}\right) \cdot \left(\frac{L_{ij} \cdot y_j}{m}\right) - \left(\frac{1}{q}\right) \cdot \left(\frac{dq}{dt}\right) \tag{7.4}$$

Here, relative growth rates are indicated by a 'hat', e.g. $\hat{n} = \dfrac{dn}{dt}\bigg/ n$.

Equation 7.4 could also be rewritten entirely in relative growth terms:

$$\hat{n} = \sum_i \sum_j \hat{L}_{ij} \cdot w_{ij} + \sum_i \sum_j \hat{y}_j \cdot w_{ij} + \sum_i \sum_j \hat{n}_i \cdot w_{ij} - \hat{q} \tag{7.5}$$

Here, weights w_{ij} ($= m_{ij}/m$) are equal to the material throughput m_{ij} ($= L_{ij} y_j n_i$) generated in activity i due to the final demand of activity j divided by the value of the national level material use m. Although equations 7.4 and 7.5 are mathematically equivalent, they lead to different decomposition indices upon integration. Liu et al. (1992) define Method 1 as the approach in which the determinants are defined in terms of the relative growth rates (Equation 7.5). Decompositions similar to Equation 7.4 are referred to as Method 2. Upon integration of the left- and right-hand side over the discrete period $t - 1$ to t, both methods result in the same general multiplicative decomposition form:

$$D_{I(m)} = \frac{n^t}{n^{t-1}} = D_{I(m)}^{IOC} \cdot D_{I(m)}^{FD} \cdot D_{I(m)}^{INT} \cdot D_{I(m)}^{PDN} \cdot D_{I(m)}^{RSD} \tag{7.6}$$

The *Ds* are used to denote various determinant effects that are identified by the superscripts (see Appendix 7.A). The subscript will be used to indicate the indicator and mathematical form. In this case, it is the multiplicative decomposition of the intensity indicator *I(m)*. The change in the indicator (no superscript) is given on the left-hand side of the equation. All decomposition subscripts and superscripts may be found in Appendix 7.A.

1a) Parametric Method 1 (conventional Divisia index)
By integrating both sides of Equation 7.5, Liu et al. (1992) found the following parametric specification:[4]

$$D_{1(m)l}^{IOC} = exp\left[\sum_i \sum_j \ln\left(\frac{L_{ij}^t}{L_{ij}^{t-1}}\right) \cdot \left[w_{ij}^{t-1} + \alpha_{ij}^{IOC} \cdot \Delta w_{ij}\right]\right]$$

$$D_{1(m)l}^{FD} = exp\left[\sum_i \sum_j \ln\left(\frac{y_j^t}{y_j^{t-1}}\right) \cdot \left[w_{ij}^{t-1} + \alpha_{ij}^{FD} \cdot \Delta w_{ij}\right]\right]$$

$$D_{1(m)l}^{INT} = exp\left[\sum_i \sum_j \ln\left(\frac{n_i^t}{n_i^{t-1}}\right) \cdot \left[w_{ij}^{t-1} + \alpha_{ij}^{INT} \cdot \Delta w_{ij}\right]\right]$$ (7.7)

$$D_{1(m)l}^{PDN} = exp\left[-\ln\left(\frac{q^t}{q^{t-1}}\right)\right]$$

A special case of the parametric Method 1 is the arithmetic mean of the weights or the conventional Divisia index or Törnqvist index (where $\alpha_{ij}^{IOC} = \alpha_j^{FD} = \alpha_i^{INT} = 0.5$).

1b) Non-parametric Method 1 (refined Divisia index)
Instead of the arithmetic mean in the parametric setting, the logarithmic mean could also be used as the weight in Method 1. This Non-parametric Method 1 index, referred to as the 'refined Divisia index' by Ang and Choi (1997), is written as follows:

$$D_{1(m)R}^{IOC} = exp\left[\sum_i \sum_j \ln\left(\frac{L_{ij}^t}{L_{ij}^{t-1}}\right) \cdot \frac{\Delta w_{ij}}{\ln\left(w_{ij}^t / w_{ij}^{t-1}\right)} \bigg/ \sum_i \sum_j \frac{\Delta w_{ij}}{\ln\left(w_{ij}^t / w_{ij}^{t-1}\right)}\right]$$

$$D_{1(m)R}^{FD} = exp\left[\sum_i \sum_j \ln\left(\frac{y_j^t}{y_j^{t-1}}\right) \cdot \frac{\Delta w_{ij}}{\ln\left(w_{ij}^t / w_{ij}^{t-1}\right)} \bigg/ \sum_i \sum_j \frac{\Delta w_{ij}}{\ln\left(w_{ij}^t / w_{ij}^{t-1}\right)}\right]$$ (7.8)

$$D_{1(m)R}^{INT} = exp\left[\sum_i \sum_j \ln\left(\frac{n_i^t}{n_i^{t-1}}\right) \cdot \frac{\Delta w_{ij}}{\ln\left(w_{ij}^t / w_{ij}^{t-1}\right)} \bigg/ \sum_i \sum_j \frac{\Delta w_{ij}}{\ln\left(w_{ij}^t / w_{ij}^{t-1}\right)}\right]$$

$$D_{1(m)R}^{PDN} = exp\left[-\ln\left(\frac{q^t}{q^{t-1}}\right)\right]$$

1c) Parametric Method 2 (Laspeyres, Paasche, Marshall-Edgeworth)
Method 1 decomposition indices are derived from Equation 7.5. Method 2 indices are created upon the integration of both sides of Equation 7.4.

$$D_{1(m)2}^{IOC} = exp\left[\sum_i \sum_j \Delta L_{ij} \cdot \left[\left(\frac{y_j^{t-1} \cdot n_i^{t-1}}{m^{t-1}}\right) + \alpha_{ij}^{IOC} \cdot \Delta\left(\frac{y_j \cdot n_i}{m}\right)\right]\right]$$

$$D_{1(m)2}^{FD} = exp\left[\sum_i \sum_j \Delta y_j \cdot \left[\left(\frac{L_{ij}^{t-1} \cdot n_i^{t-1}}{m^{t-1}}\right) + \alpha_{ij}^{FD} \cdot \Delta\left(\frac{L_{ij} \cdot n_i}{m}\right)\right]\right]$$

$$D_{1(m)2}^{INT} = exp\left[\sum_i \sum_j \Delta n_i \cdot \left[\left(\frac{L_{ij}^{t-1} \cdot y_j^{t-1}}{m^{t-1}}\right) + \alpha_{ij}^{INT} \cdot \Delta\left(\frac{L_{ij} \cdot y_j}{m}\right)\right]\right] \qquad (7.9)$$

$$D_{1(m)2}^{PDN} = exp\left[-\Delta q \cdot \left[\left(\frac{1}{q^{t-1}}\right) + \alpha^{PDN} \cdot \Delta\left(\frac{1}{q}\right)\right]\right]$$

Three special cases of Parametric Method 2 are: Laspeyres ($\alpha_{ij}^{ioc} = \alpha_{ij}^{FD} = \alpha_{ij}^{INT} = \alpha^{PDN} = 0$); Paasche ($\alpha_{ij}^{IOC} = \alpha_{ij}^{FD} = \alpha_{ij}^{INT} = \alpha^{PDN} = 1$); and Marshall-Edgeworth ($\alpha_{ij}^{IOC} = \alpha_{ij}^{FD} = \alpha_{ij}^{INT} = \alpha^{PDN} = 0.5$).

1d) Parametric Method 1 and 2 combined (adaptive weighting Divisia index)
The adaptive weighting Divisia index provides a way of setting the α-terms in the parametric methods 1 and 2, in a non-arbitrary way. It is assumed that the decomposition results are the same for Methods 1 and 2. The assumptions of the adaptive weighting Divisia index are as follows:

$$D_{1(m)1}^{IOC} = D_{i(m)2}^{IOC}$$
$$D_{1(m)1}^{FD} = D_{1(m)2}^{FD}$$
$$D_{1(m)1}^{PDN} = D_{1(m)2}^{PDN}$$
$$D_{1(m)1}^{INT} = D_{1(m)2}^{INT}$$

$$\alpha_{ij}^{IOC} \text{ (Method 1)} = \alpha_{ij}^{IOC} \text{ (Method 2)}$$
$$\alpha_{ij}^{INT} \text{ (Method 1)} = \alpha_{ij}^{INT} \text{ (Method 2)} \qquad (7.10)$$
$$\alpha_{ij}^{FD} \text{ (Method 1)} = \alpha_{ij}^{FD} \text{ (Method 2)}$$

The equality condition leads to the following unique values for the α-parameters:

$$\alpha_{ij}^{IOC} = \frac{\Delta L_{ij} \cdot \left(\frac{y_j^{t-1} \cdot n_i^{t-1}}{m^{t-1}} \right) - \ln\left(\frac{L_{ij}^{t}}{L_{ij}^{t-1}} \right) \cdot w_{ij}^{t-1}}{\Delta w_{ij} \cdot \ln\left(\frac{L_{ij}^{t}}{L_{ij}^{t-1}} \right) - \Delta\left(\frac{y_j \cdot n_i}{m} \right) \cdot \Delta L_{ij}}$$

$$\alpha_{ij}^{FD} = \frac{\Delta y_j \cdot \left(\frac{L_{ij}^{t-1} \cdot n_i^{t-1}}{m^{t-1}} \right) - \ln\left(\frac{y_j^{t}}{y_j^{t-1}} \right) \cdot w_{ij}^{t-1}}{\Delta w_{ij} \cdot \ln\left(\frac{y_j^{t}}{y_j^{t-1}} \right) - \Delta\left(\frac{L_{ij} \cdot n_i}{m} \right) \cdot \Delta y_j}$$

$$\alpha_{ij}^{INT} = \frac{\Delta r_i \cdot \left(\frac{L_{ij}^{t-1} \cdot y_j^{t-1}}{m^{t-1}} \right) - \ln\left(\frac{n_i^{t}}{n_i^{t-1}} \right) \cdot w_{ij}^{t-1}}{\Delta w_{ij} \cdot \ln\left(\frac{n_i^{t}}{n_i^{t-1}} \right) - \Delta\left(\frac{L_{ij} \cdot y_j}{m} \right) \cdot \Delta n_i}$$

$$\alpha^{PDN} = \frac{\ln\left(\frac{q^{t-1}}{q^{t}} \right) - \left(\frac{\Delta q}{q^{t-1}} \right)}{\Delta q \cdot \Delta\left(\frac{1}{q} \right)}$$

(7.11)

By definition, if these α-values are used in the parametric Methods 1 or 2, the same decomposition results are obtained.

Additive Decomposition of the Absolute Indicator

In this section the absolute use of a particular indicator is decomposed by means of additive decomposition. To avoid repetition, the derivation will be less detailed than that of the previous section. The base Equation 7.12 of material use m is:

$$m = \sum_i \sum_j L_{ij} \cdot y_j \cdot n_i$$

(7.12)

Differentiating with respect to time gives:

$$\left(\frac{dm}{dt}\right) = \sum_i \sum_j \left(\frac{dL_{ij}}{dt}\right) \cdot \left(y_j \cdot n_i\right) +$$

$$\sum_i \sum_j \left(\frac{dy_j}{dt}\right) \cdot \left(L_{ij} \cdot n_i\right) + \sum_i \sum_j \left(\frac{dn_i}{dt}\right) \cdot \left(L_{ij} \cdot y_j\right) \qquad (7.13)$$

This can also be rewritten in terms of relative growth rates:

$$\left(\frac{dm}{dt}\right) = \sum_i \sum_j \hat{L}_{ij} \cdot m_{ij} + \sum_i \sum_j \hat{y}_j \cdot m_{ij} + \sum_i \sum_j \hat{n}_i \cdot m_{ij} \qquad (7.14)$$

Integrating both sides of Equation 7.14 leads to a Method 1 decomposition, while Equation 7.13 yields a Method 2 specification. Integrating both sides of these two equations, over the discrete time period $t-1$ and t, leads to the general decomposition form:

$$D_{A(a)} = \Delta m = m^t - m^{t-1} = D_{A(a)}^{IOC} + D_{A(a)}^{FD} + D_{A(a)}^{INT} + D_{A(a)}^{RSD} \qquad (7.15)$$

2a) Parametric Method 1 (conventional Divisia index)

$$D_{A(a)1}^{IOC} = \sum_i \sum_j \ln\left(\frac{L_{ij}^t}{L_{ij}^{t-1}}\right) \cdot \left[m_{ij}^{t-1} + \alpha_{ij}^{IOC} \cdot \Delta m_{ij}\right]$$

$$D_{A(a)1}^{FD} = \sum_i \sum_j \ln\left(\frac{y_j^t}{y_j^{t-1}}\right) \cdot \left[m_{ij}^{t-1} + \alpha_{ij}^{FD} \cdot \Delta m_{ij}\right] \qquad (7.16)$$

$$D_{A(a)1}^{INT} = \sum_i \sum_j \ln\left(\frac{n_i^t}{n_i^{t-1}}\right) \cdot \left[m_{ij}^{t-1} + \alpha_{ij}^{INT} \cdot \Delta m_{ij}\right]$$

Note that, compared with the multiplicative decomposition of material use intensity, there is no production effect in this case. The conventional Divisia index sets the α-values to 0.5.

2b) Non-parametric Method 1 (refined Divisia index)
The logarithmic mean in the Method 1 setting produces the refined Divisia index.

$$D_{A(a)R}^{IOC} = \sum_i \sum_j \ln\left(\frac{L_{ij}^t}{L_{ij}^{t-1}}\right) \cdot \frac{\Delta m_{ij}}{\ln\left(m_{ij}^t / m_{ij}^{t-1}\right)}$$

$$D_{A(a)R}^{FD} = \sum_i \sum_j \ln\left(\frac{y_j^t}{y_j^{t-1}}\right) \cdot \frac{\Delta m_{ij}}{\ln\left(m_{ij}^t / m_{ij}^{t-1}\right)} \qquad (7.17)$$

$$D_{A(a)R}^{INT} = \sum_i \sum_j \ln\left(\frac{n_i^t}{n_i^{t-1}}\right) \cdot \frac{\Delta m_{ij}}{\ln\left(m_{ij}^t / m_{ij}^{t-1}\right)}$$

2c) Parametric Method 2 (Laspeyres, Paasche, Marshall-Edgeworth)
The Laspeyres, Paasche and Marshall-Edgeworth indices are used frequently in the SDA setting, but they are never specified in this parametric form.

$$D_{A(a)2}^{IOC} = \sum_i \sum_j \Delta L_{ij} \cdot \left[\left(y_j^{t-1} \cdot n_i^{t-1}\right) + \alpha_{ij}^{IOC} \cdot \Delta\left(y_j \cdot n_i\right)\right]$$

$$D_{A(a)2}^{FD} = \sum_i \sum_j \Delta y_j \cdot \left[\left(L_{ij}^{t-1} \cdot n_i^{t-1}\right) + \alpha_{ij}^{FD} \cdot \Delta\left(L_{ij} \cdot n_i\right)\right] \qquad (7.18)$$

$$D_{A(a)2}^{INT} = \sum_i \sum_j \Delta n_i \cdot \left[\left(L_{ij}^{t-1} \cdot y_j^{t-1}\right) + \alpha_{ij}^{INT} \cdot \Delta\left(L_{ij} \cdot y_j\right)\right]$$

Laspeyres, Marshall-Edgeworth and Paasche indices result if the α-parameters are set to 0, 0.5 and 1, respectively.

2d) Parametric Method 1 and 2 combined (adaptive weighting Divisia index)
The adaptive weighting Divisia index is derived by using the same assumptions as those in Equation 7.10, except for those that are specifically focused on the production effect. The resulting unique values of α are:

$$\alpha_{ij}^{IOC} = \frac{\Delta L_{ij} \cdot \left(y_j^{t-1} \cdot n_i^{t-1}\right) - \ln\left(\frac{L_{ij}^t}{L_{ij}^{t-1}}\right) \cdot m_{ij}^{t-1}}{\Delta m_{ij} \cdot \ln\left(\frac{L_{ij}^t}{L_{ij}^{t-1}}\right) - \Delta\left(y_j \cdot n_i\right) \cdot \Delta L_{ij}}$$

$$\qquad (7.19)$$

$$\alpha_{ij}^{FD} = \frac{\Delta y_j \cdot \left(L_{ij}^{t-1} \cdot n_i^{t-1}\right) - \ln\left(\frac{y_j^t}{y_j^{t-1}}\right) \cdot m_{ij}^{t-1}}{\Delta m_{ij} \cdot \ln\left(\frac{y_j^t}{y_j^{t-1}}\right) - \Delta\left(L_{ij} \cdot n_i\right) \cdot \Delta y_j}$$

$$\alpha_{ij}^{INT} = \frac{\Delta r_i \cdot \left(L_{ij}^{t-1} \cdot y_j^{t-1}\right) - ln\left(\frac{r_i^t}{r_i^{t-1}}\right) \cdot m_{ij}^{t-1}}{\Delta m_{ij} \cdot ln\left(\frac{n_i^t}{n_i^{t-1}}\right) - \Delta\left(L_{ij} \cdot y_j\right) \cdot \Delta n_i}$$

The parameter values may be substituted into the parametric methods 1 or 2.

Additive Decomposition of the Elasticity Indicator

The output elasticity[5] of material use can be found by replacing the results of the additive decomposition of material use into Equation 7.20 for the output elasticity:

$$D_{E(a)} = \frac{\Delta m}{m} \Big/ \frac{\Delta q}{q} = \left(\frac{D_{A(a)}^{IOC}}{m} \Big/ \frac{\Delta q}{q}\right) + \left(\frac{D_{A(a)}^{FD}}{m} \Big/ \frac{\Delta q}{q}\right) + \left(\frac{D_{A(a)}^{INT}}{m} \Big/ \frac{\Delta q}{q}\right) + \left(\frac{D_{A(a)}^{RSD}}{m} \Big/ \frac{\Delta q}{q}\right) \qquad (7.20)$$

3a) Laspeyres, Marshall-Edgeworth and Paasche
The Laspeyres and Marshall-Edgeworth versions of this decomposition are given in Ang and Lee (1996):

$$D_{E(a)}^{IOC} = \left(\frac{D_{A(a)2}^{IOC}}{m^{t-1} + \alpha^{IOC} \cdot \Delta m}\right) \Big/ \left(\frac{\Delta q}{q^{t-1} + \alpha^{IOC} \cdot \Delta q}\right)$$

$$D_{E(a)}^{FD} = \left(\frac{D_{A(a)2}^{FD}}{m^{t-1} + \alpha^{FD} \cdot \Delta m}\right) \Big/ \left(\frac{\Delta q}{q^{t-1} + \alpha^{FD} \cdot \Delta q}\right) \qquad (7.21)$$

$$D_{E(a)}^{INT} = \left(\frac{D_{A(a)2}^{INT}}{m^{t-1} + \alpha^{INT} \cdot \Delta m}\right) \Big/ \left(\frac{\Delta q}{q^{t-1} + \alpha^{INT} \cdot \Delta q}\right)$$

To obtain Laspeyres, Paasche and Marshall-Edgeworth indices, the α-parameters are set to 0, 1 and 0.5, respectively. Additionally, the Laspeyres, Paasche and Marshall-Edgeworth results of the additive decomposition of the absolute indicators should be used.

Additive Decomposition of the Absolute Indicator (Sun, 1998)

Sun (1998) uses the idea of splitting the residuals of a Laspeyres decomposition equally amongst the determinant variables. This procedure is only applied to additive decompositions. In the two-determinant case there is one residual term that is split equally amongst both effects. In the case of three determinants there are four residual effects which are distributed amongst the determinants according to the principle 'jointly created equally distributed'. This is consistent with the idea of a direct growth path between two discrete points in time (Vogt, 1978), and can be written as in equations 7.22. The IDA versions of these equations are given in Appendix 7.B.

$$D_{A(a)SUN}^{IOC} = \sum_i \sum_j \Delta L_{ij} \cdot y_j^{t-1} \cdot n_i^{t-1} +$$

$$\frac{1}{2} \cdot \Delta L_{ij} \left(\Delta y_j \cdot n_i^{t-1} + y_j^{t-1} \cdot \Delta n_i \right) + \frac{1}{3} \cdot \Delta L_{ij} \cdot \Delta y_j \cdot \Delta n_i$$

$$D_{A(a)SUN}^{FD} = \sum_i \sum_j L_{ij}^{t-1} \cdot \Delta y_j \cdot n_i^{t-1} +$$

$$\frac{1}{2} \cdot \Delta y_j \left(\Delta L_{ij} \cdot n_i^{t-1} + L_{ij}^{t-1} \cdot \Delta n_i \right) + \frac{1}{3} \cdot \Delta L_{ij} \cdot \Delta y_j \cdot \Delta n_i \qquad (7.22)$$

$$D_{A(a)SUN}^{INT} = \sum_i \sum_j L_{ij}^{t-1} \cdot y_j^{t-1} \cdot \Delta n_i +$$

$$\frac{1}{2} \cdot \Delta r_i \left(\Delta L_{ij} \cdot y_j^{t-1} + L_{ij}^{t-1} \cdot \Delta y_j \right) + \frac{1}{3} \cdot \Delta L_{ij} \cdot \Delta y_j \cdot \Delta n_i$$

7.4 SDA INDEX APPROACHES TRANSFERRED TO IDA

Additive Decomposition of the Absolute Indicator (Dietzenbacher and Los, 1998)

There is only one index approach that is unique to SDA and has not been implemented in the IDA (proposed in Dietzenbacher and Los, 1998). They note that, if it is assumed that each of β determinant variables can either be weighted by the Laspeyres or Paasche weights, then there are $\beta!$ different complete decompositions possible. In the IDA setting the base equation is:

$$m = \sum_i \frac{q_i}{q} \cdot \frac{m_i}{q_i} \cdot x = \sum_i h_i \cdot n_i \cdot q \qquad (7.23)$$

This may be decomposed into the following determinant effects (see Appendix 7.A for notation):

$$D_{A(a)DL} = \Delta m = m^t - m^{t-1} = D_{A(a)DL}^{STR} + D_{A(a)DL}^{INT} + D_{A(a)DL}^{PDN} \qquad (7.24)$$

Decomposing this by the method proposed in Dietzenbacher and Los (1998), the following six complete decomposition equations result:

$$D_{A(a)DL1} = \sum_i \Delta h_i \cdot n_i^t \cdot q^t + \sum_i h_i^{t-1} \cdot \Delta n_i \cdot q^t + \sum_i h_i^{t-1} \cdot n_i^{t-1} \cdot \Delta q$$

$$D_{A(a)DL2} = \sum_i \Delta h_i \cdot n_i^t \cdot q^t + \sum_i h_i^{t-1} \cdot \Delta n_i \cdot q^{t-1} + \sum_i h_i^{t-1} \cdot n_i^t \cdot \Delta q$$

$$D_{A(a)DL3} = \sum_i \Delta h_i \cdot n_i^{t-1} \cdot q^t + \sum_i h_i^t \cdot \Delta n_i \cdot q^t + \sum_i h_i^{t-1} \cdot n_i^{t-1} \cdot \Delta q$$

$$D_{A(a)DL4} = \sum_i \Delta h_i \cdot n_i^t \cdot q^{t-1} + \sum_i h_i^{t-1} \cdot \Delta n_i \cdot q^t + \sum_i h_i^t \cdot n_i^t \cdot \Delta q \qquad (7.25)$$

$$D_{A(a)DL5} = \sum_i \Delta h_i \cdot n_i^{t-1} \cdot q^{t-1} + \sum_i h_i^t \cdot \Delta n_i \cdot q^t + \sum_i h_i^t \cdot n_i^{t-1} \cdot \Delta q$$

$$D_{A(a)DL6} = \sum_i \Delta h_i \cdot n_i^{t-1} \cdot q^{t-1} + \sum_i h_i^t \cdot \Delta n_i \cdot q^{t-1} + \sum_i h_i^t \cdot n_i^t \cdot \Delta q$$

Dietzenbacher and Los (1998) suggest that, instead of finding the average of all the different index combinations (for example, if the number of determinants is very large), then the average of the two polar decompositions (*DL*1 and *DL*6 in this case) is a good estimate. The SDA versions of these equations are given in Appendix 7.B.

Multiplicative Decomposition of the Intensity Indicator (Dietzenbacher and Los, 1998)

The multiplicative version of the Dietzenbacher and Los (1998) approach is used in Dietzenbacher et al. (2000). The equation for material use intensity is:

$$r = \sum_i \frac{q_i}{q} \cdot \frac{m_i}{q_i} = \sum_i h_i \cdot n_i \qquad (7.26)$$

This may be decomposed into the following determinant effects:

$$D_{I(m)DL} = \frac{n^t}{n^{t-1}} = D_{I(m)DL}^{STR} \cdot D_{I(m)DL}^{INT} \qquad (7.27)$$

There are two complete decomposition effects:

$$D_{I(m)DL1} = \frac{\sum_i h_i^t \cdot n_i^{t-1}}{\sum_i h_i^{t-1} \cdot n_i^{t-1}} \cdot \frac{\sum_i h_i^t \cdot n_i^t}{\sum_i h_i^t \cdot n_i^{t-1}}$$

$$D_{I(m)DL2} = \frac{\sum_i h_i^t \cdot n_i^t}{\sum_i h_i^{t-1} \cdot n_i^t} \cdot \frac{\sum_i h_i^{t-1} \cdot n_i^t}{\sum_i h_i^{t-1} \cdot n_i^{t-1}}$$

(7.28)

The derivation of the additive decomposition of the material use intensity and the multiplicative decomposition of the absolute material use are easily derived and are therefore left to the reader.

7.5 A NUMERICAL EXAMPLE

In this section, a hypothetical numerical example from Ang (1999) is expanded to illustrate the differences in SDA and IDA (Table 7.3). The IO information has been added. All information is in monetary units, except for the material use, which is in kilograms. The different decomposition techniques were applied to this data and the results are shown in Table 7.4.

Table 7.3 A two-activity numerical example (year t-1 and year t)

IO(euro) (year $t-1$)	Materials	Services	Final demand	Output	Material use (kg)
Materials	3	2	5	10	30
Services	5	20	15	40	20
Value added	2	18			
Total	10	40			

IO (euro) (year t)	Materials	Services	Final demand	Output	Material use (kg)
Materials	8	2	10	20	40
Services	10	30	20	60	24
Value added	2	28			
Total	20	60			

Table 7.4 shows that the decomposition indices produce different results (for an interpretation of the different effects, see Section 7.2). Concerning the residual, the properties in Table 7.2 are confirmed: the refined Divisia, Sun (1998) and Dietzenbacher and Los (1998) approaches yield complete decompositions. A multiplicative version of the Sun (1998) approach has not

been proposed. An important conclusion is that indices that are frequently used in the literature (Laspeyres and Paasche) produce large residuals.

Interestingly, the additive decomposition results show that the approaches proposed by Sun (1998) and Dietzenbacher and Los (1998) lead to identical decomposition effects. This is a surprising outcome, considering that these approaches adopt very different a priori assumptions. It suggests that equally-distributed splitting of the residual (Sun, 1998), the mean of $n!$ index combinations (Dietzenbacher and Los, 1998), and the straight growth path proposed by Vogt (1978), all lead to the same results.

The range of results for particular determinant effects is very broad. This stresses that the choice of index is important to the decomposition results. An advantage of the Dietzenbacher and Los (1998) approach is that the minimum and maximum of decomposition forms indicates a range of results.

Table 7.4 SDA and IDA decomposition based on data in Table 7.3

Multiplicative decomposition of an intensity indicator (kg/euro)							
			Determinant effects				
Method/Index	SDA/ IDA	Total	Production Structure	Leontief	Final Demand	Intensity	Residual
Method 1							
Conventional	IDA	0.8		1.118			0.716	1.000
Divisia	SDA	0.8	0.625		1.050	1.701	0.716	1.002
Refined Divisia	IDA	0.8		1.118			0.716	1.000
	SDA	0.8	0.625		1.051	1.702	0.716	1.000
Method 2							
Laspeyres	IDA	0.8		1.133			0.756	0.934
	SDA	0.8	0.549		1.042	1.998	0.756	0.926
Marshall-	IDA	0.8		1.119			0.710	1.008
Edgeworth	SDA	0.8	0.614		1.051	1.740	0.710	1.004
Paasche	IDA	0.8		1.105			0.666	1.087
	SDA	0.8	0.687		1.059	1.515	0.666	1.089
Methods 1 & 2 combined							
Adaptive	IDA	0.8		1.118			0.716	0.999
weighting Divisia index	SDA	0.8	0.625		1.052	1.700	0.721	0.993
Dietzenbacher and Los (1998)							
Average of $n!$	IDA	0.8		1.118			0.716	1.000
decompositions	SDA	0.8	0.625		1.051	1.702	0.716	1.000
Minimum of $n!$	IDA	0.8		1.111			0.711	N/A
decompositions	SDA	0.8	0.625		1.039	1.675	0.711	N/A
Maximum of $n!$	IDA	0.8		1.125			0.720	N/A
decompositions	SDA	0.8	0.625		1.064	1.729	0.720	N/A

Table 7.4 (continued)

Additive decomposition of an absolute indicator (kg)

| Method/Index | SDA/ IDA | | Total | Production Structure | Determinant effects | | | |
					Leontief	Final Demand	Intensity	Residual
Method 1								
Conventional Divisia	IDA	14	26.8	6.4			−19.1	−0.1
	SDA	14			2.9	30.4	−19.1	−0.3
Refined Divisia	IDA	14	26.7	6.3			−19.0	0.0
	SDA	14			2.9	30.0	−18.9	0.0
Method 2								
Laspeyres	IDA	14	30.0	6.3			−14.0	−8.3
	SDA	14			2.1	34.6	−14.0	−8.7
Marshall-Edgeworth	IDA	14	27.0	6.3			−20.0	0.7
	SDA	14			2.9	30.6	−20.0	0.5
Paasche	IDA	14	24.0	6.4			−26.0	9.6
	SDA	14			3.7	26.6	−26.0	9.7
Methods 1 & 2 combined								
Adaptive weighting Divisia index	IDA	14	26.9	6.3			−18.5	−0.8
	SDA	14			2.8	30.4	−18.5	−0.7
Sun (1998)	IDA		27.2	6.6			−19.8	0.0
	SDA				3.0	30.8	−19.8	0.0
Dietzenbacher and Los (1998)								
Average of *n!* decompositions	IDA		27.2	6.6			−19.8	0.0
	SDA				3.0	30.8	−19.8	0.0
Minimum of *n!* decompositions	IDA		21.6	4.0			−14.0	N/A
	SDA				1.4	24.3	−14.0	N/A
Maximum of *n!* decompositions	IDA		33.8	10.0			−26.0	N/A
	SDA				5.4	37.9	−26.0	N/A

Additive decomposition of an elasticity indicator

	SDA/IDA		Total	Production Structure	Leontief	Final Demand	Intensity	Residual
Laspeyres	IDA	0.47	1.00	0.21			−0.47	−0.28
	SDA	0.47			0.07	1.15	−0.47	−0.29
Marshall-Edgeworth	IDA	0.53	1.03	0.24			−0.76	0.03
	SDA	0.53			0.11	1.16	−0.76	0.02
Paasche	IDA	0.58	1.00	0.27			−1.08	0.40
	SDA	0.58			0.15	1.11	−1.08	0.41

7.6 CONCLUSIONS

A number of conclusions can be drawn from the previous analysis. Firstly, there are two streams of historical decomposition methods that can analyze the determinant effects using activity level data. SDA uses the IO model while IDA uses more aggregated activity data. As a result, SDA is capable of more refined decompositions of economic and technological effects but IDA is capable of more detailed time and country studies because of the availability of data. The two fields of decomposition literature have developed rather independently. IDA is characterized by a greater variety of indicator forms, mathematical (additive and multiplicative) specifications and indices. This chapter has shown that these techniques can be transferred to SDA, and the corresponding specifications have been derived formally. In addition, it has been argued that the Dietzenbacher and Los (1998) approach used in SDA can be translated to an IDA setting. All in all, the methodological and numerical findings indicate that a careful choice of approach is needed, and possibly multiple approaches can be applied to a single problem, so as to generate a variety of perspectives on the determinants of changes in an indicator of interest. Furthermore, additional research should use the axiomatic approach of index theory to assess the index properties that are required in decomposition analyses.

APPENDIX 7.A LIST OF SYMBOLS

The superscript t refers to time period.

Country-level symbols:
m^t Total material use (kg)
q^t Total output (euro)
n^t Material use intensity of the economy (kg/euro) ($= m/q$)
β Number of sectors in the economy

Sector-level symbols:
Z_{ij}^t Deliveries of goods and services of activity i to activity j (euro)
A_{ij}^t IO coefficients matrix. The amount of input from activity i required per unit output of activity j
L_{ij}^t Leontief inverse. The direct and indirect effect on the output of activity i per unit of change of demand of activity j ($= (I - A_{ij}^t)^{-1}$)
m_{ij}^t Material use by activity i due to demand for products from activity j (kg)
m_i^t Material use by activity i (kg)

w_{ij}^t Material use weights. Material use in activity i due to demand for products from activity j as a proportion of the total material use (kg) ($= m_{ij}/m$)

w_i^t Material use weights. Material use in activity i as a proportion of the total material use (kg) ($= m_i/m$)

q_i^t Output of activity i (euro)

y_j^t Final demand of activity j (euro)

n_i^t Material use intensity of activity i (kg/euro) ($= m_i/q_i$)

h_i^t Output share. Activity i output as a proportion of total output ($=q_i/q$)

Superscripts of parameters α_{ij}:

STR   Structural effect

INT   Intensity effect

PDN   Production effect

IOC   IO coefficients effect

FD   Final demand effect

Superscripts of decomposition variable D:

(Variable without a superscript is equal to the total change of material use)

STR   Structural effect

INT   Intensity effect

PDN   Production effect

IOC   IO coefficients effect

FD   Final demand effect

RSD   Residual effect

Subscripts of decomposition variable D:

First Subscript (Indicator type)

I Intensity

A Absolute

E Elasticity

Second Subscript (Decomposition type)

(a)   Additive

(m)   Multiplicative

Third Subscript (Decomposition index)

I Parametric Divisia index Method 1

R Refined Divisia index (Non-parametric Method 1)

2 Parametric Divisia index Method 2

A Adaptive weighting Divisia index

SUN   Index approach proposed in Sun (1998)

DL   Index approach proposed in Dietzenbacher and Los (1998)

APPENDIX 7.B DECOMPOSITION FORMULAE

This appendix presents decomposition formula that are derived or taken from the literature (Ang, 1999, Sun, 1998 and Dietzenbacher and Los, 1998).

IDA: Multiplicative Decomposition of the Intensity Indicator

1a) Parametric Method 1

$$D_{I(m)1}^{STR} = exp\left[\sum_i ln\left(\frac{h_i^t}{h_i^{t-1}}\right)\cdot\left[w_i^{t-1} + \alpha_i^{STR}\cdot\Delta w_i\right]\right]$$

$$D_{I(m)1}^{INT} = exp\left[\sum_i ln\left(\frac{n_i^t}{n_i^{t-1}}\right)\cdot\left[w_i^{t-1} + \alpha_i^{INT}\cdot\Delta w_i\right]\right]$$

1b) Non-parametric Method 1

$$D_{I(m)R}^{STR} = exp\left[\sum_i ln\left(\frac{h_i^t}{h_i^{t-1}}\right)\cdot\left(\frac{\Delta w_i}{ln\left(w_i^t/w_i^{t-1}\right)}\bigg/\sum_i\frac{\Delta w_i}{ln\left(w_i^t/w_i^{t-1}\right)}\right)\right]$$

$$D_{I(m)R}^{INT} = exp\left[\sum_i ln\left(\frac{n_i^t}{n_i^{t-1}}\right)\cdot\left(\frac{\Delta w_i}{ln\left(w_i^t/w_i^{t-1}\right)}\bigg/\sum_i\frac{\Delta w_i}{ln\left(w_i^t/w_i^{t-1}\right)}\right)\right]$$

1c) Parametric Method 2

$$D_{I(m)2}^{STR} = exp\left[\sum_i \Delta h_i\cdot\left[\frac{n_i^{t-1}}{n^{t-1}} + \alpha_i^{STR}\cdot\Delta\left(\frac{n_i}{n}\right)\right]\right]$$

$$D_{I(m)2}^{INT} = exp\left[\sum_i \Delta n_i\cdot\left[\frac{q_i^{t-1}}{n^{t-1}} + \alpha_i^{INT}\cdot\Delta\left(\frac{q_i}{n}\right)\right]\right]$$

1d) Parametric Methods 1 and 2 combined

$$\alpha_i^{STR} = \frac{\Delta h_i\cdot\left(\frac{n_i^{t-1}}{n^{t-1}}\right) - ln\left(\frac{h_i^t}{h_i^{t-1}}\right)\cdot w_i^{t-1}}{\Delta w_i\cdot ln\frac{h_i^t}{h_i^{t-1}} - \Delta\left(\frac{n_i}{n}\right)\cdot\Delta h_i}$$

$$\alpha_i^{INT} = \frac{\Delta r_i \cdot \left(\dfrac{q_i^{t-1}}{n^{t-1}} \right) - ln\left(\dfrac{n_i^t}{n_i^{t-1}} \right) \cdot w_i^{t-1}}{\Delta w_i \cdot ln\left(\dfrac{n_i^t}{n_i^{t-1}} \right) - \Delta\left(\dfrac{q_i}{n} \right) \cdot \Delta n_i}$$

IDA: Additive Decomposition of the Absolute Indicator

2a) Parametric Method 1

$$D_{A(a)1}^{STR} = \sum_i ln\left(\frac{h_i^t}{h_i^{t-1}} \right) \cdot \left[m_i^{t-1} + \alpha_i^{STR} \cdot \Delta m_i \right]$$

$$D_{A(a)1}^{INT} = \sum_i ln\left(\frac{n_i^t}{n_i^{t-1}} \right) \cdot \left[m_i^{t-1} + \alpha_i^{INT} \cdot \Delta m_i \right]$$

$$D_{A(a)1}^{PDN} = \sum_i ln\left(\frac{q^t}{q^{t-1}} \right) \cdot \left[m_i^{t-1} + \alpha_i^{PDN} \cdot \Delta m_i \right]$$

2b) Non-parametric Method 1

$$D_{A(a)R}^{STR} = \sum_i ln\left(\frac{s_i^t}{s_i^{t-1}} \right) \cdot \left[\frac{\Delta m_i}{ln\left(m_i^t / m_i^{t-1} \right)} \right]$$

$$D_{A(a)R}^{INT} = \sum_i ln\left(\frac{r_i^t}{r_i^{t-1}} \right) \cdot \left[\frac{\Delta m_i}{ln\left(m_i^t / m_i^{t-1} \right)} \right]$$

$$D_{A(a)R}^{PDN} = \sum_i ln\left(\frac{q^t}{q^{t-1}} \right) \cdot \left[\frac{\Delta m_i}{ln\left(m_i^t / m_i^{t-1} \right)} \right]$$

2c) Parametric Method 2

$$D_{A(a)2}^{STR} = \sum_i \Delta h_i \cdot \left[n_i^{t-1} \cdot q^{t-1} + \alpha_i^{STR} \cdot \Delta(n_i \cdot q) \right]$$

$$D_{A(a)2}^{INT} = \sum_i \Delta n_i \cdot \left[h_i^{t-1} \cdot q^{t-1} + \alpha_i^{INT} \cdot \Delta(h_i \cdot q) \right]$$

$$D_{A(a)2}^{PDN} = \sum_i \Delta q \cdot \left[h_i^{t-1} \cdot n_i^{t-1} + \alpha_i^{PDN} \cdot \Delta(h_i \cdot n_i) \right]$$

2d) Parametric Methods 1 and 2 combined

$$\alpha_i^{STR} = \frac{\Delta h_i \cdot \left(n_i^{t-1} \cdot q^{t-1}\right) - \ln\left(\frac{h_i^t}{h_i^{t-1}}\right) \cdot m_i^{t-1}}{\Delta m_i \cdot \ln\left(\frac{h_i^t}{h_i^{t-1}}\right) - \Delta(n_i \cdot q) \cdot \Delta h_i}$$

$$\alpha_i^{INT} = \frac{\Delta n_i \cdot \left(h_i^{t-1} \cdot q^{t-1}\right) - \ln\left(\frac{n_i^t}{n_i^{t-1}}\right) \cdot m_i^{t-1}}{\Delta m_i \cdot \ln\left(\frac{n_i^t}{n_i^{t-1}}\right) - \Delta(h_i \cdot q) \cdot \Delta n_i}$$

$$\alpha_i^{PDN} = \frac{\Delta q \cdot \left(n_i^{t-1} \cdot h_i^{t-1}\right) - \ln\left(\frac{q^t}{q^{t-1}}\right) \cdot m_i^{t-1}}{\Delta m_i \cdot \ln\left(\frac{q^t}{q^{t-1}}\right) - \Delta(n_i \cdot h_i) \cdot \Delta q}$$

IDA: Additive Decomposition of the Elasticity Indicator

$$D_{E(a)}^{STR} = \left(\frac{D_{A(a)2}^{STR}(\alpha^{STR})}{m^{t-1} + \alpha^{STR} \cdot \Delta m}\right) \Big/ \left(\frac{\Delta q}{q^{t-1} + \alpha^{STR} \cdot \Delta q}\right)$$

$$D_{E(a)}^{INT} = \left(\frac{D_{A(a)2}^{INT}(\alpha^{INT})}{m^{t-1} + \alpha^{INT} \cdot \Delta m}\right) \Big/ \left(\frac{\Delta q}{q^{t-1} + \alpha^{INT} \cdot \Delta q}\right)$$

$$D_{E(a)}^{PDN} = \left(\frac{D_{A(a)2}^{PDN}(\alpha^{PDN})}{m^{t-1} + \alpha^{PDN} \cdot \Delta m}\right) \Big/ \left(\frac{\Delta q}{q^{t-1} + \alpha^{PDN} \cdot \Delta q}\right)$$

IDA: Additive Decomposition of the Absolute Indicator (Sun, 1998)

$$D_{A(a)SUN}^{STR} = \sum_i \Delta h_i \cdot n_i^{t-1} \cdot q^{t-1} +$$

$$\frac{1}{2} \cdot \Delta h_i \left(\Delta n_i \cdot q^{t-1} + n_i^{t-1} \cdot \Delta q\right) + \frac{1}{3} \cdot \Delta h_i \cdot \Delta n_i \cdot \Delta q$$

$$D_{A(a)SUN}^{INT} = \sum_i \Delta n_i \cdot h_i^{t-1} \cdot q^{t-1} +$$

$$\frac{1}{2} \cdot \Delta n_i \left(\Delta h_i \cdot q^{t-1} + h_i^{t-1} \cdot \Delta q \right) + \frac{1}{3} \cdot \Delta h_i \cdot \Delta n_i \cdot \Delta q$$

$$D_{A(a)SUN}^{PDN} = \sum_i \Delta q \cdot h_i^{t-1} \cdot n_i^{t-1} +$$

$$\frac{1}{2} \cdot \Delta q \cdot \left(\Delta h_i \cdot n_i^{t-1} + h_i^{t-1} \cdot \Delta n_i \right) + \frac{1}{3} \cdot \Delta h_i \cdot \Delta n_i \cdot \Delta q$$

SDA: Additive Decomposition of the Absolute Indicator (Dietzenbacher and Los, 1998)

$$D_{A(a)DL1} = \sum_i \Delta L_{ij} \cdot y_j^t \cdot n_i^t + \sum_i L_{ij}^{t-1} \cdot \Delta y_j \cdot n_i^t + \sum_i L_{ij}^{t-1} \cdot y_j^{t-1} \cdot \Delta n_i$$

$$D_{A(a)DL2} = \sum_i \Delta L_{ij} \cdot y_j^t \cdot n_i^t + \sum_i L_{ij}^{t-1} \cdot \Delta y_j \cdot n_i^{t-1} + \sum_i L_{ij}^{t-1} \cdot y_j^t \cdot \Delta n_i$$

$$D_{A(a)DL3} = \sum_i \Delta L_{ij} \cdot y_j^{t-1} \cdot n_i^t + \sum_i L_{ij}^t \cdot \Delta y_j \cdot n_i^t + \sum_i L_{ij}^t \cdot y_j^{t-1} \cdot \Delta n_i$$

$$D_{A(a)DL4} = \sum_i \Delta L_{ij} \cdot y_j^t \cdot n_i^{t-1} + \sum_i L_{ij}^{t-1} \cdot \Delta y_j \cdot n_i^{t-1} + \sum_i L_{ij}^t \cdot y_j^t \cdot \Delta n_i$$

$$D_{A(a)DL5} = \sum_i \Delta L_{ij} \cdot y_j^{t-1} \cdot n_i^{t-1} + \sum_i L_{ij}^t \cdot \Delta y_j \cdot n_i^t + \sum_i L_{ij}^t \cdot y_j^{t-1} \cdot \Delta n_i$$

$$D_{A(a)DL6} = \sum_i \Delta L_{ij} \cdot y_j^{t-1} \cdot n_i^{t-1} + \sum_i L_{ij}^t \cdot \Delta y_j \cdot n_i^{t-1} + \sum_i L_{ij}^t \cdot y_j^t \cdot \Delta n_i$$

SDA: Multiplicative decomposition of the intensity indicator (Dietzenbacher and Los, 1998) [6]

$$D_{I(m)DL1} = \frac{\dfrac{\sum_i \sum_j L_{ij}^t \cdot y_j^{t-1} \cdot n_i^{t-1}}{q^{t-1}}}{\dfrac{\sum_i \sum_j L_{ij}^{t-1} \cdot y_j^{t-1} \cdot n_i^{t-1}}{q^{t-1}}} \cdot \frac{\dfrac{\sum_i \sum_j L_{ij}^t \cdot y_j^t \cdot n_i^{t-1}}{q^{t-1}}}{\dfrac{\sum_i \sum_j L_{ij}^t \cdot y_j^{t-1} \cdot r_i^{t-1}}{q^{t-1}}} \cdot$$

$$\frac{\dfrac{\sum_i \sum_j L_{ij}^t \cdot y_j^t \cdot n_i^t}{q^{t-1}}}{\dfrac{\sum_i \sum_j L_{ij}^t \cdot y_j^t \cdot n_i^{t-1}}{q^{t-1}}} \cdot \frac{\dfrac{\sum_i \sum_j L_{ij}^t \cdot y_j^t \cdot n_i^t}{q^t}}{\dfrac{\sum_i \sum_j L_{ij}^t \cdot y_j^t \cdot n_i^t}{q^{t-1}}}$$

$$D_{I(m)DL24} = \cfrac{\cfrac{\sum_i \sum_j L_{ij}^t \cdot y_j^t \cdot n_i^t}{q^t}}{\cfrac{\sum_i \sum_j L_{ij}^{t-1} \cdot y_j^t \cdot n_i^t}{q^t}} \cdot \cfrac{\cfrac{\sum_i \sum_j L_{ij}^{t-1} \cdot y_j^t \cdot n_i^t}{q^t}}{\cfrac{\sum_i \sum_j L_{ij}^{t-1} \cdot y_j^{t-1} \cdot n_i^t}{q^t}} \cdot$$

$$\cfrac{\cfrac{\sum_i \sum_j L_{ij}^{t-1} \cdot y_j^{t-1} \cdot n_i^t}{q^t}}{\cfrac{\sum_i \sum_j L_{ij}^{t-1} \cdot y_j^{t-1} \cdot n_i^{t-1}}{q^t}} \cdot \cfrac{\cfrac{\sum_i \sum_j L_{ij}^{t-1} \cdot y_j^{t-1} \cdot n_i^{t-1}}{q^t}}{\cfrac{\sum_i \sum_j L_{ij}^{t-1} \cdot y_j^{t-1} \cdot n_i^{t-1}}{q^{t-1}}}$$

NOTES

1. This chapter has been published as Hoekstra and van den Bergh (2003). However, the names of some variables have been changed to match those used in this book (r has been replaced by n; x has been replaced by q; s has been replaced by h; and n has been replaced by β). Furthermore, here, the 'Leontief effect' is referred to as the 'IO coefficients effect'. Superscripts for the determinant effects have been changed to capital letters.
2. These effects can be split into sub-effects. For example, if there are β production sectors in the economy, then the IO coefficients effect is an aggregate of $\beta \times \beta$ sub-effects. For instance, the IO coefficients effect has been split into input 'substitution' and 'technological' effects (Rose and Chen, 1991a; Casler and Rose, 1998). The possibilities for further decomposition of the IDA model are limited.
3. Milana (2000) introduces Cobb-Douglas and Törnqvist indices into the SDA setting, in an attempt to couple index theory and SDA. However, he discusses this in the context of price IO models and these indices are therefore not discussed here.
4. Although mathematical details are not given in Liu et al., (1992), this parametric specification seems to be based on the integral form of the mean value theorem. Assuming $L_{ij}(t)$ and $w_{ij}(t)$ are continuous on $[t-1, t]$ and $L_{ij} > 0$ on $(t-1, t)$, then there is some point c between $t-1$ and t, such that:

$$\sum_i \sum_j \int_{t-1}^{t} L_{ij}(\tau) \cdot w_{ij}(\tau) d\tau = \sum_i \sum_j w_{ij}(c) \cdot \int_{t-1}^{t} L_{ij}(\tau) d\tau$$

The point c can also be written in the following parametric form:

$$w_{ij}(c) = w_{ij}^{t-1} + \alpha_{ij} \cdot \Delta w_{ij} \quad \text{where} \quad 0 \le \alpha_{ij} \ge 1$$

5. Ang and Lee (1996) also refer to it as the 'energy coefficient' in their study of energy issues.
6. For simplicity only the two polar decomposition forms are presented.

8. Structural Decomposition Analysis of Iron and Steel and Plastics

8.1 INTRODUCTION[1]

The majority of studies on environmental structural decomposition analysis (SDA) that were reviewed in Chapter 6 analyze energy use or emissions related to fossil fuel combustion. Only four of the studies listed in Table 6.3 deal with other types of physical flows: Rose et al. (1996) analyze the changes in plastics, rubber, glass, iron and steel, and non-ferrous metals for the United States for the period 1972–1982; Moll et al. (1998a, b) study an aggregate indicator, Total Material Requirement (TMR), for Germany for the period 1980–1990; and Wier and Hasler (1999) examine nitrogen loading in Denmark for the period 1966–1988. This chapter investigates bulk-materials, which is why Rose et al. (1996) will be reviewed in detail in this chapter.[2]

So far, SDA has therefore contributed little to the analysis of the historical driving forces of bulk-materials other than fossil fuels. The main purpose of this chapter is, therefore, to present a new SDA for iron and steel and plastics in the Netherlands for the period 1990–1997.[3] The hybrid IO tables (HIOTs), the construction of which is described in Chapter 5, are used for these calculations.

Iron and steel and plastics have been chosen in this study because they are used in large quantities as well as in a wide variety of applications. They end up in consumer products, investment goods and intermediate inputs. Furthermore, production and consumption of iron and steel, and plastic products are related to various environmental problems, such as global warming, toxic pollution, resource depletion and waste disposal. SDA can assess the impact of structural, technological and demand changes on these material flows, and this provides insight into the driving forces of the associated environmental problems.

This chapter also discusses the effect of the accounting assumptions of the IO framework on SDA results. It is suggested that changes in the IO coefficient matrix are sometimes caused by changes in the organization of production chains, rather than by technological changes. To restrict the impact of these assumptions the results, adaptations to the data are used.

The organization of this chapter is as follows. The empirical results from Rose et al. (1996) are discussed in Section 8.2. Section 8.3 discusses the implications of the accounting system on SDA results. In Section 8.4, the development of iron and steel, and plastic products in the Netherlands is summarized for the period 1990–1997. Section 8.5 discusses four SDAs, which help to understand the development of physical output and value added. Section 8.6 evaluates the adjustments proposed in Section 8.3. Section 8.7 concludes.

8.2 SDA STUDIES OF BULK-MATERIALS

In this section, the results reported by Rose et al. (1996) are discussed. Since this is the only SDA of individual bulk-materials, it is reviewed in detail. Furthermore, the results are compared with two related studies, which investigate energy use and carbon dioxide emissions for the same period and country (Rose and Chen, 1991a, and Casler and Rose, 1998, respectively). This comparison provides insight into the difference between the driving forces of bulk-materials and physical flows related to energy.

Rose et al. (1996) perform an SDA using a closed IO model, where the intermediates are divided into capital, labor, energy, materials and other materials (KLEMO) aggregates. The results of this study, which are reported in Table 8.1, depict the relative contribution, in percentages, of each of the determinant effects. The last row indicates the percentage increase or decrease in material use. Absolute dematerialization is exhibited for glass (−6 percent), iron and steel (−30 percent) and non-ferrous metals (−7 percent) while the use of plastics (16 percent) and rubber (25 percent) increased over the period 1972–1982.

The first two effects depicted in the table are the final demand level (FDL) and mix (FDM) effects. The FDL effect indicates the influence of overall economic growth on materials use. The FDM captures the influence of the changes in the final demand package (see also Section 6.3). The FDM effect is negative for all materials, except for rubber. This indicates that the shift in the final demand package has contributed to lower use of most materials through direct and indirect demand. The FDM effect for iron and steel is particularly large, and is nearly large enough to counterbalance the positive effect of the FDL effect. However, the sum of FDL and FDM effects: the net final demand effect, is positive for all materials because of the large positive FDL effects.

A wide range of technological change (TC) effects is shown in the table. Significant results were obtained for technological changes in capital and labor, which contribute towards increasing materials use. These technological changes in capital and labor are induced effects that arise because of the use of a closed IO model. In this type of model, the columns for investment and consumption, which are final demand categories in the open IO model, are included in the IO coefficient matrix. The corresponding rows of wage and capital depreciation of the primary inputs are also incorporated in the intermediate input matrix.

Table 8.1 SDA of material use, United States, 1972–1982 (%)

Decomposition effects	Plastic	Rubber	Glass	Iron and steel	Non-ferrous metals	Average
Final demand effects						
Level of final demand (FDL)	119	78	330	57	281	185
Mix of final demand (FDM)	−25	2	−64	−47	−18	−72
Total final demand effects*	94	80	266	10	263	114
Technological change (TC)						
TC in capital	54	36	145	26	124	84
TC in labor	56	34	149	20	92	70
TC in energy	15	10	39	6	29	21
Linkage TC in materials	−6	−1	−1	−1	13	0
Direct TC in materials	2	−100	−249	−45	−220	−147
TC in intermediates	2	6	48	7	3	15
Linkage material substitution	51	6	−2	−8	−13	−3
Direct material substitution	26	115	−117	−36	15	0
Intermediate substitution	−120	−66	−302	−76	−214	−195
Interfuel substitution	4	3	11	2	8	6
KLEMO substitution	−77	−23	−85	−4	−200	−64
Total TC *	7	20	−364	−109	−363	−214
Total	100	100	−100	−100	−100	−100
FDM/FDL*	−0.21	0.05	−0.21	−0.82	−0.05	−0.38
TC/FDL*	0.05	0.20	−1.05	−1.88	−1.32	−1.15
% change	16	25	−6	−30	−7	−10

Note: The rows with asterisks have been added to the table reported in Rose et al. (1996). The sum of the percentages does not always add up to 100% or −100% because of rounding errors.

Source: Rose et al. (1996).

The dominant downward pressure on material use resulting from the TC effect is caused by intermediate substitution, direct technological change in materials, and KLEMO substitution. The intermediate substitution effect indicates that the structural change in intermediate inputs led to less material use. The direct TC effect on materials reflects the conservation of materials. KLEMO substitution indicates that shifts in these aggregates of intermediate inputs have led to less material use through direct and indirect demand. Note that the direct material substitution effect indicates a shift from iron and steel and glass to rubber, plastics and, to a lesser extent, non-ferrous metals. The aggregate results for all materials shows that it is a zero-sum effect.

Two ratios have been calculated for the table: the FDM/FDL and TC/FDL.[4] The FDL effect is a good numeraire because it is the same, in percentage terms, for all materials.[5] These ratios can therefore be used to assess the relative importance of the FDM and TC effects for each material, as well as allowing for comparison with other studies.

The ratios of materials that exhibit absolute dematerialization, and those that do not, differ. Absolute dematerialization seems to have arisen because of the large negative TC effect, which is larger than the positive FDL effect, that is, the ratio is smaller than -1. This is the case for glass, iron and steel and non-ferrous metals. Although the absolute dematerialization of these materials is further enhanced by sizable FDM effects, these are not large enough, in themselves, to outweigh the FDL effect.

Comparing the absolute values of the ratios, the importance of the decomposition effects becomes apparent. For the materials that experience absolute dematerialization, the ranking of the absolute size of the effects is TC, FDL, FDM. For plastics, the order is FDL, FDM, TC. For rubber, it is FDL, TC, FDM. The overall impression, which is bolstered by the weighted average results, is that, for this period, the most important driving force was technology followed by the effect of economic growth (FDL). The FDM effect is least important in this study.

Are the driving forces of material flows different from those of energy consumption or carbon dioxide emissions? Rose and Chen (1991a) and Casler and Rose (1998) decompose energy demand and carbon dioxide (CO_2) emissions, respectively. These studies use similar decomposition methods for the same period in the United States, which make these three studies suited for a comparison. Table 8.2 is based on the results that are presented in these two studies.

There are a number of similarities and differences between the three studies. First, consider the total results for material use, energy use and CO_2 emissions denoted by the 'average', 'weighted average' and 'total' respectively in Tables 8.1, 8.2 and 8.3. The FDM/FDL and TC/FDL ratios are all negative, indicating that these effects are helping to alleviate the upward pressure of the FDL effect. However, the relative importance of the determinant effects is different. The ratios indicate that the ranking of the absolute values of the determinant effects for total energy use is FDL, TC, FDM, while for total CO_2 emissions it is FDL, FDM, TC. For material demand this ranking was TC, FDL, FDM. The TC effects of material use are therefore more important for this period in the United States.

Table 8.2 SDA of energy demand for the United States, 1972–1982

Decomposition effect	Energy use				
	Coal	Petroleum	Natural gas	Electricity	Weighted average
FDL	66	510	88	65	1846
FDM	−45	−159	−46	−10	−798
Total	22	350	43	55	1048
TC	78	−450	−143	45	−948
Total	100	−100	−100	100	100
FDM/FDL	−0.67	−0.31	−0.52	−0.16	−0.43
TC/FDL	1.18	−0.88	−1.62	0.70	−0.51
% change	28	−4	−20	27	1

Source: Tables 3 and 4 of Rose and Chen (1991a).

Table 8.3 SDA of CO_2 emissions for the United States, 1972–1982

Decomposition effect	CO_2 emissions			
	Coal	Petroleum	Natural gas	Total
FDL	51	156	53	441
FDM	−33	−94	−46	−300
Total	18	62	7	141
TC	82	−162	−107	−241
Total	100	−100	−100	−100
FDM/FDL	−0.65	−0.60	−0.87	−0.68
TC/FDL	1.60	−1.04	−2.02	−0.55
% change	23	−7	−19	−2

Source: Tables II and III of Casler and Rose (1998).

Further analysis of the ratios of the individual materials and energy carriers within each study leads to number of general conclusions:

- TC effects are nearly always more important than FDM effects because the absolute value of the TC/FDL ratio is always larger than the FDM/FDL ratio (the only exception is rubber).
- The FDM effect helped to reduce environmental pressures in all three studies, because the FDM/FDL ratio is nearly always negative (the only exception is rubber).
- TC effects are important driving forces for increase and decreases in environmental pressures, as indicated by the range of TC/FDL ratios (−2.02 to 1.60). The FDM effects are smaller, and nearly all negative. The range of the FDM/FDL ratio is −0.87 to 0.05.

For this period, the physical economy of the United States seems to have experienced a shift from iron and steel and glass to plastics, rubber and non-ferrous metals, and a shift from petroleum and natural gas to coal. All three studies show the influence of the extraordinary oil crises experienced in that decade. The shifts in the environmental variables of the three studies have probably been caused (relative) energy price changes and regulatory policies.

8.3 IO ACCOUNTING AND SDA

Before the SDA for iron and steel and plastics in the Netherlands (1990–1997) is presented, we will take a closer look at the implications of the accounting system of the IO framework on SDA results.

The focus of the IO model, and therefore SDA, is output, which is equal to the sum of final and intermediate demand. Estimates of final demand are based on source data, such as international trade statistics, budget surveys and investment accounts. Estimates of intermediate inputs are based on production statistics, which are derived from questionnaires completed by staff at the institutional production units of the economy – companies. It is therefore assumed in this accounting scheme that these production statistics provide a good estimate of the production processes in the economy. However, when IO tables for two years are compared in SDA, the differences are not necessarily caused by technological change in the production processes. It is possible that the technology remains the same while the individual steps in the production process are divided differently amongst the companies. The SDA results can therefore be affected by changes in the organizational structure of the economy, which are captured by the IO accounting system. Appendix 8.A provides and example.

The problem arises because value or mass associated with intermediate goods and services are recorded several times as they are passed along from company to company. The long-term changes in output investigated by SDA could, therefore, be caused by a relative increase or decrease in the number of steps in the production chain. Primary input and final demand in the MIOT, and raw materials, final demand and wastes in the PIOT, are only counted once because these are the 'source' and 'destination' of value and mass.[6]

The seriousness of this issue for SDA has not yet been investigated. However, the recommendations proposed in Appendix 8.A are adopted in the subsequent SDA calculations. First, the results will only be discussed per commodity group. Second, the diagonals will be set to zero and the row and column totals adjusted accordingly.[7] This is because the diagonals are most likely to be affected by change in the organizational structure, as the diagonals are caused by the aggregation of similar commodities.

For example, Table 5.13 shows that, in 1990, the input of basic iron and steel, $0.66*10^9$ kg, was used to produce a total output of $5.60*10^9$ kg of basic iron and steel, which corresponds to an IO coefficient of 0.117. However, in 1997, this coefficient had decreased to 0.105 (see Table 5.14). This could be caused by technological changes, but it is also possible that there were fewer companies in the production chain of basic iron and steel in 1997. By assuming that both coefficients are zero, the influence of these organizational changes is excluded. A drawback of this type of adaptation is that interesting technological changes may also be excluded from the resulting calculations. The empirical results of applying a zero diagonal are discussed in Section 8.6.

8.4 DEVELOPMENT OF IRON AND STEEL AND PLASTICS

Chapter 5 describes the construction of HIOTs for iron and steel and plastics for the Netherlands for 1990 and 1997. Tables 5.13 and 5.14 distinguish 46 monetary rows and ten physical products of iron and steel or plastics. In Table 8.4, the development of physical output and value added for the physical commodities is summarized. In the last the last column the type of dematerialization that has occurred has been specified. Note that many definitions of dematerialization have been proposed. The indicator used here provides a measure of the economic activity (value added) to a measure of physical output (10^9 kg) of the production process. If the growth rate of value added increases while the physical output decreases, this is referred to as 'absolute dematerialization'. If the physical growth rate is positive but smaller than the growth rate of value added, this is referred to as 'relative dematerialization'. Finally, if the physical growth rate exceeds the value added growth rate, this is referred to as 'rematerialization'.

Table 8.4 The development of physical output and value added of iron and steel and plastic products in the Netherlands (1990–1997)

Product group	Abbreviation	Domestic output (10⁹ kg)			Value added (million 1997 euros)			Type of dematerialization
		1990	1997	%	1990	1997	%	
Basic plastics	Basc.Plas.	3.48	5.11	47	736	1403	91	relative dematerialization
Plastic products	Plas.Prod.	1.09	1.42	30	1220	1472	21	rematerialization
Basic iron and steel	Basc.Iron.	4.94	6.33	28	1226	1329	8	rematerialization
Iron and steel products	Iron.Prod.	2.80	3.92	40	1965	2259	15	rematerialization
Machines	Machine.	0.96	1.18	22	3262	3619	11	rematerialization
Office equipment and computers	Off.Comp.	0.07	0.15	124	78	244	212	relative dematerialization
Electrical appliances	Elec.Appl.	0.26	0.51	92	934	899	−4	rematerialization
Electronics	Electron.	0.19	0.51	169	419	514	23	rematerialization
Cars and engines	Cars.Engi.	0.56	0.63	14	950	1367	44	relative dematerialization
Transportation equipment	Trans.Equ.	0.41	0.29	−29	399	425	7	absolute dematerialization

Note: Percentage change with respect to 1990. The output totals are different from those in Tables 5.13 and 5.14 because the diagonals have been subtracted from output.

Note that both relative dematerialization and rematerialization coincide with increasing absolute material throughput, and therefore with increasing environmental pressures. Only absolute dematerialization lowers environmental pressures. However, even if absolute dematerialization occurs, this does not mean that the level of material use is sustainable. It is still possible that environmental or sustainable resource use limits are exceeded in periods when material use is diminishing. Absolute dematerialization is a necessary but not a sufficient condition for sustainable development.

The table shows that all commodities experienced growth in physical output, except for transportation equipment. Electrical appliances experienced a decrease in real value added. The most important commodities in terms of mass are basic iron and steel, basic plastics and iron and steel products. However, in terms of value added, machines are about twice as important as basic iron and steel. The physical output of office equipment and computers, electrical appliances and electronics shows a particularly high growth rate. The increase in value added is particularly high for office equipment and computers and basic plastics.

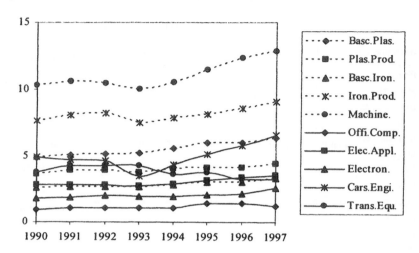

Figure 8.1 Domestic production of commodities (10^9 euros, prices 1997)

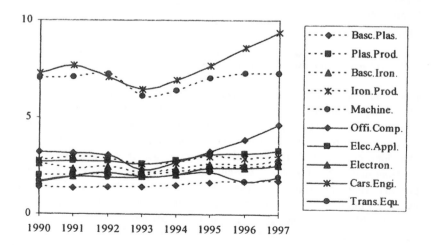

Figure 8.2 Imports of commodities (10^9 euros, prices 1997)

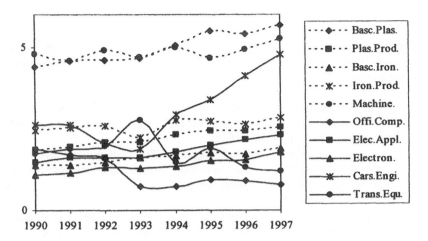

Figure 8.3 Exports of commodities (10^9 euros, prices 1997)

Overall, the table suggests that 1990–1997 was a period of rematerialization for these commodities in the Netherlands. Six of the ten production activities earned less in 1997, in real terms, per kg output than in 1990. Among these are basic iron and steel, iron and steel products and plastic products, which are all very large in terms of their physical output. Three activities – namely, basic plastics, office equipment and cars and engines – underwent relative dematerialization. Only transportation equipment experienced absolute dematerialization for this period.[8] To understand the developments of the ten commodities, the developments of domestic production, imports and exports for the period 1990–1997 have been charted in Figures 8.1 to 8.3, respectively.

The figures show that over the 7-year period, most of the commodities have grown in terms of domestic production, imports and exports. Some of the commodities experienced decreases in these categories in the middle of the period because of an economic slowdown. This particularly affected cars and engines and machines. Machines and iron and steel products are the most important commodities in terms of the value of domestic production. Cars and engines and machines are the largest commodity groups, in terms of inbound trade. Exports are dominated by basic plastics, machines and the rapidly growing cars and engines commodity group. Also notable is the growth pattern of the export of transportation equipment. This increased over 1992–1993, when the export of other commodities was decreasing, but the total period 1990–1997 is characterized by an erratic downward trend.

8.5 SDA OF IRON AND STEEL AND PLASTICS

This section presents an analysis of four SDAs that investigate the rematerialization and dematerialization of iron and steel and plastics products in the Netherlands (1990–1997). The four SDAs are:

1. *Decomposition of output.* The change in output is decomposed into IO coefficients (IOC), final demand level (FDL), final demand mix (FDM) and import substitution (IS) effects.
2. *Decomposition of final demand categories.* The final demand effect that is found in the previous decomposition is split into category effects: exports, household consumption, government consumption, investments and stock changes effects.
3. *Detailed decomposition of final demand categories.* The final demand category effects that are found in the previous decomposition are split into level and mix effects.
4. *Decomposition of value added.* The change in value added is decomposed into value added coefficient, IOC, final demand and IS.

To study dematerialization, it is necessary to find the driving forces of physical output, which is the aim of the first three calculations. It is also necessary to find the sources of value added growth, which is done in the fourth decomposition.

Decomposition of Output

Equation 8.1 decomposes the change in the physical output (Δx) into four effects: the IOC ($\Delta L \cdot y$), FDL ($L \cdot \Delta y^{lev}$), FDM ($\Delta L \cdot y^{mix}$), and IS ($L \cdot \Delta b$) effects. The first three effects were discussed earlier in Section 6.3 and above in Section 8.2. The import substitution effect occurs because of the use of an 'IO table including imports', where imports are recorded as negative final demand (see Box 5.1). The advantage of this framework is that the changes in the intermediate demand can be interpreted as technological changes that are unaffected by import substitution. The effect of shifts in imports is captured by the import substitution effect. In this type of IO model, the production processes of domestic and imported goods are assumed to be the same.

Equation 8.1 is applied to the data in Tables 5.13 and 5.14. The index approach proposed by Dietzenbacher and Los (1996) is used in these calculations, because the discussion in Chapter 7 showed that this is commonly used in SDA. Furthermore, Chapter 7 showed that this approach yielded equivalent results to the Sun (1998) approach, which is based on the attractive assumption that there is a straight line between two discrete points.

For the sake of brevity, the decomposition equations are not specified (see Chapter 7 for the derivation of these type of equations). The SDA results for the physical commodities are presented in Table 8.5.[9] In addition, this table records the FDM/FDL and IOC/FDL ratios (where IOC is the only TC effect in this decomposition).

$$\Delta q = \Delta L \cdot y + L \cdot \Delta y^{lev} + L \cdot \Delta y^{mix} + L \cdot \Delta b \qquad (8.1)$$

Where $q = L \cdot y = L \cdot \left(y^{lev} \cdot y^{mix} - b \right)$ is the IO model 'including imports'. The explanation of the symbols is as follows:

x	Output
L	Leontief inverse
y	Final demand
y^{lev}	Final demand level
y^{mix}	Final demand mix
m	Imports

The FDL effect in Table 8.5 reflects the influence of economic growth on physical output. For cars and engines, the level effect is the largest, in relative terms: namely, 416 percent. This product group is relatively small in terms of its total change in the physical output. The level effect is responsible for a $2.63*10^9$ kg increase in the output of basic iron and steel. The level effect is least important for electronics: 34 percent of the physical output growth is attributable to it. In fact, the FDM effect is larger than the FDL effect for this commodity group.

The FDM effect exhibits negative effects for transportation equipment (−192 percent), machines (−77 percent) and basic iron and steel (−15 percent). This indicates that the relative shift in the final demand package of products is leading, through direct and indirect demand, to reductions in the output of these goods. However, the FDM effect contributes towards increasing office equipment and computers (77 percent) and basic plastics use (58 percent).

Eight out of ten of the IOC effects are positive, that is, the intermediate input structure has shifted towards production processes that use these physical products, either directly or indirectly. Only cars and engines and transportation equipment have (small) negative IOC effects. The shifts in intermediate demand have contributed to 43 percent and 50 percent of the growth in physical output of basic iron and steel and electrical appliances, respectively.

The import substitution effects (IS) show that increased imports of iron and steel and plastic products has led to lower output levels than would have occurred without this increase. For many products, it is the most influential driving force that exerts downward pressure on the physical output. The exception is transportation equipment, which saw a decrease in imports.

Table 8.5 Decomposition of output (10^9 kg and %)

Product group	Final demand level (FDL)	Final demand mix (FDM)	IO coefficient (IOC)	Import substitution (IS)	Change in output	FDM/ FDL	IOC/ FDL
Prim.Plas	1.31	0.94	0.06	−0.68	1.63	0.72	0.04
	81%	58%	4%	−42%	100%		
Plas.Prod.	0.48	0.13	0.03	−0.31	0.33	0.26	0.06
	146%	39%	8%	−93%	100%		
Prim.Iron	2.63	−0.20	0.59	−1.63	1.38	−0.08	0.22
	190%	−15%	43%	−118%	100%		
Iron.Prod	1.00	0.24	0.33	−0.45	1.12	0.24	0.33
	89%	21%	29%	−40%	100%		
Machine.	0.40	−0.16	0.02	−0.04	0.21	−0.41	0.04
	188%	−77%	8%	−19%	100%		
Off.Comp.	0.04	0.05	0.01	−0.02	0.08	1.43	0.39
	45%	64%	17%	−26%	100%		
Elec.Appl.	0.17	0.11	0.12	−0.15	0.24	0.62	0.72
	69%	43%	50%	−62%	100%		
Electron.	0.11	0.14	0.10	−0.02	0.32	1.24	0.89
	34%	42%	30%	−6%	100%		
Cars.Engi.	0.33	0.01	−0.02	−0.24	0.08	0.03	−0.05
	416%	10%	−23%	−304%	100%		
Trans.Equ.	0.09	−0.23	−0.02	0.03	−0.12	−2.40	−0.17
	80%	−192%	−13%	25%	−100%		

Note: The percentage values are relative to the change in commodity output.

Comparison with Rose et al. (1996)

The results for the United States (1972–1982), reported in Table 8.1, differ from those for the Netherlands (1990–1997) in Table 8.5. First, consider the results for plastics. For the United States (Table 8.1), the FDM/FDL is negative, while TC/FDL has a small positive value. Our results show that FDM/FDL and IOC/FDL are both positive for basic plastics and plastic products. The FDM/FDL effect for basic plastics is particularly large.

For iron and steel, according to Rose et al. (1996), the FDM/FDL and TC/FDL ratios are both negative. The TC/FDL ratio is less than −1. The results for basic iron and steel and iron and steel products in Table 8.5 are different. The IOC/FDL ratios suggest that the technological driving forces have reversed, and have started causing increased use of materials. The FDM/FDL ratio is positive for iron and steel products, negative for basic iron and steel, for the Netherlands. In both studies, the FDL is an important driving force for increased material use. There could be three reasons for the differences in the studies:

1. *Period.* There could be differences in the driving forces of materials for the 1970s and 1990s.
2. *Country.* The Netherlands and the United States are different countries that could be experiencing different structural changes. For example, international trade flows are much less important for the United States.
3. *Decomposition method.* The indices used by the two studies are different. Furthermore, the calculations for the United States are based on a closed KLEMO model, while the study for the Netherlands uses an open IO model. Other differences in the SDA application, such as the use of IO tables including and excluding imports, could influence the results.

The most likely reason for the differing results is the period under investigation, particularly since the studies show that 1972–1982 is a period of absolute dematerialization, while 1990–1997 is a period of rematerialization. It is less likely that structural changes are different in both countries, to the extent of the results shown. The decomposition methods are more likely to affect relative magnitudes than the sign of the results.

Decomposition of Final Demand

The previous decomposition of output has underlined the importance of final demand effects. An additional SDA, shown in Equation 8.2, takes a closer look at the influence of changes in separate categories of final demand: exports ($L \cdot \Delta y^{exp}$), household consumption ($L \cdot \Delta y^{cons}$), government consumption ($L \cdot \Delta y^{gov}$), investments ($L \cdot \Delta y^{inv}$), and stocks ($L \cdot \Delta y^{stock}$). In Equation 8.2, the IOC effect and IS effect are included, but, since these effects have already been discussed in the previous decomposition, they are not included in the results in Table 8.6.

$$\Delta q =$$
$$\Delta L \cdot y + L \cdot \Delta y^{exp} + L \cdot \Delta y^{cons} + L \cdot \Delta y^{gov} + \qquad (8.2)$$
$$L \cdot \Delta y^{inv} + L \cdot \Delta y^{stock} + L \cdot \Delta b$$

New symbols used in this equation denote the following:

y^{exp}	Exports
y^{cons}	Household consumption
y^{gov}	Government consumption
y^{inv}	Investment
y^{stock}	Stocks

Table 8.6 Decomposition of final demand (10^9 kg and %)

Product group	Export	Household consumption	Government consumption	Investments	Stock	Final demand effect
Prim.Plas	2.11	0.10	0.00	0.06	−0.02	2.25
	94%	4%	0%	2%	−1%	100%
Plas.Prod.	0.50	0.07	0.00	0.04	−0.01	0.61
	83%	12%	1%	7%	−2%	100%
Prim.Iron	1.94	0.27	0.02	0.38	−0.18	2.43
	80%	11%	1%	15%	−7%	100%
Iron.Prod	0.85	0.13	0.02	0.29	−0.04	1.24
	68%	10%	1%	23%	−3%	100%
Machine.	0.15	0.06	0.00	0.09	−0.06	0.24
	63%	24%	2%	38%	−26%	100%
Off.Comp.	0.04	0.00	0.00	0.05	0.00	0.09
	41%	4%	0%	53%	0%	100%
Elec.Appl.	0.23	0.02	0.00	0.03	−0.01	0.27
	83%	9%	1%	10%	−2%	100%
Electron.	0.19	0.03	0.00	0.03	0.00	0.25
	78%	11%	0%	11%	0%	100%
Cars.Engi.	0.24	0.06	0.00	0.09	−0.05	0.33
	72%	17%	0%	26%	−15%	100%
Trans.Equ.	−0.03	0.01	0.00	−0.11	0.00	−0.13
	−26%	7%	1%	−81%	−1%	−100%

Note: The percentage values are relative to the final demand effect per commodity. The final demand effect is the sum of the FDM and FDL effects of Table 8.5.

The results show that exports are the largest driving force of iron and steel and plastic products output, which is not surprising for a small open economy such as the Netherlands. The exception is transportation equipment, which exhibits a negative export effect. This contributes to the absolute dematerialization that is observed for transportation equipment in Table 8.4. However, the main driving force of the dematerialization of this commodity is the investment effect. The export effect dominates the other category effects for all other commodity groups. Significant investment effects are observed for office equipment and computers (53 percent) and machines (38 percent). Note the large effect of investment on basic iron and steel (15 percent), which is an indirect effect. The effects of changes in household consumption, government consumption and stock changes are rather small.

Detailed Decomposition of Final Demand

The effect of the individual final demand categories can decomposed further into level and mix effects as shown in Equation 8.3 (see Section 6.3 for details). The variables are the same as those of the previous decomposition of final demand, but have a mix or lev superscript. The IO effect and IS effects are included in the equation, but since these effects have already been discussed in the output decomposition, they are not included in the results in Table 8.7.

$$
\begin{aligned}
\Delta q = \\
\Delta L \cdot y + L \cdot \Delta y^{exp,lev} + L \cdot \Delta y^{exp,mix} + L \cdot \Delta y^{cons,lev} + L \cdot \Delta y^{cons,mix} \\
+ L \cdot \Delta y^{gov,lev} + L \cdot \Delta y^{gov,mix} + L \cdot \Delta y^{inv,lev} + L \cdot \Delta y^{inv,mix} \\
+ L \cdot \Delta y^{stock,lev} + L \cdot \Delta y^{stock,mix} + L \cdot \Delta b
\end{aligned} \tag{8.3}
$$

New symbols used in this equation denote the following:

$y^{exp,lev}$	Export level
$y^{exp,mix}$	Export mix
$y^{cons,lev}$	Household consumption level
$y^{cons,mix}$	Household consumption mix
$y^{gov,lev}$	Government consumption level
$y^{gov,mix}$	Government consumption mix
$y^{inv,lev}$	Investment level
$y^{inv,mix}$	Investment mix
$y^{stock,lev}$	Stock level
$y^{stock,mix}$	Stock mix

The table shows that all level effects are positive, except for some of the effects of stock changes. The level effects are generally larger than the corresponding mix effects. The main exceptions concern office equipment and computers, for which the investment mix effect exceeds the investment level effects, which reflects the fact that the mix of investment goods has shifted in such a way that it has led to increases in the output of computers. For electronics too, the export mix effect is greater than the export level effect.

The household consumption effects are only a small driving force in the overall material throughput. Compared to the other categories of final demand it plays a minor role in the explanation of changes in material use. Nevertheless, it is interesting to see the influence of changes in consumption patterns. Nearly all consumption mix effects are leading to a small reduction in physical output. However, although the Dutch consumption package is causing lower demand for these physical products, the level of consumption has increased to such an extent that the net consumption effect is an increase for all commodities. This shows that, for this empirical application, the absolute quantity of consumption overrides any positive effect from a shift in the consumption package. This tempers the hope that some growth optimists may have that consumption could contribute to lowering of environmental strains.

Table 8.7 Detailed decomposition of final demand (10^9 kg and %)[10]

Product group	Exports		Household consumption		Government consumption		Investments		Stocks		
	Mix	Level	Mix	Level	Mix	Level	Mix	Level	Mix	Level	Total
Prim.Plas	0.56	1.56	−0.04	0.14	0.00	0.01	−0.05	0.10	0.03	−0.05	2.25
	25%	69%	−2%	6%	0%	0%	−2%	5%	1%	−2%	100%
Plas.Prod.	0.09	0.41	−0.02	0.10	0.00	0.00	−0.04	0.08	0.01	−0.02	0.61
	16%	67%	−4%	16%	0%	1%	−6%	13%	2%	−4%	100%
Prim.Iron	−0.50	2.44	−0.03	0.29	0.00	0.03	−0.14	0.52	0.00	−0.18	2.43
	−21%	101%	−1%	12%	0%	1%	−6%	21%	0%	−7%	100%
Iron.Prod	0.16	0.69	−0.01	0.14	0.00	0.02	0.00	0.29	−0.01	−0.03	1.24
	13%	55%	−1%	11%	0%	1%	0%	23%	−1%	−2%	100%
Machine.	−0.11	0.25	0.00	0.06	0.00	0.01	−0.04	0.12	−0.10	0.04	0.24
	−45%	108%	−2%	26%	−1%	2%	−15%	53%	−44%	17%	100%
Off.Comp.	0.01	0.03	0.00	0.00	0.00	0.00	0.04	0.01	0.00	0.00	0.09
	12%	29%	1%	4%	0%	1%	40%	13%	1%	0%	100%
Elec.Appl.	0.11	0.12	0.00	0.03	0.00	0.00	−0.02	0.04	0.00	−0.01	0.27
	39%	44%	−2%	11%	0%	1%	−5%	15%	0%	−2%	100%
Electron.	0.10	0.09	0.01	0.02	0.00	0.00	0.01	0.02	0.00	0.00	0.25
	41%	37%	3%	8%	0%	1%	3%	8%	−1%	1%	100%
Cars.Engi.	0.05	0.19	−0.01	0.07	0.00	0.00	−0.01	0.09	−0.03	−0.02	0.33
	15%	57%	−4%	22%	0%	0%	−2%	28%	−10%	−5%	100%
Trans.Equ.	−0.08	0.04	0.00	0.01	0.00	0.00	−0.14	0.04	0.01	−0.01	−0.13
	−57%	31%	−4%	10%	−1%	2%	−109%	28%	7%	−8%	−100%

Note: The percentage values are relative to the final demand effect per commodity.

Decomposition of Value Added

Equation 8.4 decomposes the change in value added (Δv) into a value added coefficient ($\Delta u \cdot L \cdot y$), an IO coefficient ($u \cdot \Delta L \cdot y$), a final demand ($u \cdot L \cdot \Delta y$) and an IS effect ($u \cdot L \cdot \Delta m$). The value added coefficient is equal to the ratio of value added and output. Results are presented in Table 8.8.

$$\Delta v = \Delta u \cdot L \cdot y + u \cdot \Delta L \cdot y + u \cdot L \cdot \Delta y + u \cdot L \cdot \Delta m \qquad (8.4)$$

New symbols used in this equation denote the following:
v	Value added
u	Value added coefficient
y	Final demand

Table 8.8 Decomposition of value added (million 1997 euros and %)

Product group	Value added coefficient	IO coefficient	Final demand	Import substitution	Change in value added
Prim..Plas.	271	14	548	−166	667
	41%	2%	82%	−25%	100%
Plas.Prod	−104	30	658	−332	252
	−41%	12%	261%	−132%	100%
Prim.Iron.	−214	135	556	−374	103
	−208%	131%	541%	−364%	100%
Iron.Prod.	−425	210	796	−288	294
	−145%	72%	271%	−98%	100%
Machine.	−325	54	761	−132	357
	−91%	15%	213%	−37%	100%
Off.Comp.	50	20	126	−30	166
	30%	12%	76%	−18%	100%
Elec.Appl.	−670	318	717	−400	−35
	−1917%	910%	2049%	−1143%	−100%
Electron.	−418	155	390	−32	95
	−440%	163%	411%	−33%	100%
Cars.Engi.	266	−35	646	−460	417
	64%	−8%	155%	−110%	100%
Trans.Equ.	169	−19	−160	36	26
	640%	−71%	−606%	137%	100%
Total	−1400	882	5038	−2179	2342
	−60%	38%	215%	−93%	100%

Note: The percentage values are relative to the change in value added per commodity.

Table 8.8 includes a row that indicates the total impact of each decomposition effect on the ten commodities. The value added coefficient effect contributes −60 percent to the total value added growth of these ten commodities. In other words, the overall earnings per physical output are decreasing and are responsible for a significant downward pressure on the total value added of physical commodities. Nevertheless, the final demand effect leads to sufficient growth in value added to overcome the value added coefficient effect.

The six commodities that experience rematerialization (see Table 8.4) all have a negative value added coefficient effect because these are earning less per kilogram over the period 1990–1997. The commodities that exhibit relative and absolute dematerialization have a positive value added coefficient effect. The IS effect is large and negative for many commodities: it shows that increasing imports have reduced domestic earnings.

What do the SDA results tell us about dematerialization? Table 8.4 shows that six commodities exhibited rematerialization, three experienced relative dematerialization and only one shows absolute dematerialization. The SDA results can help to explain these developments. Relative dematerialization has two components: change in physical output and change in value added. Absolute dematerialization is only achieved through changes in the physical output.

The growth in physical output is caused primarily by the export level effect. This is the most important driving force for increased material use for eight out of ten of the physical commodities. Furthermore, the export mix effect is positive for seven out of ten commodities. The investment and IOC effects are an important source of growth for a few of the commodities. The growth of physical output is lowered mainly by the growth in imports. However, this negative impact is always dominated by the export effect. The final demand is the most important driving force of value added. However, the value added coefficient plays an important role in diminishing value added for the commodities that experience rematerialization.

8.6 SENSITIVITY ANALYSIS OF DATA ADAPTATIONS

In Section 8.3, the influence of the accounting assumptions on SDA results was discussed. It was recommended that excluding the diagonals could reduce the problems caused by this assumption. To assess the effect of this procedure, the SDA calculations for Equation 8.1 are repeated by replacing the diagonals. The results are shown in Table 8.9.

The results of Tables 8.5 and 8.9 are very similar, which implies that the adaptation has little influence on these SDA results. The main difference is that the change in output in Table 8.9 is different because the diagonals are included. Three of the decomposition effects of Table 8.9 have a different sign than they have in Table 8.5. However, these are all relatively small IOC effects for basic plastics, cars and engines and electronics.

Table 8.9 Decomposition of output (including IO diagonals) (10^9 kg and %)

Product Group	Final demand level (FDL)	Final demand mix (FDM)	IO coefficient (IOC)	Import substitution effect (IS)	Change in output
Prim.Plas.	1.40	1.01	0.17	−0.73	1.85
	76%	54%	9%	−39%	100%
Plas.Prod	0.53	0.14	−0.01	−0.34	0.32
	164%	43%	−3%	−105%	100%
Prim.Iron	2.96	−0.23	0.58	−1.84	1.47
	201%	−16%	39%	−125%	100%
Iron.Prod	1.18	0.28	0.52	−0.53	1.45
	81%	19%	36%	−36%	100%
Machine.	0.50	−0.20	0.01	−0.05	0.25
	198%	−81%	3%	−20%	100%
Off.Equip.	0.04	0.06	0.02	−0.02	0.09
	42%	60%	23%	−24%	100%
Elec.Appl.	0.21	0.13	0.15	−0.19	0.31
	70%	43%	50%	−63%	100%
Electron.	0.14	0.18	−0.03	−0.03	0.26
	54%	68%	−12%	−10%	100%
Cars.Engi	0.47	0.01	0.06	−0.35	0.20
	239%	6%	30%	−174%	100%
Trans.Equ.	0.10	−0.25	−0.01	0.03	−0.12
	84%	−203%	−8%	27%	−100%

Note: The percentage values are relative to the change in commodity output.

8.7 CONCLUSIONS

This chapter has analyzed the driving forces of the use of bulk-materials through structural decomposition analysis (SDA). The empirical results of Rose et al. (1996), which analyses the use of plastics, rubber, glass, iron and steel and non-ferrous metals (United States 1972–1982), were reviewed. The general conclusion is that the technological changes (TC) effect was the most important driving force for overall reductions in material use. The final demand level (FDL) effect was the largest driving force for increased material use. The final demand mix (FDM) effect was generally small but negative, that is, it contributed to lower material use. Similar studies for the United States show that the TC effect is less important for energy and CO_2 emissions.

This chapter introduced a new SDA study, which analysed the use of iron and steel and plastics. Four SDA calculations were presented for the Netherlands for the period 1990–1997. Overall, this was a period of rematerialization. Only one commodity group, transportation equipment, experiences absolute dematerialization over this period. Three commodity groups experienced relative dematerialization, while the other six commodities exhibited rematerialization.

The first three decomposition calculations analyze the driving forces of output. The simplest decomposition of output shows that economic growth - the FDL effect - contributes most to physical output growth. Nevertheless, the FDM effect and IO coefficients (IOC) effect also contribute to increases in output for seven and eight commodities, respectively. The import substitution (IS) effect contributes to lower physical output for nine out of ten commodities. In the subsequent decompositions of the final demand categories, it becomes clear that the change in the level of exports is the largest driving force for eight of the ten commodities. Although increase in import substitution led to lower physical output, these effects were always outweighed by the export effect. Changes in the other categories of final demand - household consumption, government consumption, investments and stocks - generally have little impact on output. Nevertheless, the investment effect and TC effect are large for some of the commodities.

The SDA results for value added show that changes in final demand are the largest driving force. However, for some commodities less value added is being created per kilogram, which reduces the value added growth. These are the six commodities that experience rematerialization. Overall, the value added coefficient is responsible for a 60 percent reduction in value added.

The results of the basic decomposition of output are different from those of Rose et al. (1996). While the United States' study suggests that TC and FDM are contributing to lower environmental pressures, they are generally driving forces for increased physical throughput for our study. The difference in the results could be caused by the time period, country or decomposition method

The influence of accounting practices on SDA results was also discussed in this chapter. It is argued that changes in intermediate demand could be caused by organizational rather than technological changes. This could affect SDA calculations. Recommendations include that the results should be discussed separately for each individual commodity. Furthermore, the diagonals should be set to zero and the corresponding output adjusted, to negate some of the organizational changes in the economy. The drawback of this procedure is that it might eliminate actual technological changes in the production structure from the SDA results. However, the empirical evaluation shows that, for this data, the adaptations have little impact on the results.

APPENDIX 8.A EFFECT OF IO ACCOUNTING

This appendix shows that changes in the intermediate input requirements are sometimes caused by changes in the organization of the production process rather than by technological change. The reason for this is that it is assumed that production statistics provide a good estimate of the production processes.

Tables 8.A.1 and 8.A.2 provide a numerical example of PIOTs for two years. Table 8.A.1 shows that, in year $t - 1$, a raw material is mined directly from nature. This material is used to produce a final product. In both these parts of the production process, wastes are produced. Table 8.A.2 shows that, in year t, the economy has doubled compared with $t - 1$. In addition, the production process of the final product has been split into two steps, one creating an intermediate product, and the other using this intermediate to make the final product, that is, specialization has occurred.

Table 8.A.1 PIOT for year t − 1

PIOT	Primary product	Intermediate product	Final product	Consumers	Total	Unit
Primary product	0	0	130	0	130	ktons
Intermediate product	0	0	0	0	0	ktons
Final product	0	0	0	100	100	ktons
Raw material	150	0	0		150	ktons
Wastes	−20	0	−30		−50	ktons
Total	130	0	100	200		ktons

Table 8.A.2 PIOT for year t

PIOT	Primary product	Intermediate product	Final product	Consumers	Total	Unit
Primary product	0	260	0	0	260	ktons
Intermediate product	0	0	240	0	240	ktons
Final product	0	0	0	200	200	ktons
Raw material	300	0	0		300	ktons
Wastes	−40	−20	−40		−100	ktons
Total	260	240	200	200		ktons

No technological change has occurred in this example. In year $t - 1$, 150 units of raw material are required to produce 100 units of final product and 50 units of waste. In year t, this technological relationship remains unchanged, although the size of the economy has increased by 100 percent. However, the total mass of physical output increases from 230 (130 + 100) ktons to 700 (260 + 240 + 200) ktons, an increase of 204 percent. This is because the accounting system records the output of each company of the production process, rather than taking a production process as a whole.

The SDA results are provided in Table 8.A.3. The decomposition uses the physical IO coefficients and the index approach of Dietzenbacher and Los (1998). The results indicate, correctly, that the increase in final demand has caused growth in output. However, an IO coefficient effect is also observed, while the discussion above shows that this is not caused by technological changes. These changes are caused by the organizational changes that were described above. This problem is also relevant for monetary SDA.

Table 8.A.3 SDA results

SDA effects/ Commodity	IO coefficient effect (IOC)	Final demand effect (FD)	Total	Units
Primary product	0	130	130	ktons
Intermediate product	180	60	240	ktons
Final product	0	100	100	ktons
Total	180	290	470	ktons

Note that the results for primary and final products are correct. It is only the decomposition of intermediate product, and the sum total of the commodities, which erroneously indicate a technological change. A conclusion that is implied by this example is, therefore, that the SDA results per commodity group are less likely to be affected by this problem than the total SDA results for the economy.

The aggregation scheme can also play a part in the influence of the accounting assumptions. For example, assume that the intermediate and final products are classified in the same commodity group. The resulting aggregate IO tables for year $t - 1$ and t are shown in Tables 8.A.4 and 8.A.5, respectively. Note that the diagonal of the table for year t has increased from 0 to 240 due to the aggregation. The SDA results of these aggregate tables are shown in Table 8.A.6.

The SDA results of Table 8.A.6 are consistent with the results in Table 8.A.3. Now assume that the diagonals of Tables 8.A.4 and 8.A.5 are set to zero, and the row and columns are adjusted. The SDA results are provided in Table 8.A.7.

Table 8.A.4 Aggregated PIOT for year t−1

PIOT	Primary product	Intermediate +final product	Consumers	Total	Unit
Primary product	0	130	0	130	ktons
Intermediate + final product	0	0	100	100	ktons
Raw material	150	0		150	ktons
Wastes	−20	−30		−50	ktons
Total	130	100	200		ktons

Table 8.A.5 Aggregated PIOT for year t

PIOT	Primary product	Intermediate +final product	Consumers	Total	Unit
Primary product	0	260	0	260	ktons
Intermediate + final product	0	240	200	440	ktons
Raw material	300	0		300	ktons
Wastes	−40	−60		−100	ktons
Total	260	240	200		ktons

Table 8.A.6 Aggregate SDA results

SDA effects/ Commodity	IOC	FD	Total	Units
Primary product	0	130	130	ktons
Intermediate + final product	180	160	340	ktons
Total	180	290	470	ktons

Table 8.A.7 Aggregate SDA results with diagonals set to zero

SDA effects/ Commodity	IOC	FD	Total	Units
Primary product	0	130	130	ktons
Intermediate + final product	0	100	100	ktons
Total	0	230	230	ktons

In this case, the SDA results show that there is a 100 percent increase in output, which is consistent with the growth of the economy. Furthermore, the output increase is correctly ascribed only to the final demand effect. The recommendation that is implied by this result is that the diagonals should be set to zero. However, it should be noted that this is a numerical example in which no technological changes occur. In real economies, organizational and technological changes will occur simultaneously. Setting the diagonals to zero could, therefore, lead to the exclusion of genuine technological changes from the SDA result.

NOTES

1. This chapter is based on Hoekstra and van den Bergh (2005).
2. Moll et al. (1998a, b) will not be reviewed because of our reservations about TMR, which were discussed in Section 1.4. Wier and Hasler (1999) do not study bulk-materials and will therefore not be reviewed.
3. Farla (2000) uses IDA to decompose energy use in the Netherlands (1980–1995). One of the determinant effects that is used is the influence of dematerialization on energy use. This chapter investigates the driving forces of dematerialization, rather than the effect of dematerialization on other indicators.
4. If the sum of the two ratios is less than −1, then the material use has decreased, that is, absolute dematerialization has occurred.
5. Rose et al. (1996) report that the level effect is not precisely the same for all materials because of rounding errors and problems in obtaining constant price tables.
6. This is why economic indicators are based on the value of primary inputs or final demand, rather than on economic output.
7. By setting the diagonals to zero, the auxiliary inputs (see Chapter 4) of the physical rows are set to zero. Since these inputs are not passed on to other companies, they do not cause double counting. Setting the diagonals to the auxiliary inputs' value would therefore be preferable, if this information were available. However, since auxiliary inputs of iron and steel and plastics products are much smaller than structural inputs (see Konijn et al., 1995), the procedure adopted here seems justified.
8. Table 8.1 shows that Rose et al. (1996) report absolute dematerialization for iron and steel. Table 8.3 shows that basic iron and steel and iron and steel products in this study are experiencing rematerialization.
9. The results of the 46 other commodities have been excluded.
10. Note that, in this decomposition specification, the sum of the mix effects of all categories of final demand is not equal to the aggregate FDM effect in Table 8.5. This also holds for the level effects. However, the sum of mix and level effect of each individual final demand category is equal to the results per category in Table 8.6.

9. Forecasting and Backcasting Scenarios

9.1 INTRODUCTION

This chapter explores the possibilities of using SDA results as a basis for scenario analysis. The aim is to use the SDA results for the Netherlands (1990–1997), obtained in Chapter 8, to create forecasting and backcasting scenarios to the year 2030. The forecasting scenarios include projections of current trends ('business-as-usual' – BaU), as well as the 'isolated-effects', 'adjusted-BaU' and 'BaU-with-limits' projections. One backcasting scenario, 'target analysis', is proposed.

The organization of this chapter is as follows. In Section 9.2, the use of SDA and other decomposition approaches in scenario analysis is discussed. Section 9.3 presents the BaU scenarios for the ten physical commodities studied in the previous chapter. The three forecasting scenarios are introduced in Section 9.4. In Section 9.5, one type of backcasting approach is explained. Section 9.6 concludes.

9.2 SCENARIO ANALYSIS USING SDA RESULTS

Scenario analysis is common in the IO literature. A variety of studies, such as Duchin and Lange et al. (1994), have already been discussed in Section 2.4. However, scenario analysis in the SDA setting, or in other decomposition methods, is rare. To our knowledge, only two SDA studies and one index decomposition analysis (IDA) study deal with scenario analysis. In the first environmental SDA study, Leontief and Ford (1972) projected the increase of air pollutants to 1980. This increase was calculated using estimates of the expected change in final demand and emission coefficients from the past. Siegel et al. (1995) provide a conceptual framework for SDA policy models, but it is not applied empirically. In the IDA setting, Ang and Lee (1996) produce several projections that are based on changing one of the determinant effects, while keeping others constant.

The scenarios that are proposed in this chapter will project physical output for the period 1997–2030. Rienstra (1998) distinguishes two types of scenario analysis:

- Forecasting scenarios: These types of projections predict future outcome based on assumptions about current and future developments. Usually, no development goal is set, that is, no value judgment is made about the outcome of the scenario. Extrapolation of historical developments is a common forecasting approach.
- Backcasting scenarios: In this type of scenario a target is defined for a future year without taking account of current trends. Potential paths that lead to this target are then calculated. Restrictions can be set on the degree to which certain factors can change.

Table 9.1 Summary of forecasting and backcasting scenarios

Name	Physical flows	Assumption
Business-as-usual (BaU) (Section 9.3)	Ten commodities of iron and steel and plastics	Linear extrapolation of 1990–1997 determinant effects.
Isolated-effects (Section 9.4)	Basic plastics and basic iron and steel	All determinant effects are assumed to be zero, except one which is given the 1990–1997 value.
Adjusted-BaU (Section 9.4)	Basic plastics and basic iron and steel	All determinant effects are at 1990–1997 levels, except one which is adapted in the optimistic and pessimistic scenario.
BaU-with-limits (Section 9.4)	Basic plastics and basic iron and steel	Absolute and relative limits are introduced to show how these affect the BaU scenario.
Target analysis (Section 9.5)	Basic plastics and basic iron and steel	Given a certain target, all combinations of determinant effects that achieve this target are plotted in a curve.

The forecasting and backcasting scenarios that are proposed in this chapter are summarized in Table 9.1. All the scenarios use 2030 as the projection year. The business-as-usual (BaU) scenario, which extrapolates the 1990–1997 trends linearly to 2030, is discussed in Section 9.3. These projections are carried out for all ten physical commodities studied in Chapter 8. Three forecasting scenario analyses, discussed in Section 9.4, focus only on the use of basic plastics and basic iron and steel. The isolated-effects sets one of the determinant effects to the level of 1990–1997, while setting all other decomposition effects to zero. The adjusted-BaU projects what would happen if one of the SDA results changes, while the other determinant effects remain the same as for the period 1990–1997. A pessimistic and optimistic scenario is proposed. The BaU-with-limits shows what happens when the BaU developments are restricted by physical, monetary, technological, logistical, social and consumption limits within the economic system. One backcasting scenario, target analysis is proposed in Section 9.5. This curve records all the combinations of determinant effects that can achieve a certain policy target. It is shown for basic plastics and basic iron and steel.

9.3 BUSINESS-AS-USUAL (BAU)

The physical output in year t can be projected using the SDA effects, as shown in Equation 9.1 (based on the decomposition Equation 8.2):

$$q^t = q^{97} +$$

$$\alpha^{IOC} \cdot (t-1997) \cdot \frac{IOC^{90,97}}{1997-1990} + \alpha^{FDE} \cdot (t-1997) \cdot \frac{FDE^{90,97}}{1997-1990} +$$

$$\alpha^{FDC} \cdot (t-1997) \cdot \frac{FDC^{90,97}}{1997-1990} + \alpha^{FDG} \cdot (t-1997) \cdot \frac{FDG^{90,97}}{1997-1990} + \quad (9.1)$$

$$\alpha^{FDI} \cdot (t-1997) \cdot \frac{FDI^{90,97}}{1997-1990} + \alpha^{FDS} \cdot (t-1997) \cdot \frac{FDS^{90,97}}{1997-1990} +$$

$$\alpha^{IS} \cdot (t-1997) \cdot \frac{IS^{90,97}}{1997-1990}$$

t	Year
q^t	Output of in year t
q^{97}	Output in year 1997
$IOC^{90,97}$	IO coefficient effect (1990–1997)
$FDE^{90,97}$	Final demand export effect (1990–1997)
$FDC^{90,97}$	Final demand private consumption effect (1990–1997)
$FDG^{90,97}$	Final demand government consumption effect (1990–1997)
$FDI^{90,97}$	Final demand investment effect (1990–1997)
$FDS^{90,97}$	Final demand stock effect (1990–1997)
$IS^{90,97}$	Import substitution effect (1990–1997)
α^λ	Coefficients of decomposition effect λ in the forecasting scenario

For the business-as-usual (BaU) scenario, the values of all α-terms are assumed to be 1, that is, $\alpha^{IOC} = \alpha^{FDE} = \alpha^{FDC} = \alpha^{FDG} = \alpha^{FDI} = \alpha^{IS} = 1$. Only α^{FDS} is set equal to zero, because it is assumed that in the long run, no stock changes will occur. The SDA results are derived from tables 8.5 and 8.6, and the resulting scenario for the ten physical commodities is shown in Figure 9.1. The value added results from Table 8.8 are used to make the projections in Figure 9.2.

Figure 9.1 indicates that, in terms of mass, the primary commodities are the most important. By 2030, the BaU scenario indicates that demand for basic plastics converges slowly with the demand for basic iron and steel, to a level of approximately 13 000 million kg. This signifies that, if current trends persist, the use of basic plastics, and basic iron and steel will approximately triple over the period 1990–2030. The physical output of transportation equipment decreases to the extent that the BaU scenario leads to negative values. This is clearly not possible, since output must be non-negative. In BaU-with-limits scenarios, these types of restrictions on developments are incorporated in the projections.

From a monetary point of view, basic iron and steel is much less important. Figure 9.2 shows that machines and iron and steel products are large contributors of value added to the economy. By 2030, due to its rapid growth rate, basic plastics has become the second largest commodity group in terms of value added. Earnings for electrical appliances are projected to decrease over the period 1990–1997.

In Figure 9.3, the BaU scenario for the ratio of value added and physical output is depicted. This figure shows what will happen to the value added (in 1997 euros) per kilogram, if the 1990–1997 trends continue. Transportation equipment is not included because the physical output turns negative, thereby distorting the ratios. The ratio of the value added per kilogram is growing for cars and engines and office equipment and computers, while it falls rapidly for electrical appliances, machines and electronics.

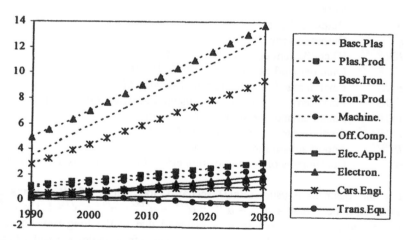

Note: For abbreviations see Table 8.4

Figure 9.1 Business-as-usual: output (10^9 kg)

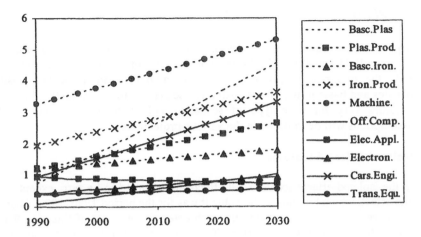

Note: For abbreviations see Table 8.4

Figure 9.2 Business-as-usual: value added (10⁹ kg)

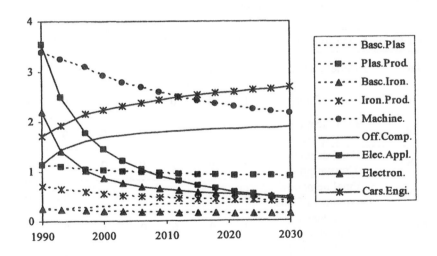

Note: For abbreviations see Table 8.4

Figure 9.3 Business-as-usual: ratio value added and output (euro/10⁹ kg)

9.4 FORECASTING SCENARIOS

This section proposes three types of forecasting scenarios: isolated-effects, adjusted-BaU and BaU-with-limits. For the sake of clarity in the scenarios, only the two most important physical commodities are projected: basic plastics and basic iron and steel. All three scenarios use Equation 9.1, but the α-values vary for each type of scenario, and in some cases additional assumptions will be imposed in the various projections.

Isolated-Effects Scenarios

In the isolated-effects scenario, all effects are assumed to be zero, except for one effect, which remains at the value it was for the period 1990–1997. There are therefore six scenarios, one for each determinant effect of Equation 9.1, except for the stock change effect. The values of the α-coefficients that are used in the scenarios are summarized in Table 9.2. The necessary decomposition data is obtained from tables 8.5 and 8.6. The resulting projections are shown in figures 9.4 and 9.5 for basic plastics and basic iron and steel, respectively. The BaU scenario is also included for comparison.

Table 9.2 Isolated-effects: α-values

Scenario	Scenario in words	α^{IOC}	α^{FDE}	α^{FDC}	α^{FDG}	α^{FDI}	α^{FDS}	α^{IS}
BaU	Business-as-usual	1	1	1	1	1	1	1
IOC	IO coefficient	1	0	0	0	0	0	0
FDE	Final demand-Export	0	1	0	0	0	0	0
FDC	Final demand-Consumption	0	0	1	0	0	0	0
FDG	Final demand-Government Cons.	0	0	0	1	0	0	0
FDI	Final demand-Investment	0	0	0	0	1	0	0
IS	Final demand-Import Substitution	0	0	0	0	0	0	1

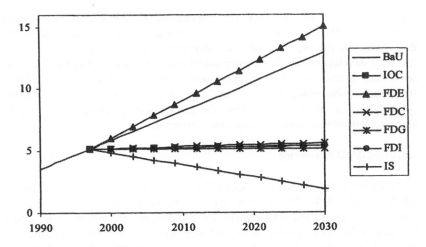

Note: For abbreviations see Table 9.2

Figure 9.4 Isolated-effects: basic plastics (10^9 kg)

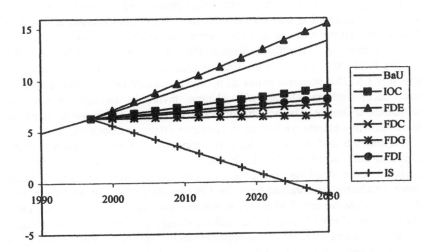

Note: For abbreviations see Table 9.2

Figure 9.5 Isolated-effects: basic iron and steel (10^9 kg)

Figures 9.4 and 9.5 illustrate the importance of the export and import substitution effects. The BaU scenario is also included in these figures, and this shows that the export effect leads to projections that are close to or above the BaU developments. The import substitution scenario shows considerable reductions in the domestic output of basic plastics. For basic iron and steel, the import substitution effect is so large that it leads to negative output projections. For all other scenarios, the use of basic plastics and basic iron and steel exhibits a stabilization or small increase.

Adjusted-BaU Scenarios

In the adjusted-BaU scenarios, SDA effects are assumed to remain constant at the level of 1990–1997, except for one decomposition effect, which is increased or decreased. Since there are six determinant effects in Equation 9.1, this yields six scenarios. A seventh scenario is included which allows for all the determinant effects to change. The BaU scenario is also included for comparison. The determinant effect that is adjusted in each projection is treated differently in the optimistic or pessimistic versions scenarios.

For the optimistic scenarios, it is assumed that the decomposition effects that contribute to lower material use (that is, negative) will double (that is, $\alpha = 2$ in Equation 9.1) for the 1997–2030 period, while other determinant effects are assumed to remain constant ($\alpha = 1$). Decomposition effects that lead to increasing material use are assumed to decrease by 50 percent ($\alpha = 0.5$). For example, if the IO-coefficient effect is −0.1 then it will become −0.2 for the 1997–2030 period. If the final demand effect is 0.8 then it is assumed that it is 1.6. This scenario paints an optimistic picture of the future, assuming that decomposition effects will change favorably through policies or autonomous change. The pessimistic scenario assumes the opposite: negative decomposition effects are halved and positive effects are doubled.

Figures 9.6 and 9.7 show the optimistic and pessimistic versions of the adjusted-BaU scenarios for basic plastics. Note that, in the optimistic scenario, even if all decomposition effects change favorably, only a fairly modest reduction is obtained from the 1997 levels. In fact, the projected level of primary plastic for 2030 is still above the level in 1990. In the pessimistic scenario, in which all determinant effects change for the worse, the demand for basic plastics increases from approximately 3500 to 25 500 million kg, a sevenfold increase. BaU only projected a threefold increase.

The results for basic iron and steel are different from those for basic plastics, as is shown in Figures 9.8 and 9.9. The optimistic scenario shows that if all decomposition effects change favorably then the output of iron and steel reduces to the point that negative output is projected. In the pessimistic scenario, there is a sixfold increase in basic iron and steel.

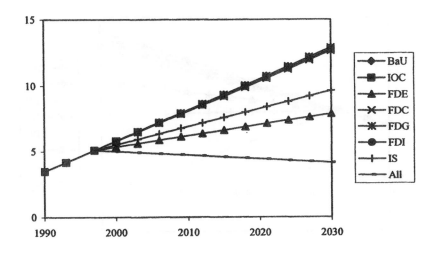

Note: For abbreviations see Table 9.2

Figure 9.6 Optimistic adjusted-BaU: basic plastics (10^9 kg)

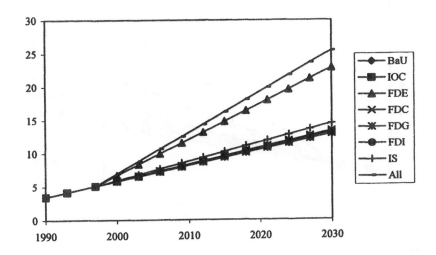

Note: For abbreviations see Table 9.2

Figure 9.7 Pessimistic adjusted-BaU: basic plastics (10^9 kg)

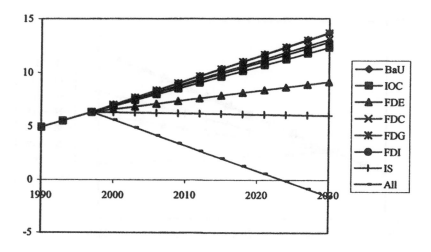

Note: For abbreviations see Table 9.2

Figure 9.8 Optimistic adjusted-BaU: basic iron and steel (10⁹ kg)

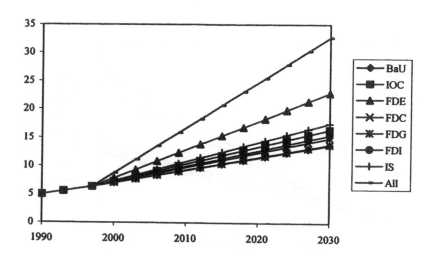

Note: For abbreviations see Table 9.2

Figure 9.9 Pessimistic adjusted-BaU: basic iron and steel (10⁹ kg)

BaU-with-Limits Scenarios

Scenarios can cause implausible or impossible outcomes. For example, Figures 9.1, 9.5 and 9.8 include projections that forecast negative output, which is impossible. There are sometimes limits to the absolute values of variables. Sometimes it is the relative changes in variables that are limited. There are several types of restrictive limits that can be identified:

- Physical limits: This includes the material balance principle.
- Monetary limits: Output, intermediate inputs and final demand should be greater than, or equal to, zero.
- Technological limits: Technologies have absolute limits, but changes can be limited by lock-in effects and path dependence.
- Logistical limits: Transportation infrastructure cannot increase indefinitely, which restricts the level of imports and exports.
- Social limits: Certain developments are socially or politically infeasible.
- Consumption limits: There are physical limits on consumption of goods.

Some of these restrictions, such as non-negativity restrictions, are hard limits that cannot be exceeded. Some of the limits are soft, that is, the resistance to certain developments increases as the limit is approached. To illustrate the BaU-with-limits scenario, several hypothetical limits are proposed in Table 9.3. The resulting scenarios for basic plastics and basic iron and steel are shown in Figure 9.10. In these scenarios, the SDA decomposition effects follow BaU until the limits are reached, after which the effect is assumed to remain constant at the level dictated by the restriction.

Figure 9.10 shows that the limits proposed are reached in 2012 and beyond. In the case of basic iron and steel, the output actually decreases because the limit for imports is reached later than the restrictions for exports. The non-negativity physical limits are never reached. The consumption limit is restrictive but has little impact on output growth.

Table 9.3 Hypothetical limits for the BaU-with-limits scenario

Limits	Description
Physical	The intermediate and final demand use of primary metals and plastics must be non-negative.
Logistical	Export and import of basic plastics can increase by 200% relative to 1990. Export and import of basic iron and steel can increase by 150% relative to 1990.
Consumption	Consumer final demand for plastic products can increase by a factor of 3, a factor of 2 for iron and steel products.

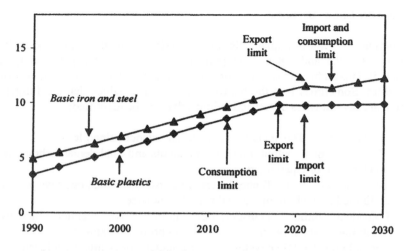

Figure 9.10 BaU-with-limits: basic plastic, basic iron and steel (10^9 kg)

9.5 BACKCASTING SCENARIO

Target Analysis

This section proposes a backcasting scenario. A dematerialization target is set, and then the paths that lead to this outcome are calculated. The target for the backcasting scenario in this section is provided by von Weiszäcker et al. (1997). Their aim was to reduce the resource use by 50 percent, while doubling the associated level of wealth. In our scenario, the target of halving material use in 2030 is adopted. All SDA effects that can achieve this target together form a curve. Table 9.4 summarizes the information that is required to produce this curve. The columns are discussed from left to right. The levels for 1990 and 1997 are provided, as well as the target, which is equal to 50 percent of the value in 1990. The appropriate reduction that is required is the difference between the value in 1997 and the target. The annual reduction is calculated by dividing the reduction by 33 years, because the reduction has to be achieved over the period 1997–2030. The SDA results that were obtained for 1990–1997 are also shown in Table 9.4. The IO coefficient effects (IOC) and the export effect (FDE) are shown, given that the other effects are assumed to be constant. Figure 9.11 depicts the target analysis for the IO coefficient effect and the final demand-export effect.[1]

Table 9.4 Levels, targets and SDA results

	Physical output information					Annual SDA results (1990–1997)		
	1990	1997	Target	Reduction	Annual reduction	IO coefficient effect	Export effect	Other effects
Basic plastics	3.48	5.11	1.74	−3.37	−0.10	0.01	0.30	−0.07
Primary metals	4.94	6.33	2.47	−3.86	−0.12	0.08	0.28	−0.14

Target analysis is capable of confronting the actual SDA results with the policy target. The SDA results for 1990–1997 are shown in Figure 9.11. Comparison with the curve shows that the trend for this 7-year period is insufficient to achieve the reductions required for halving resource use.

Potentially, target analysis could prove to be a particularly useful tool for the analysis of multiple year decompositions. Figure 9.12 shows how SDA results for the periods $[t − 1, t]$ and $[t, t + 1]$ can be compared with the target line. The SDA result for $[t − 1, t]$ is represented by the (0) point in the figure. Furthermore, the figure shows five potential SDA results for the subsequent period. These indicate the following:

(1) Divergence from the policy target because of determinant effect 2
(2) Divergence from the policy target because of determinant effect 1
(3) Convergence to the policy target because of determinant effect 2
(4) Convergence to the policy target because of determinant effect 1
(5) Convergence to the policy target because of both determinant effects

Note that, in these multiple year SDAs, the target curve is endogenous. Since the target is an absolute value that has to be met in a certain fixed year in the future, the annual reductions that are required will increase for every year that the decomposition results are above the target line. This is represented in Figure 9.12 by the shift downwards by the target curve.

9.6 CONCLUSIONS

This chapter has shown that both forecasting and backcasting scenarios can be generated using results from a two-year SDA. The business-as-usual (BaU) forecasting scenario indicates that, given the current structural changes, the demand for basic plastics and basic iron and steel will approximately triple for the period 1990–2030. The isolated-effects scenario

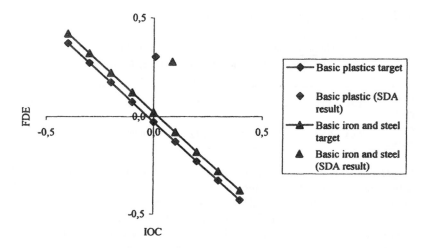

Figure 9.11 Target analysis: IOC vs. FDE

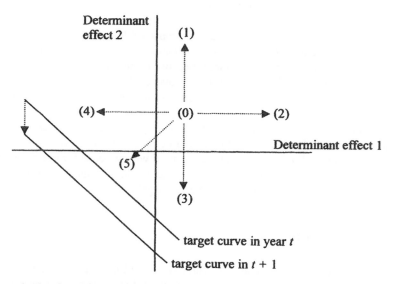

Figure 9.12 A hypothetical target analysis

analyzes the impact if one decomposition effect is kept at the 1990–1997 level, the other effects are set to zero. The resulting scenarios illustrate the importance of the export effect and the import substitution effects. The adjusted BaU forecasting scenario keeps all the decomposition effects at the 1990–1997 values, except one effect, which increases or decreases. In the optimistic scenario, the use of basic plastics stabilizes, while basic iron and steel use reduces to zero. However, in the pessimistic scenario, these commodities are projected to increase sevenfold. The BaU-with-limits sets restrictions on the physical, monetary, technological, logistical, social and consumption variables. Since the limits proposed in this chapter are hypothetical, the results are only illustrations of this type of scenario analysis. The target curve records all the combinations of decomposition effects that achieve a given target. It can be used to confront the decomposition results for a given period with the target. This target analysis shows that the decomposition effects for 1990–1997 are not sufficient to achieve the halving of resource use in 2030.

Overall the results of the forecasting scenario analyses show that, under a wide range of assumptions, the trend of increasing material use will continue in future. Only under certain optimistic assumptions about the development of the determinant effects do the scenarios exhibit reductions in the use of basic iron and steel and plastics. The backcasting scenario shows that the current determinant effects are insufficient to achieve the aim of halving the use of these materials.

Finally, a number of aspects should be kept in mind when developing scenario analysis using SDA results. First, the development of SDA scenario analysis is particularly useful when SDA for multiple years are used. This provides insights about the second derivative of developments over time, which could lead to non-linear projection paths. Furthermore, the convergence towards some the limits discussed in the BaU-with-limits scenario may become apparent from data from multiple years. Second, IO coefficients and primary input coefficients are interdependent, as the sum of intermediate input coefficients and primary input coefficients in a column of an IO table equals 1. By projecting SDA effects, the scenario may violate this restriction. This dependent determinants problem was identified in the historical SDA setting by Dietzenbacher and Los (2000).

NOTE

1. The scales of Figure 9.11 can also be expressed in percentages of the SDA results for 1990–1997. This provides insight into the relative increases required to achieve the target.

10. Summary and Conclusions

The motivation for the research reported in this book is to understand the relationship between structural change in the economy and the extraction and emission of materials. This will render insights into the way that economic activities give rise to environmental problems, and, indirectly, into what type of policies can alleviate them. The input–output (IO) framework served as the basis for the approach adopted in this book, because it distinguishes between individual components of the economy, such as technology, exports, imports, consumption and investments. Furthermore, the IO table and model are capable of simultaneously accommodating monetary and physical units in hybrid models. The physical information can be obtained from physical IO tables (PIOTs). The structure of the PIOT is extensively discussed and elaborated in this book.

To assess the impact of structural changes, IO tables from several years can be analyzed using structural decomposition analysis (SDA). The methods and techniques used in the SDA literature were critically reviewed. Moreover, decomposition forms and indices which are common in a similar method, index decomposition analysis (IDA), were transferred to SDA, and vice versa.

The effect of structural change on the physical economy was analyzed specifically for iron and steel and plastics, in the Netherlands (1990–1997). The construction of hybrid IO tables (HIOT) for 1990 and 1997 was described in detail. The resulting physical data generally show a pattern of rematerialization, which was explained on the basis of several SDA specifications. The remainder of this chapter will summarize and draw a number of conclusions from Chapters 1 to 9.

Chapter 1 introduced the general context of this book. In particular, three issues in environmental economics were discussed: the growth debate, economic models that include material flows and economic-environmental accounting frameworks. The growth debate concerns the question of whether economic growth can continue indefinitely, without exceeding environmental limits. Pessimists dispute that this is possible, while optimists are confident that economic growth is a requirement for environmental improvement.

There are many types of economic models that include material flows:

material flow analysis (MFA), substance flow analysis (SFA), material-product (M-P) chain analysis, life cycle assessment (LCA), macroeconomic models and IO models. Furthermore, concepts such as 'industrial metabolism' and 'industrial ecology' have been proposed. This book discusses and implements IO models – in particular the hybrid IO models – which are capable of using monetary, physical and other units simultaneously.

The issue of economic-environmental accounting frameworks has been addressed extensively in the IO framework. A variety of set ups have been implemented to record physical flows within the economic system and between the economy and the environment. This book focuses on one of these accounting frameworks: namely, the physical IO table (PIOT).

Section 1.5 introduced the four objectives of this book, which will be discussed below as they arise. In general the book can be divided into Chapters 2 to 5, which discuss various topics related to IO models of environmental issues and Chapters 6 to 9 which deal with issues related to SDA.

Chapter 2 is an introduction to IO tables and models. The structure of IO tables and the homogeneous product and fixed coefficient assumptions of the IO model were discussed. Two types of applications of the IO model were presented: impact analysis and imputation to final demand. A brief review of the literature that has applied IO models to environmental issues was reviewed. One particular model, which uses multiple units, was discussed in detail. This 'hybrids' or 'mixed-units' IO model provides a better description of the technological relationships in a production process because the commodity is measured in its own natural unit. It was further shown that, in the case of non-uniform prices, the hybrid model maintains the mass balance principle, where the corresponding monetary model fails. For each production activity, the output should be recorded in the natural unit, which is the unit which best describes the technological or consumptive demand for a product. These units can be mass, energy, other physical measures, or units specific to services. In cases where the natural unit is difficult to establish or data is unavailable, it can be necessary to use the monetary data.

Chapter 3 discussed the theoretical aspects of constructing IO tables from supply and use tables (SUT). These are industry-by-commodity accounts that record the production and consumption of goods and services. Four types of supply and use tables were discussed: monetary, physical, energy and hybrid tables. The monetary SUT, in current prices, are financially balanced, that is, the commodity and industry totals of both tables are equal. The mass and energy SUT are balanced in kilograms and Joules, respectively, because of the laws of conservation of mass and energy. This holds for both the industry and commodity dimensions. However, the hybrid supply and use table is only balanced in the commodity dimension.

It was shown that SUT in constant prices do not balance for either the commodity or industry dimensions, although this is commonly assumed in the production of SUT in constant prices. However, the empirical results suggest that in the Netherlands, for the period 1990–1997, the discrepancy was not large.

SUT can be used to produce industry-by-industry, commodity-by-commodity or activity-by activity IO tables. However, the assumptions that are used to make these IO tables sometimes do not correspond with the assumptions of the IO model. This chapter showed that only those IO tables that are produced using the activity technology model are consistent with IO modeling assumptions. However, such an IO table requires additional information about input requirements beyond what is contained in the SUT. Another type of IO table that is often used is the commodity-by-commodity IO table, which is produced using the commodity technology assumption. However, negative elements arise because of measurement errors, heterogeneous production processes, commodity aggregation, and non-uniform prices. These reasons were illustrated, using a numerical example, and appropriate remedies were suggested.

Chapter 4 deals with Objective 1 of this book, which was (Section 1.5): Explore and elaborate the physical IO tables (PIOT) as an economic-environmental accounting framework.

The PIOT framework provides an accounting system to record the physical flows within the economy and between the economy and environment. PIOTs have been produced for the Netherlands, Germany, Denmark, Italy, Finland, and for the European Union as a whole. The basic PIOT, which was used by all studies except the Dutch one, is similar to the accounting structure of the traditional monetary IO table.

The extended PIOT for the Netherlands distinguishes between structural and auxiliary production processes. The *structural production process* includes all inputs and outputs associated with the production of a physical product. An example is nuts and bolts that are used in the production of cars. The *auxiliary production process* refers to all other physical inputs and outputs that facilitate the production process, but which are not intended to be part of the physical product. A prime example of an auxiliary input is fossil fuel used for energy purposes.

Production processes include two other types of physical flows. First, the investment goods facilitate the production process, but unlike the auxiliary inputs, are used over multiple years. Examples of an investment good are machines and buildings. Second, unwanted physical flows can enter and leave a production process. The best example is packaging that is used for the structural inputs, auxiliary inputs and investment goods that are used in a production process.

Chapter 4 used the basic and extended PIOTs, as well as other insights, to produce the full PIOT. The framework includes all relevant aspects of material flows such as product flows, packaging, recycling, landfilling, incineration, raw material extraction and emissions. A detailed numerical example was provided to illustrate the implementation of the accounting system. The numerical example was also used to show the types of environmental information and indicators that could be obtained from a full PIOT. This includes information about environmental pressures, chemical composition of products, element cycles in the economy and dematerialization indicators. Finally, the chapter shows that the PIOT data can be used in IO modeling applications such as impact analysis and imputation to final demand.

Chapter 5 deals with Objective 3 of this book, which is (Section 1.5): Construct Hybrid IO tables for iron and steel and plastic products for the Netherlands for 1990 and 1997.

This chapter discusses the construction of HIOTs from hybrid SUT for the Netherlands for two years, 1990 and 1997. The construction of these tables was based on the theoretical discussion in Chapter 3. However, the construction of an activity-by-activity IO table was beyond the scope of this book because of the information requirements. The IO tables that were produced are commodity-by-commodity IO tables based on the commodity technology assumption.

The construction procedure consists of six steps. In Step 1 the monetary SUT for 1990 and 1997 in constant prices of 1997 were produced. Step 2 involved the construction of the physical SUT. In Step 3, the data of the monetary and physical tables were combined to provide hybrid SUT. These hybrid tables were made square in Step 4. In Step 5, the commodity technology assumption was applied to the SUT to produce hybrid commodity-by-commodity IO tables. Finally, in Step 6, the negative elements that arose in Step 5 were analyzed, and adjustments were made to construct non-negative hybrid commodity-by-commodity IO tables. The end result is an IO table with ten commodities in physical units (kg) and 46 other goods and services in monetary units (euros in 1997 prices).

Chapter 6 deals with the main point of Objective 2 of this book, which is (Section 1.5): Investigate structural decomposition analysis as a tool to identify the influence of structural change on physical flows.

The chapter introduced environmental structural decomposition analysis (SDA). The methods and techniques that are available were reviewed. These include the choice of multiplicative or additive decomposition; absolute, intensity or elasticity decompositions; hybrid or physical coefficient models; choice of indices; and the treatment of imports. In addition, the ways to decompose the sub-effects of the IO coefficients effect and final demand effect were considered. Finally, there is the choice of using open or closed IO models as a basis for the SDA. Decomposition based on the closed IO model is sometimes referred to as the 'KLEM specification', which links SDA to neoclassical approaches.

Approximately 34 SDA studies have applied SDA to environmental issues. These address issues such as energy use, carbon dioxide (CO_2) emissions, acidifying emissions, nitrogen loading and demand for bulk-materials. There are large differences in the decomposition methods used and the countries and time periods covered, which makes comparison difficult. General statements about the importance of certain decomposition effects are, therefore, difficult to make. However, the results for energy use and CO_2 emissions suggest that economic growth, as captured by the final demand level (FDL) effect, nearly always exceeds the downward-pushing effects of technological change (TC) and final demand mix (FDM) effects. Nevertheless, results for individual energy carriers or the results at a sector level deviate from this pattern. Other environmental variables, such as sulphur dioxide and material demand, exhibit technological effects that create greater downward pressure than economic growth creates upward pressure, for some periods and countries.

Chapter 7 deals with Objective 2a of this book, which is (Section 1.5): In particular, compare methods and techniques used in SDA with other decomposition methods.

In this chapter, the relationship between SDA and a related decomposition method called index decomposition analysis (IDA) was discussed. IDA does not use IO data, but restricts itself to using aggregate sector-level information. Therefore, IDA is incapable of the same level of detail of decomposition of technological and demand relationships as SDA. An advantage of IDA is the fact that the less detailed data is often available as longer time series. Moreover, the IDA literature has seen more developments in terms of specific decomposition methods and techniques used. A larger variety of decomposition indicators, forms and indices have been suggested in this setting. Chapter 7 showed how the IDA techniques and indices could be transferred to the SDA setting. Furthermore, one of the index approaches of SDA was transferred to the IDA setting. Each index has certain properties, but no 'ideal' with all advantageous properties exists. The differences between the various methods, techniques and indices were illustrated using a numerical example.

Chapter 8 deals with Objective 4 of this book, which is (Section 1.5): Investigate the structural changes that have contributed to the use of iron and steel and plastics in the Netherlands, for the period 1990–1997.

The data constructed for 1990 and 1997 in Chapter 5 for ten physical commodities of iron and steel and plastics shows that six experience rematerialization, three exhibit relative dematerialization and only one shows absolute dematerialization. The structural changes that cause these developments were analyzed in four SDAs of the increases in physical output and of value added growth.

The SDA results show that the main source of upward pressure was the growth in the level of exports, which was the largest driving force for increased output for eight of the ten commodities. The mix effect of exports, which analyzes the impact of the shift in the export package also contributed to output growth in seven out of ten of the commodities. The period 1990–1997 also experienced increased imports, which caused great downward pressure on output. Nevertheless, this never exceeded the upward pressure of increased exports. The other components of final demand, private consumption, government consumption, investments and stocks are generally small, although they exhibited larger effects for a couple of commodities. Value added, in real terms, grows for nine out of ten commodities. SDA showed that the growth in value added was subdued by the reduction in the value added per kg of commodities. The decomposition shows that the value added would have been 60 percent higher had these margins been maintained.

The results obtained here differ from those in a previous study for the United States (1972–1982), which found that technological changes had contributed to the dematerialization of iron and steel commodities, to the extent that it exceeded the upward pressures of economic growth. In our calculations, IO coefficient effects contribute to increased material use for eight out of the ten commodities. Similarly, the final demand mix effect of iron and steel was negative for the United States, while for the Netherlands it was positive for seven out of ten commodities. These differences could be caused by the deviation in the time period or country. In addition, the use of an open IO model for the Netherlands, and a closed IO model for the United States, may also have affected the results. Although the differences in country and method are difficult to quantify, the time period is the most likely source of the difference in the results.

Finally, the chapter discussed the influence of the accounting assumptions on SDA. It was shown that changes in the organization of the production chains in the economy, such as mergers or break ups into specialized firms, could affect SDA results. As a remedy, it was suggested that the results of the physical output should be discussed only for each individual commodity. Furthermore, the diagonals of the HIOTs were set to zero, and the output adjusted accordingly. In a sensitivity analysis of this procedure, it was shown that the latter modification has little influence on the results of this data set.

Chapter 9 deals with Objective 2b of this book, which is (Section 1.5): In particular, develop forecasting and backcasting scenario analysis based on SDA results.

In this chapter, the SDA results from Chapter 8 were used to perform forecasting and backcasting scenario analyses. The Business-as-usual (BaU) forecasts suggest that over the period 1990–2030, if current trends persist, the use of basic plastics and basic iron and steel will triple in physical terms. Three forecasting methods and one backcasting method were examined for these goods. In the isolated-effects forecasting scenario, all decomposition effects were assumed to be zero, except one, which was assigned the same value as that for the period 1990–1997. In the adjusted-BaU forecasting scenario, all decomposition effects were assumed to continue unchanged until 2030, except one, which was assumed to accelerate or decelerate, depending on whether an optimistic or pessimistic projection was intended. The demand for basic plastics and basic iron and steel increases sevenfold in the pessimistic scenario. In the BaU-with-limits scenario, restrictions are placed on physical, monetary, technological, logistical, social and consumption variables. Finally, target analysis backcasting scenario, shows all combinations of decomposition effects that can achieve a certain policy target. Such a curve was used to compare decomposition results with a policy target. In our case, it was shown that the developments for the period 1990–1997 were not compatible with a target of halving resource use.

This book has covered many aspects of analyzing the relationship between structural change and the physical economy. The accounting system of the physical economy was discussed in the context of a physical IO table. Furthermore, the construction and use of HIOTs and models received detailed attention. The methods and techniques used in structural decomposition analysis were reviewed and elaborated, including the development of scenario analysis using SDA results. All these aspects were brought together in an application of hybrid IO data for iron and steel and plastic commodities, for the Netherlands, in the period 1990–1997.

References

Adriaanse, A., S. Bringezu, Y. Moriguchi, E. Rodenburg, D. Rogich and H. Schutz (1997), *Resource Flows: The Materials Basis of Industrial Economies*, World Resources Institute, Washington DC.

Alcántara, V. and J. Roca (1995), 'Energy and CO_2 emissions in Spain: methodology of analysis and some results for 1980–1990', *Energy Economics*, **17** (3), 221–30.

Allenby, B.R. and D.J. Richards (eds) (1994), *The Greening of Industrial Ecosystems*, National Academy Press, Washington DC.

Almon, C. (2000), 'Product-to-product tables via product technology with no negative flows' *Economic Systems Research*, **12** (1), 27–43.

Ang, B.W. (1994), 'Decomposition of industrial energy consumption: the energy intensity approach', *Energy Economics*, **16** (3), 163–174.

Ang, B.W. (1999), 'Decomposition methodology in energy demand and environmental analysis', in J.C.J.M. van den Bergh (ed.), *Handbook of Environmental and Resource Economics*, Edward Elgar, Cheltenham, pp. 1146–63.

Ang, B.W. and K.H. Choi (1997), 'Decomposition of aggregate energy and gas emissions intensities for industry: a refined Divisia index method', *Energy Journal*, **18** (3), 59–73.

Ang, B.W. and P.W. Lee (1996), 'Decomposition of industrial energy consumption: the energy coefficient approach', *Energy Economics*, **18**, 129–43.

Ang, B.W. and F.Q. Zhang (2000), 'A survey of index decomposition analysis in energy and environmental studies'. *Energy*, **25**, 1149–76.

Ayres, R.U. (1978), *Resources, Environment, and Economics: Applications of the Materials/Energy Balance Principle*, John Wiley and Sons, New York.

Ayres, R.U. and A.V. Kneese (1969), 'Production, consumption and externalities', *American Economic Review*, **59**, 282–97.

Ayres, R.U. and U.E. Simonis (1994), *Industrial Metabolism, Restructuring for Sustainable Development*, United Nations University Press, Tokyo.

Ayres, R.U., L.A. Ayres and B. Warr (2005), 'Is the US economy dematerializing? Main indicators and drivers', in J.C.J.M. van den Bergh and M.A. Janssen (eds), *Economics of Industrial Ecology: Materials,*

Structural Change, and Spatial Scales, MIT Press, Cambridge, MA.

Balk, B.M. (1995), 'Axiomatic price index theory: a survey', *International Statistical Review*, 63, 69–93.

Battjes, J.J. (1999), 'Dynamic modelling of energy stocks and flows in the economy (An energy accounting approach)', PhD thesis University of Groningen, The Netherlands.

Beckerman, W. (1999), 'A pro-growth perspective', in J.C.J.M. van den Bergh (ed.), *Handbook of Environmental and Resource Economics*, Edward Elgar, Cheltenham, pp. 867–94.

Bergh, J.C.J.M. van den (1999), 'Materials, capital, direct/indirect substitution and mass balance production functions', *Land Economics*, 75 (4), 547–61.

Bergh, J.C.J.M. van den and P. Nijkamp (1994), 'Dynamic macro modelling and materials balance', *Economic Modelling*, 11, 283–307.

Bergh, J.C.J.M. van den and R. de Mooij (1999), 'An assessment of the growth debate', in J.C.J.M. van den Bergh (ed.), *Handbook of Environmental and Resource Economics*, Edward Elgar, Cheltenham, pp. 643–55

Beukering, P.J.H. van (2001), *Recycling, International Trade and the Environment: An Empirical Analysis*, Kluwer Publishers, Dordrecht.

Boer, S. de, W. van Nunspeet and T. Takema (1999), 'Supply and use table in current and constant prices for the Netherlands: an experience of fifteen years', Report NA-092, Statistics Netherlands, Voorburg/Heerlen.

Bos, F. (2003), 'The National Accounts as a tool for analysis and policy: past, present and future', PhD thesis, University of Twente, Enschede.

Boulding, K.E. (1966), 'The economics of the coming spaceship earth', in H. Jarret (ed.), *Environmental Quality in the Growing Economy*, Baltimore, MD, Johns Hopkins University Press, pp. 3–14.

Bouman, M., R. Heijungs, E. van der Voet, J.C.J.M. van den Bergh and G. Huppes (2000), 'Material flows and economic models: an analytical comparison of SFA, LCA and partial equilibrium models', *Ecological Economics*, 32, 195–216.

Boyd, G., J.F. McDonald, M. Ross and D.A. Hanson (1987), 'Separating the changing composition of U.S. manufacturing production from energy efficiency improvements: a Divisia index approach', *Energy Journal*, 8 (2), 77–96.

Bruijn, S.M. de and J.B. Opschoor (1997), 'Developments in the throughput-income relationship: theoretical and empirical observations', *Ecological Economics*, 20, 255–68.

Bruijn, S.M. de and R.J. Heintz (1999), 'The environmental Kuznets curve hypothesis', in J.C.J.M. van den Bergh (ed.), *Handbook of Environmental and Resource Economics*, Edward Elgar, Cheltenham, pp. 656–77.

Bullard III, C.W. and R.A. Herendeen (1975), 'The energy cost of goods and services', *Energy Policy*, 1 (4), 268–77.

Casler, S.D. (2001), 'Interaction terms and structural decomposition: an application to the defense cost of oil', in M. L. Lahr and E. Dietzenbacher (eds), *Input–Output: Frontiers and Extensions*, Palgrave Publishers Ltd, Basingstoke, Hampshire.

Casler, S.D. and A.Z. Rose (1998), 'Carbon dioxide emissions in the U.S. economy', *Environmental and Resource Economics*, 11 (3–4), 349–63.

Casler, S.D. and A. Rose (1999), 'Structural decomposition analysis: a microeconomic integration', Thoughts on SDA Workshop, Tinbergen Institute, Amsterdam.

Casler, S.D. and S. Wilbur (1984), 'Energy input–output analysis: a simple guide', *Resources and Energy*, 6, 187–201.

CBS (Centraal Bureau voor de Statistiek) (1992), 'Bedrijfsafvalstoffen 1990', Afdeling Milieustatistieken, Voorburg/Heerlen, The Netherlands.

CBS (Centraal Bureau voor de Statistiek) (1998), 'Bedrijfsafvalstoffen 1996', Afdeling Milieustatistieken, Voorburg/Heerlen, The Netherlands.

CBS (Centraal Bureau voor de Statistiek) (2000), 'Bedrijfsafvalstoffen 1998', Afdeling Milieustatistieken, Voorburg/Heerlen, The Netherlands.

CBS (Centraal Bureau voor de Statistiek) (2001), 'IJzer,staal en kunststoffen in de Nederlandse economie, 1990 en 1997', Nota nr. 01753-01-MNR, Sector Nationale Rekeningen, Voorburg, The Netherlands.

Chang, Y.F. and S.J. Lin (1998), 'Structural decomposition of industrial CO_2 emission in Taiwan: an input–output approach', *Energy Policy*, 26 (1), 5–12.

Chen, C.Y. and A. Rose (1990), 'A structural decomposition analysis of changes in energy demand in Taiwan: 1971–1984', *Energy Journal*, 11 (1), 127–46.

Chen, C.Y. and R.H. Wu (1994), 'Sources of change in industrial electricity use in the Taiwan economy, 1976–86', *Energy Economics*, 16 (2), 115–20.

Chertow, M.R. (2000), 'Industrial symbiosis: literature and taxonomy', *Annual Review of Energy and the Environment*, 25, 313–37.

Chung, H.S. (1998), 'Industrial structure and source of carbon dioxide emissions in East Asia: estimation and comparison', *Energy and Environment*, 9 (5), 509–33.

Cleveland, C.J. and M. Ruth (1997), 'Indicators of dematerialization and the intensity of use', *Journal of Industrial Ecology* 2 (3), 15–50.

Common, M.S. and U. Salma (1992), 'Accounting for changes in Australian carbon dioxide emissions', *Energy Economics*, 13, 217–25.

Cumberland, J.H. (1966), 'A regional inter-industry model for analysis of development objectives', *Papers of the Regional Science Association*, 17,

65–95.

Dalen, J. van and W. Sluis (2002), *WINADJUST*, Statistics Netherlands, Voorburg, The Netherlands.

Daly, H.E. (1968), 'On economics of a life science', *Journal of Political Economy*, **76** (3), 392–406.

Daly, H.E. (1977), Steady-state Economics, 1st edition, Island Press, Washington, DC.

Daly, H.E. (1991), Steady-state Economics, 2nd edition, Island Press, Washington, DC.

Daly, H.E. (1999), 'Steady-state Economics: avoiding uneconomic growth', in J.C.J.M. van den Bergh (ed.), *Handbook of Environmental and Resource Economics*, Edward Elgar, Cheltenham, pp. 635–42.

Dellink, R., M. Bennis and H. Verbruggen (1996), 'Sustainable economic structures: scenarios for sustainability in the Netherlands', IVM-report W96/27, Institute for Environmental Studies, Free University, Amsterdam.

Dietzenbacher, E. (2005), 'Waste treatment in physical input-output analysis', Working paper, University of Groningen, Groningen.

Dietzenbacher, E. and R. Hoekstra (2002), 'The RAS structural decomposition approach', in G.J.D. Hewings, M. Sonis and D.E. Boyce (eds), *Trade, Networks and Hierarchies*, Springer-Verlag, Berlin.

Dietzenbacher, E. and B. Los (1998), 'Structural decomposition techniques: sense and sensitivity', *Economic Systems Research*, **10** (4), 307–23.

Dietzenbacher, E. and B. Los (2000), 'Structural decomposition analyses with dependent determinants', *Economic Systems Research*, **12** (4), 497–514.

Dietzenbacher, E., S. Giljum, K. Hubacek and S. Suh (2005), 'Physical input-output analysis and disposal to nature', Working paper, University of Groningen, Groningen.

Dietzenbacher, E., A. Hoen and B. Los (2000), 'Labor productivity in Western Europe 1975–1985: an intercountry, interindustry analysis', *Journal of Regional Science*, **40**, 425–52.

Duchin, F. and G. M. Lange (1998), 'Prospects for recycling of plastics in the United States', *Structural Change and Economic Dynamics*, **9**, 307–31.

Duchin, F. and G.M. Lange with K. Thonstad and A. Idenburg (1994), *The Future of the Environment: Ecological Economics and Technological Change*, Oxford University Press, New York/Oxford.

Duchin, F. and A. E. Steenge (1999), 'Input–output analysis, technology and the environment', in J.C.J.M. van den Bergh (ed.), *Handbook of Environmental and Resource Economic*, Edward Elgar, Cheltenham, pp. 1037–59.

Economic Systems Research (1998), Special issue on I/O models of environmental issues, June 1998.

Eurostat (1998), *Iron and Steel Yearly Statistics 1998*, Eurostat, Luxembourg.

Eurostat (2001), *Economy-wide Material Flow Accounts and Derived Indicators: A Methodological Guide*, Eurostat, Luxembourg.

Fankhauser, S. and D. McCoy (1995), 'Modelling the economic consequences of environmental policies', in H. Folmer, H. Landis Gabel and H. Opschoor (eds), *Principles of Environmental and Resource Economics*, Edward Elgar, Aldershot UK and Brookfield US, pp. 253–275.

Farla, J.C.M. (2000), 'Physical indicators of energy efficiency', PhD thesis, University of Utrecht, Utrecht, The Netherlands.

Ferrer, G. and R.U. Ayres (2000), 'The impact of remanufacturing in the economy', *Ecological Economics*, 32, 413–29.

Fisher, I. (1922), *The Making of Index Numbers: A Study of their Varieties, Tests and Reliability*, Houghton Mifflin, Boston.

Garbaccio, R. F. M.S. Ho and D.W. Jorgenson (1999), 'Why has the energy–output ratio fallen in China?', *Energy Journal*, 20 (3), 63–91.

Georgescu-Roegen, N. (1971), *The Entropy Law and the Economic Process*, Harvard University Press, Cambridge MA.

Giljum, S. and K. Hubacek (2001), 'International trade, material flows and land use: developing a physical trade balance for the European Union', Interim Report IR-01-059, IIASA, Laxenburg.

Giljum, S. and K. Hubacek (2004), 'Approaches of physical input–output analysis to estimate primary material inputs of production and consumption', *Economic Systems Research*, 16 (3), 301–10.

Gould, B.W. and S.N. Kulshreshtha (1986), 'An interindustry analysis of structural change and energy use linkages in the Saskatchewan economy', *Energy Economics*, 8, 186–96.

Gowdy, J.M. and J.L. Miller (1987), 'Technological and demand change in energy use: an input–output analysis', *Environment and Planning A*, 19, 1387–98.

Graedel, T.E. and B.R. Allenby (1995), *Industrial Ecology*, Prentice Hall, Englewood Cliffs, NJ.

Gravgård-Pedersen, O. (1999), *Physical Input–Output Tables for Denmark. Products and Materials 1990, Air Emissions 1990–92*, Statistics Denmark, ISBN 87-501-1076-4, Kopenhagen.

Griliches, Z. (1994), 'Productivity, R&D, and the data constraint', *American Economic Review*, 84 (1), 1–23.

Gross, L.S. and E.C.H. Veendorp (1990), 'Growth with exhaustible resources and a materials balance production function', *Natural Resource Modeling*, 4, 77–94.

Grossman, G.M. and A.B. Krueger (1995), 'Economic growth and the environment', *Quarterly Journal of Economics*, 110, 353–77.

Guinée, J.B. (1995), 'Development of a methodology for the environmental life-cycle assessment of products – with a case study on margarines', PhD thesis, Centre for Environmental Science (CML), Leiden University, The Netherlands.

Haan, M. de (2001), 'A structural decomposition analysis of pollution in the Netherlands', *Economic System Research*, 13 (2), 181–96.

Haan, M. de (2004), 'Accounting for goods and for bads. Measuring environmental pressure in a national accounts framework', PhD thesis, Statistics Netherlands (CBS), Voorburg, The Netherlands.

Hamilton, C. (1997), 'The sustainability of logging in Indonesia's tropical forests: a dynamic input–output analysis', *Ecological Economics*, 21, 183–95.

Han, X. and T.K. Lakshmanan (1994), 'Structural changes and energy consumption in the Japanese economy 1975–85: an input–output analysis', *Energy Journal*, 15 (3), 165–88.

Hansen, E. (1995), *Environmental Prioritising of Industrial Products*. Environmental project No. 281, The Danish Environmental Protection Agency (in Danish).

Heijungs, R. and S. Suh (2001), *The Computational Structure of Life Cycle Assessment*, Kluwer Academic Publishers, Dordrecht.

Hoekstra, R. and J.C.J.M. van den Bergh (2002), 'Structural decomposition analysis of physical flows in the economy', *Environmental and Resource Economics*, 23, 357–78.

Hoekstra, R. and J.C.J.M. van den Bergh (2003), 'Comparing structural and index decomposition analysis', *Energy Economics*, 25, 39–64.

Hoekstra, R. and J.C.J.M. van den Bergh (2005), 'Structural decomposition analysis of iron and steel and of plastics', in J.C.J.M. van den Bergh and M.A. Janssen (eds), *Economics of Industrial Ecology: Materials, Structural Change, and Spatial Scales*, MIT Press, Cambridge, MA.

Hoen, A.R. (1999), 'An input–output analysis of European integration', PhD thesis, University of Groningen, Systems, Organization and Managment (SOM), The Netherlands.

Huang, G.H., W.P. Anderson and B.W. Baetz (1994), 'Environmental input–output analysis and its application to regional solid-waste management planning', *Journal of Environmental Management*, 42, 63–79.

Hubacek, K. and S. Giljum (2003), 'Applying physical input–output analysis to estimate land appropriation (ecological footprints) of international trade activities', *Ecological Economics*, 44, 137–51.

Idenburg, A.M. (1993), 'Gearing production models to ecological economic analysis: a case study, within the input–output framework, of fuels for road transport', PhD thesis, Universiteit Twente, Enschede, The Netherlands.

Idenburg, A.M. and A.E. Steenge (1991), 'Environmental policy in single-product and joint production input–output models', in F. Dietz, F. van der Ploeg and J. van der Straaten (eds), *Environmental Policy and the Economy*, Elsevier, Dordrecht.

IISI (International Iron and Steel Institute) (1998), *Steel Statistical Yearbook*, Brussels, Belgium.

Isard, W. (1972), *Ecological-Economic Analysis for Regional Development*, The Free Press, New York.

Jacobsen, H.K. (2000), 'Energy demand, structural change and trade: a decomposition analysis of the Danish manufacturing industry', *Economic Systems Research*, **12** (3), 319–43.

James, D.E., H.M.A. Jansen and J.B. Opschoor (1978), *Economic Approaches to Environmental Problems: Techniques and Results of Empirical Analysis*, Elsevier Scientific Publishing, Amsterdam/Oxford/New York.

Johnson, M. and J. Bennet (1981), 'Regional environmental and economic impact evaluation', *Regional Science and Urban Economics*, **11** (2, May), 215–30.

Joosten, L.A.J. (2001), 'The industrial metabolism of plastics: analysis of material flows, energy consumption and CO_2 emissions in the lifecycle of plastics', PhD thesis, University of Utrecht, Utrecht, The Netherlands.

Kagawa, S. and H. Inamura (2000), 'Structural decomposition of energy consumption based on a hybrid rectangular I–O framework: Japan's Case', 13th International Conference on Input–Output Techniques, Macerata, Italy.

Kagawa, S. and H. Inamura (2001), 'A structural decomposition of energy consumption based on a hybrid rectangular I–O framework: Japan's Case', *Economic Systems Research*, **13** (4), 339–63.

Kagawa, S., H. Inamura and Y. Moriguchi (2002), 'The invisible multipliers of joint-products', *Economic Systems Research*, **14** (2), 185–203.

Kagawa, S. and H. Inamura (2004), 'A spatial structural decomposition analysis of Chinese and Japanese Energy Demand: 1985–1990', *Economic Systems Research*, **16** (3), 279–99.

Kandelaars, P.P.A.A.H. (1998), *Economic Models of Material-product Chains for Environmental Policy Analysis*, Kluwer Academic Publishers, Dordrecht, The Netherlands.

Kandelaars, P.P.A.A.H. and J.C.J.M. van den Bergh (2001), 'A survey of material flows in economic models', *International Journal of Sustainable Development*, **4** (3), 282–303.

Kleijn, R. (2001), 'Adding it all up: the sense and non-sense of bulk-MFA', *Journal of Industrial Ecology*, **4** (2), 7–8.

Konijn, P.J.A. (1994), 'The make and use of commodities by industries: on the compilation of input–output data from the National Accounts', PhD thesis, Universiteit Twente, Enschede, The Netherlands.

Konijn, P.J.A. and S. de Boer (1993), 'Een homogene input–outputtabel voor Nederland, 1990. Een beschrijving van de economie in 316 produktieprocessen', Notanr:184–93-PS.E8/int BPA:11191–93-PS.E8/int, National Accounts Department, Statistics Netherlands, The Netherlands.

Konijn, P.J.A. and A.E. Steenge (1995), 'Compilation of input–output data from the national accounts', *Economic Systems Research*, 7 (1), 31–45.

Konijn, P.J.A., S. de Boer and J. van Dalen (1995), 'Material flows and input–output analysis: methodological description and empirical results', Notanr: 006–95-EIN.PNR/int BPA-nr: 698–95-EIN.PNR/int, Sector National Accounts, Statistics Netherlands, The Netherlands.

Konijn, P.J.A., S. de Boer and J. van Dalen (1997), 'Input–output analysis of material flows with application to iron, steel and zinc', *Structural Change and Economic Dynamics*, 8, 129–53.

Kratterl, A. and K. Kratena (1990), *Reale Input–Output Tabelle und ökologischer Kreislauf*, Physica-Verlag, Heidelberg.

Kruk, R. van der (1999a), 'An input–output structural decomposition analysis of the energy demand of 9 OECD countries', MSc. thesis, Erasmus University, Rotterdam, The Netherlands.

Kruk, R. van der (1999b), 'Decomposition uniqueness: the basic additive identity splitting method', Thoughts on SDA Workshop, Tinbergen Institute, Amsterdam.

Kuczynski, M. and R.L. Meek (1972), *Quesnay's Tableau Économique*, MacMillan, London.

Kurz, H. and N. Salvadori (2000), 'Economic dynamics in a simple model with exhaustible resources and a given real wage rate', *Structural Change and Economic Dynamics*, 11, 167–79.

Lenzen, M. (2001), 'Errors in conventional and input–output life-cycle inventories', *Journal of Industrial Ecology*, 4 (4), 127–48.

Leontief, W. (1936), 'Quantitative input and output relations in the economic system of the United States', *Review of Economics and Statistics*, **XVIII** (3, August), 105–125.

Leontief, W. (1941), '*The Structure of the American Economy, 1919–1929: an Empirical Application of Equilibrium Analysis*', Harvard University Press, Cambridge MA.

Leontief, W. (1966), *Input–Output Economics*, Oxford University Press, New York.

Leontief, W. (1970), 'Environmental repercussions and the economic structure: an input–output approach', *Review of Economics and Statistics*, 52 (3, August), 262–71.

Leontief, W. and D. Ford (1972), 'Air pollution and economic structure:

empirical results of input–output computations', in A. Brody and A. P. Carter (eds), *Input–Output Techniques*, American Elsevier, New York, pp. 9–30.

Leontief, W. A. Carter and P. Petri (1977), *Future of the World Economy*, Oxford University Press, New York.

Lin, X. (1996), *China's Energy Strategy: Economic Structure, Technological Choices, and Energy Consumption*, Praeger, Westport, CT.

Lin, X. and K. R. Polenske (1995), 'Input–output anatomy of China's energy use changes in the 1980s', *Economic Systems Research*, 7 (1), 67–84.

Linden, J.A van der and E. Dietzenbacher (1995), 'The determinants of structural change in the European Union: a new application of RAS', SOM Research report (95D36), University of Groningen, Groningen, The Netherlands.

Liu, X.Q., B.W. Ang and H.L. Ong (1992), 'The application of the Divisia index to the decomposition of changes in industrial energy consumption', *Energy Journal*, 13 (4), 161–77.

Londero, E. (2001), 'By-products', *Economic Systems Research*, 13 (1), 35–46.

Los, B. (2001), 'Endogenous growth and structural change in a dynamic I/O model', *Economic Systems Research*, 8, 129–53.

Luptacik, M. and B. Böhm (1999), 'A consistent formulation of the Leontief pollution model', *Economic Systems Research*, 11 (3), 263–75.

Machado, G., R. Schaeffer and E. Worrell (2001), 'Energy and carbon embodied in the international trade of Brazil: an input–output analysis'. *Ecological Economics*, 39 (3), 409–24.

Maddison (2001), *The World Economy: A Millennial Perspective*, OECD, Paris.

Mäenpää, I. (2002), 'Physical input–output tables of Finland 1995 – solutions to some basic methodological problems', 14th International conference on input–output techniques, Montreal, Canada.

Mäenpää, I. and J. Muukkonen (2001), 'Physical input–output in Finland: methods, preliminary results and tasks ahead', Conference on economic growth, material flows and environmental pressure, Stockholm, Sweden.

Mannaerts, H.J.B.M. (2000), 'STREAM: Substances throughput related to economic activity model: a partial equilibrium model for material flows in the economy', Research Memorandum No 165, Netherlands Bureau for Economic Policy Analysis (CPB), The Netherlands.

Meadows, D.H., D.L. Meadows, J. Randers and W.W. Behrens II (1972), *The Limits to Growth*, Universe Books, New York.

Milana, C. (2000), 'The input–output structural decomposition analysis of "flexible" production systems', in E. Dietzenbacher and M.L. Lahr (eds), *Input–Output Analysis: Frontiers and Extensions*, MacMillan Publishers,

London, pp. 349–80.

Miller, R.E. and P.D. Blair (1985), *Input–Output Analysis: Foundations and Extensions*, Prentice-Hall, Englewood-Cliffs, NJ.

Mokyr, J. (ed.) (1999), *The British Industrial Revolution: An Economic Perspective*, Westview Press, Boulder.

Moll, S., F. Hinterberger, A. Femia and S. Bringezu (1998a), 'Ein Input–output-Ansatz zur Analyse des stofflichen Ressourcenverbrauchs einer Nationalökonmie: Ein Beitrag zur Methodik der volkswirtschaftlichen Materialintensitätsanalyse, 6. Stuttgarter Input–Output Workshop, Stuttgart.

Moll, S., F. Hinterberger, A. Femia and S. Bringezu (1998b), 'An input–output approach to analyse the total material requirement (TMR) of national economies', Conaccount Workshop: Ecologizing Societal Metabolism, Designing Scenarios for Sustainable Materials Management, Amsterdam.

Mukhopadhyay, K. and D. Chakraborty (1999), 'India's energy consumption changes during 1973/74 to 1991/92', *Economic Systems Research*, 11 (4), 423–37.

Nakamura, S. (1999), 'An interindustry approach to analyzing economic and environmental effects of the recycling of waste', *Ecological Economics*, 28, 133–45.

Nebbia, G. (2000), 'Contabilià monetaria e contabilità ambientale', *Economia Pubblica*, 30 (6), 5–33.

NFK (Nederlandse Federatie van Kunststoffen) (1997), 'Kunststof recycling 1996: Inzameling en herverwerking, materiaalstromen in kaart - Ontwikkelingen naar 2000', Leidschendam, The Netherlands.

Nooij, M. de, R. van der Kruk and D. van Soest (2003), 'International comparisons of domestic energy consumption', *Energy Economics*, 25 (4), 359–73.

Oosterhaven, J. and A.R. Hoen (1998), 'Preferences, technology, trade and real income changes in the European Union - an intercountry decomposition analysis for 1975–1985', *Annals of Regional Science*, 21, 505–24.

Opschoor, J.B. (1994), 'Chain management in environmental policy: analytical and evaluative concepts', in J.B. Opschoor and R.K. Turner (eds), *Economic Incentives and Environmental Policies*, Kluwer Academic Publishers, Dordrecht, The Netherlands.

OTA (Office of Technology Assessment) (1990), *Energy Use and the Economy*, USGPO, Washington DC.

Perman, R., Y. Ma and J. McGilvray (1996), *Natural Resource and Environmental Economics*, Addison, Wesley Longman Limited, London and New York.

Perrings, C. (1987), *Economy and Environment – a Theoretical Essay on the Interdependence of Economic and Environmental Systems*, Cambridge University Press, Cambridge.

Pløger, E. (1984), 'The effects of structural changes on Danish energy consumption', 5th IIASA Task Force Meeting on input–output modeling, Laxenburg, Austria, pp. 211–20.

Proops, J.L.R., M. Faber and G. Wagenhals (1993), *Reducing CO_2 Emissions: a Comparative Input–Output Study for Germany and the UK*, Springer-Verlag, Heidelberg.

Quesnay, F. (1766), 'Analyse du Tableau Économique', *Journal d'Agriculture, du commerce et des finance.*

Richardson, H. (1972), *Input–Output and Regional Economics*, John Wiley and Sons (Halsted Press), New York.

Rienstra, S.A. (1998), 'Options and barriers for sustainable transport policies: a scenario approach', PhD thesis, Free University, Amsterdam, The Netherlands.

RIVM (Rijksinstituut voor Volksgezondheid en Milieuhygiene) (1989), Diverse informatie documenten, Direct Afvalstoffen, The Netherlands.

Rose, A. (1999), 'Input–output decomposition analysis of energy and the environment', in J.C.J.M. van den Bergh (ed.), *Handbook of Environmental and Resource Economics*, Edward Elgar, Cheltenham. pp. 1164–79.

Rose, A. and S.D. Casler (1996), 'Input–output structural decomposition analysis: a critical appraisal', *Economic Systems Research*, **8** (1), 33–62.

Rose, A. and C.Y. Chen (1991a), 'Sources of change in energy use in the U.S. Economy, 1972–1982', *Resources and Energy*, **13**, 1–21.

Rose, A. and C.Y. Chen (1991b), 'Modeling the responsiveness of energy use to changing economic conditions', Conference Paper, International Association for Energy Economics.

Rose, A.Z. and S-M Lin (1995), 'Regrets or no regrets – that is the question: is conservation a costless CO_2 mitigation strategy?', *Energy Journal*, **16** (3), 67–87.

Rose, A. and W. Miernyk (1989), 'Input–output analysis: the first fifty years', *Economic Systems Research*, **1** (2), 229–71.

Rose, A., C.Y. Chen and G. Adams (1996), 'Structural decomposition analysis of changes in material demand', Working paper, Pennsylvania State University.

Ruth, M. (1993), *Integrating Economics, Ecology and Thermodynamics*, Kluwer Academic Publishers, Dordrecht, the Netherlands.

Ruth, M. (1999), 'Physical principles and environmental economic analysis', in J.C.J.M. van den Bergh (ed.), *Handbook of Environmental and Resource Economics*, Edward Elgar, Cheltenham, pp. 855–66.

Schaffer, A. (2001), 'ECOLogical Input–output analysis: ECOLIO: a model for conventional and ecological key sector analysis', PhD thesis, University of Karlsruhe, Germany.

SEEA (System of Environmental and Economic Accounting) (2002), *System of Environmetal and Economic Accounting 2000*, London Group on Environmental Accounting.

Seibel, (2003) 'Decomposition analysis of carbon dioxide-emission changes in Germany – Conceptual framework and empirical results', Working Papers and Studies, European Communities, Luxembourg.

Siegel, P.B., J. Alwang and T.G. Johnson (1995), 'Decomposing sources of regional growth with an I/O model: a framework for policy analysis', *International Regional Science Review*, **18** (3), 331–53.

Socolow, R., C. Andrews, F. Berkhout and V. Thomas (1994), *Industrial Ecology and Global Change*, Cambridge University Press, Cambridge.

Stahmer, C., M. Kuhn and N. Braun (1997), 'Physical input–output tables for Germany, 1990', Working Paper No. 2/1998/B/1, German Federal Statistical Office.

Steenge, A. E. (1978), 'Environmental repercussions and the economic structure: further comments', *Review of Economics and Statistics*, **60**, 482–86.

Structural Change and Economic Dynamics (1999), Special issue on the NAMEA, **10**.

Stone, R. (1961), *Input–Output and National Accounts*, OECD, Paris.

Suh, S., G. Huppes and H. Udo de Haes (2002), 'Environmental impacts of domestic and imported commodities in the U.S. economy', 14th International Conference on Input–Output Techniques, Montreal, Canada.

Suh, S. (2004a), 'A note on the calculus for physical input–output analysis and its application to land appropriation of international trade activities', *Ecological Economics*, **48** (1), 9–17.

Suh, S. (2004b), 'Materials and energy flows in industry and ecosystem networks. Life-cycle assessment, input-output analysis, material flow analysis, ecological network flow analysis, and their combinations for industrial ecology', PhD thesis, Institute of Environmental Studies (CML), University of Leiden, The Netherlands.

Sun, J.W. (1998), 'Changes in energy consumption and energy intensity: a complete decomposition model', *Energy Economics*, **20** (1), 85–100.

Tiwari, P. (2000), 'An analysis of sectoral energy intensity in India', *Energy Policy*, **28**, 771–8.

Turner, R.K, D.W. Pearce and I. Bateman (1992), *Environmental Economics: an Elementary Introduction*. Johns Hopkins University Press, Baltimore.

UN (United Nations) (1997), *Iron and Steel Statistics*, Economic Commission for Europe, Geneva, Switzerland.

UN (United Nations) (1968), *System of National Accounts*.

UN (United Nations) (1993), *Input–Output Tables and Analysis*, Series F, no. 2, Rev. 3, New York.

Victor, P.A. (1972), *Pollution: Economy and Environment*, George Allen and Unwin Ltd, London.

Voet, E. van der (1996), 'Substances from cradle to grave: developments of a methodology for the analysis of substance flows through the economy and the environment of a region', PhD thesis, Centre of Environmental Science, Leiden University, The Netherlands.

Vogt, A. (1978), 'Divisia indices on different paths', in W. Eichhorn, R. Henn, O. Opitz and R.W. Shepard (eds), *Theory and Applications of Economic Indices*, Physica-Verlag, Wurzburg, pp. 297–305.

Vogt, A. and J. Barta (1997), *The Making of Tests of Index Numbers: Mathematical Methods of Descriptive Statistics*, Springer-Verlag, Heidelberg.

Vollebregt, M. and J. van Dalen (2002), 'Deriving homogeneous input–output tables from supply and use tables', Report of Statistics Netherlands (CBS), Division of macro-economic statistics and dissemination (MSP), Voorburg, The Netherlands.

WCED (World Commission on Environment and Development) (1987), *Our Common Future*, Oxford University Press, Oxford/New York.

Weizsäcker, E. von, A.B. Lovins and L.H. Lovins (1997), *Factor Four: Doubling Wealth – Halving Resource Use, a Report to the Club of Rome*, Earthscan, London.

Wier, M. (1998), 'Sources of changes in emissions from energy: a structural decomposition analysis', *Economic Systems Research*, **10** (2), 99–112.

Wier, M. and B. Hasler (1999), 'Accounting for nitrogen in Denmark – a structural decomposition analysis', *Ecological Economics*, **30**, 317–31.

Wilting, H. (1996), 'An energy perspective on economic activities', PhD thesis, University of Groningen, The Netherlands.

WRI (World Resources Institute) (2000), *Weight of Nations: Material Outflows from Industrial Economies*, World Resources Institute, Washington DC.

Wyckoff, A.W. and J.M. Roop (1994), 'The embodiment of carbon in imports of manufactured products: implications for international greenhouse gas emissions', *Energy Policy*, (March), 187–94.

Zheng, Y. (2000), 'Sources of China's energy use changes in the 1990s', 13th International Conference on Input–Output Techniques, Macerata, Italy.

Index

Printed and bound by CPI Group (UK) Ltd, Croydon, CR0 4YY

23/04/2025

14660963-0003